150 Key Concepts in

art

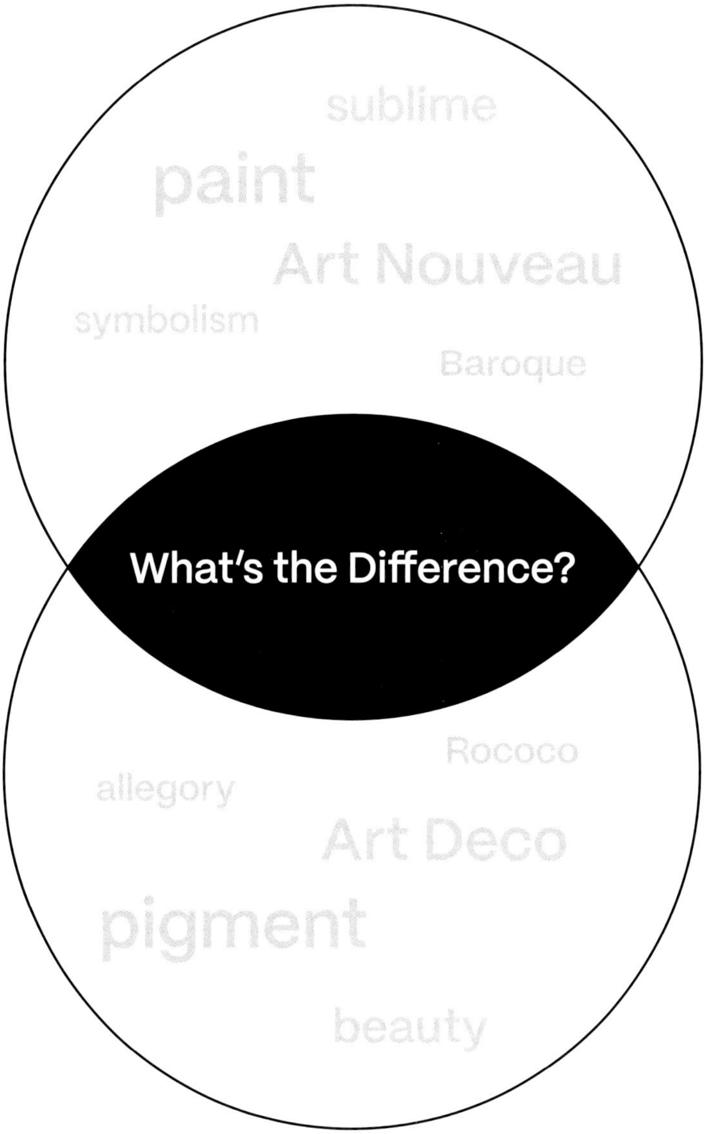

IVY PRESS

introduction

Part of a series of accessible reference books, *What's the Difference? 150 Key Concepts in Art* explores the nuanced world of art terminology. Within these pages, you can take a closer look at the subtle yet often significant differences between terms, words and concepts that are often confused, misunderstood or even misused.

Art is full of language that is both fascinating and frustrating. What exactly is the difference between tone and shadow, or assemblage and collage? How does Impressionism differ from Post-Impressionism? Are paint and pigment the same thing? What are scumbling, glazing, distortion and foreshortening – and are any of them related? Addressing 150 pairs of commonly conflated terms, words and concepts, this book provides straightforward explanations that clarify meaning without oversimplifying. The book offers clear definitions, historical context where relevant and comparisons or examples that bring the distinctions to life. Wherever possible, technical jargon is avoided, ensuring that explanations remain approachable without sacrificing accuracy.

This book is a focused guide, an invitation to explore art through language. Divided into four sections – on movements, techniques, materials and concepts – the book is easy to navigate. For example, the first section includes entries on Early and High Renaissance, Impressionism and Post-Impressionism, Photorealism and Hyper-realism and many more. You will find out the similarities and differences between Minoan and Mycenaean art, Cubism and Futurism, and Dada and Surrealism, and be able to put them all into context.

The second section examines technical terms, such as modelling and carving, and fresco and mural. It clarifies ideas that many of us have heard of, but do not necessarily understand in detail. The next two sections, materials and concepts, delve deeper into words and terms such as mosaic and tilework, and watercolour and gouache. These sections not only make distinctions but also open up a greater awareness and enjoyment of art throughout history.

Whether you are interested in art for study and a future career, or simply enjoy looking at it; whether you are a teacher or an avid gallery-goer, this book is for you. You can read it from cover to cover, dip in at random or use it as a quick reference whenever needed. Key works are illustrated, but you can also use this book as a starting point for your own investigations, researching further the artists and works named.

What's the Difference? 150 Key Concepts in Art is about clarity. When we understand the language of art, we can engage with it more deeply, and so often, understanding the differences between terms can open up a whole new way of looking and seeing.

how to use this book

Each double-page spread is designed to make the concepts clear and accessible. Expert text explains each key term, from the basic idea to the nuanced concept.

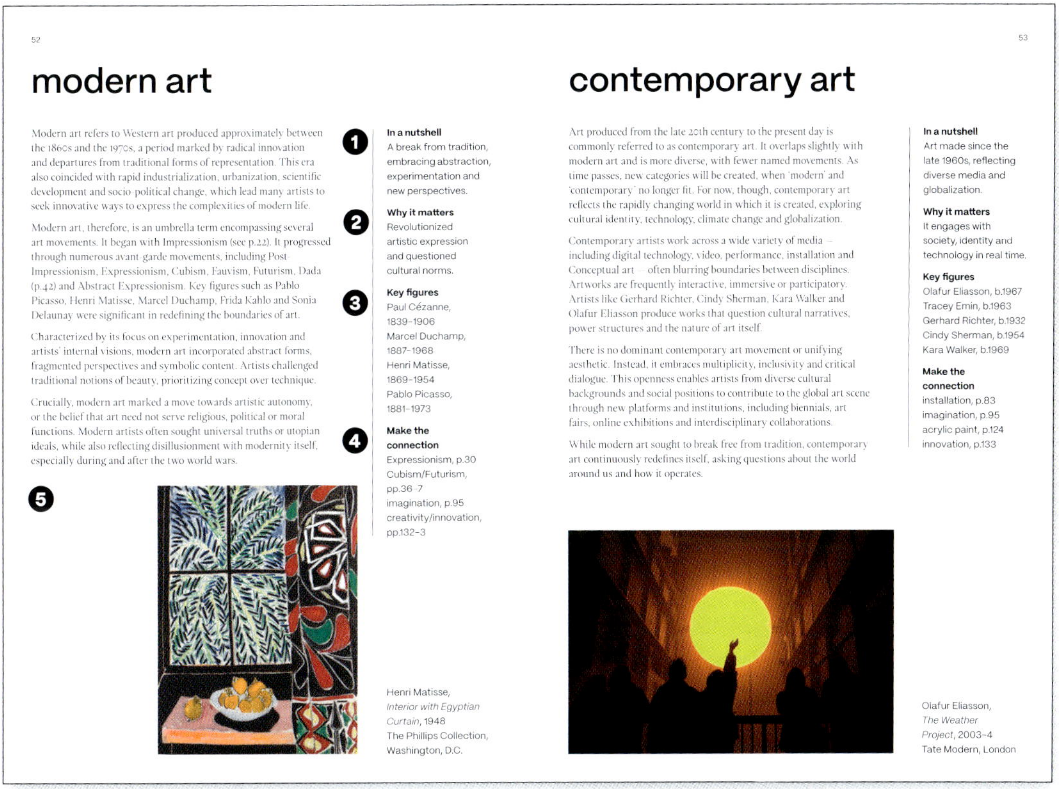
52

modern art

Modern art refers to Western art produced approximately between the 1860s and the 1970s, a period marked by radical innovation and departures from traditional forms of representation. This era also coincided with rapid industrialization, urbanization, scientific development and socio-political change, which lead many artists to seek innovative ways to express the complexities of modern life.

Modern art, therefore, is an umbrella term encompassing several art movements. It began with Impressionism (see p.22). It progressed through numerous avant-garde movements, including Post-Impressionism, Expressionism, Cubism, Fauvism, Futurism, Dada (p.42) and Abstract Expressionism. Key figures such as Pablo Picasso, Henri Matisse, Marcel Duchamp, Frida Kahlo and Sonia Delaunay were significant in redefining the boundaries of art.

Characterized by its focus on experimentation, innovation and artists' internal visions, modern art incorporated abstract forms, fragmented perspectives and symbolic content. Artists challenged traditional notions of beauty, prioritizing concept over technique.

Crucially, modern art marked a move towards artistic autonomy, or the belief that art need not serve religious, political or moral functions. Modern artists often sought universal truths or utopian ideals, while also reflecting disillusionment with modernity itself, especially during and after the two world wars.

1 **In a nutshell**
A break from tradition, embracing abstraction, experimentation and new perspectives.

2 **Why it matters**
Revolutionized artistic expression and questioned cultural norms.

3 **Key figures**
Paul Cézanne, 1839–1906
Marcel Duchamp, 1887–1968
Henri Matisse, 1869–1954
Pablo Picasso, 1881–1973

4 **Make the connection**
Expressionism, p.30
Cubism/Futurism, pp.36–7
imagination, p.95
creativity/innovation, pp.132–3

5

Henri Matisse, *Interior with Egyptian Curtain*, 1948
The Phillips Collection, Washington, D.C.

53

contemporary art

Art produced from the late 20th century to the present day is commonly referred to as contemporary art. It overlaps slightly with modern art and is more diverse, with fewer named movements. As time passes, new categories will be created, when 'modern' and 'contemporary' no longer fit. For now, though, contemporary art reflects the rapidly changing world in which it is created, exploring cultural identity, technology, climate change and globalization.

Contemporary artists work across a wide variety of media – including digital technology, video, performance, installation and Conceptual art – often blurring boundaries between disciplines. Artworks are frequently interactive, immersive or participatory. Artists like Gerhard Richter, Cindy Sherman, Kara Walker and Olafur Eliasson produce works that question cultural narratives, power structures and the nature of art itself.

There is no dominant contemporary art movement or unifying aesthetic. Instead, it embraces multiplicity, inclusivity and critical dialogue. This openness enables artists from diverse cultural backgrounds and social positions to contribute to the global art scene through new platforms and institutions, including biennials, art fairs, online exhibitions and interdisciplinary collaborations.

While modern art sought to break free from tradition, contemporary art continuously redefines itself, asking questions about the world around us and how it operates.

In a nutshell
Art made since the late 1960s, reflecting diverse media and globalization.

Why it matters
It engages with society, identity and technology in real time.

Key figures
Olafur Eliasson, b.1967
Tracey Emin, b.1963
Gerhard Richter, b.1932
Cindy Sherman, b.1954
Kara Walker, b.1969

Make the connection
installation, p.83
imagination, p.95
acrylic paint, p.124
innovation, p.133

Olafur Eliasson, *The Weather Project*, 2003–4
Tate Modern, London

1 *In a nutshell* is a single-sentence summary of each concept.

2 *Why it matters* gives the broader art-historical context.

3 *Key figures* names those all-important folk engaged in the debate.

4 *Make the connection* helps you to trace key concepts across the book.

5 Images support the terms and concepts, further clarifying the explanations.

Minoan art

Flourishing mainly on the island of Crete from approximately 3000 BCE to 1450 BCE, Minoan art is renowned for its elegance, fluidity and naturalism (meaning lifelike representation without embellishment). Characterized by vibrant depictions of figures and rituals, the art reflects a peaceful society that valued beauty, nature and custom rather than dominance or warfare. Minoan artists worked with a range of media, including fresco, decorated ceramics, metalwork, symbolic seals and jewellery. As the Minoan writing systems, Cretan Hieroglyphic and Linear A, remain undeciphered, it is not known whether artisans signed or recorded their works.

One of the most distinctive features of Minoan art is its tradition of dynamic wall painting, as found at Knossos on Crete and Akrotiri on the island of Santorini. Many of these paintings depict lively scenes of marine life (such as dolphins), acrobatics (such as bull-leaping, see below) and ceremonial processions. Figures are often shown in profile, with stylized yet graceful forms and movements. Adhering to standard gender conventions in ancient art, men are typically depicted with reddish-brown skin, while women are often pale. The decoration of Minoan pottery evolved from simple geometric patterns to ornate, naturalistic motifs (recurring elements or ideas), particularly representing marine themes.

Overall, Minoan art is distinguished by its optimism, lightness and apparent love of nature, suggesting a comparatively peaceful and prosperous society.

In a nutshell
Vibrant, naturalistic and graceful, Minoan art reflects a peaceful, nature-loving island culture.

Why it matters
Influenced later Greek art and offers insights into early European civilization, ritual and aesthetics.

Make the connection
fresco, p.64
buon fresco/fresco secco, pp.66–7
pigment, p.111

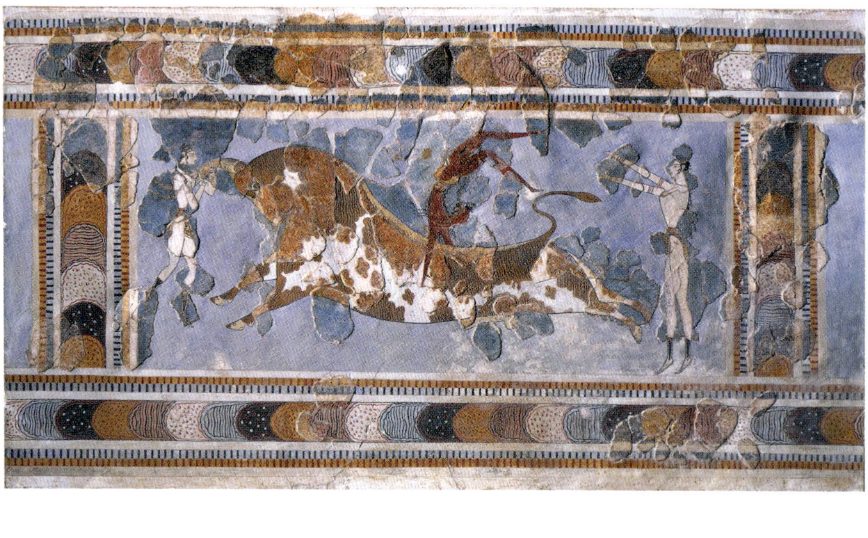

Restored fresco depicting bull-leaping ritual, from the Palace of Knossos, c.1450–1450 BCE
Heraklion Archaeological Museum

Mycenaean art

If Minoan art reflects a peaceful civilization, Mycenaean art, which developed on mainland Greece between approximately 1600 BCE and 1100 BCE, reflects a society structured around kingship, military prowess and fortified palaces, in which warfare, power and prestige were key. Through early trade and cultural contact, the Mycenaeans adopted and adapted many Minoan motifs, but infused them with a more formal, military character.

Grand Mycenaean palaces and castles were adorned with frescoes and opulent gold jewellery that conveyed prosperity and influence. Architecture and monumental sculpture played a significant role, with fortified palace complexes like Mycenae and Tiryns featuring Cyclopean masonry – a method of construction that utilized enormous stones without mortar – and grand entrances. This emphasis on defence contrasts with the open, airy Minoan palaces.

Mycenaean wall paintings retain Minoan techniques but often depict chariot processions, hunting and war scenes. Figures are typically more rigid than in Minoan art. Mycenaean pottery features stylized motifs and sometimes marine or geometric designs, but with less naturalism than their Minoan counterparts. Goldwork – as seen in the 'Mask of Agamemnon' (below) and on weapons and jewellery – reveals exceptional craftsmanship and a focus on status and the afterlife.

In a nutshell
Blending practicality with splendour and intricacy, Mycenaean art was often focused on warriors, nature and mythology.

Why it matters
Combined Minoan and Classical Greek aesthetics, giving us valuable insights into Bronze Age beliefs, trade and social hierarchy.

Make the connection
buon fresco/fresco secco, pp.66–7
contrast, p.92

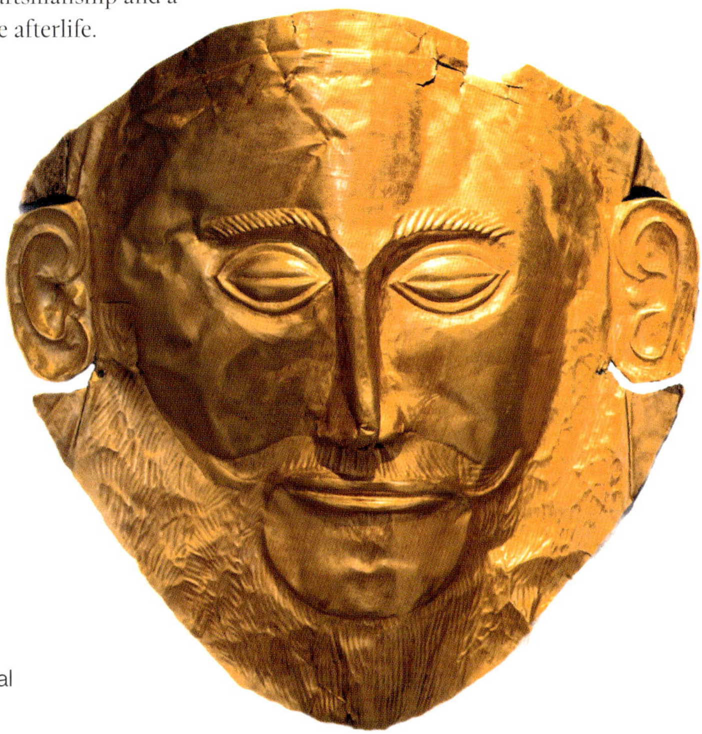

Gold funerary mask, known as the 'Mask of Agamemnon', *c.*1550–1500 BCE
National Archaeological Museum of Athens

ancient Roman art

Reflecting the political might and cultural diversity of the evolving Roman Empire, the art of this era (*c*.500 BCE – 476 CE) was a powerful tool of communication. Drawing on ancient Greek precedents, Roman artists developed styles emphasizing realism, narrative and public messaging.

Roman portraiture is notable for its realism, particularly in the busts of senators and emperors, which conveyed authority and character. In contrast with the idealized forms of ancient Greek art, Roman portraits often depicted age and imperfections as signs of virtue.

Advances in Roman engineering, notably the development of concrete and the use of arches, allowed architects to build on an unprecedented scale. These innovations made it possible to construct enduring landmarks such as vast aqueducts, basilicas and domes. Interiors and public spaces were richly decorated. Wall paintings and mosaics adorned villas, bathhouses and temples, ranging from lifelike frescoes to intricate mythological scenes. Beyond painting, the decorative arts flourished: finely crafted cameos, glass vessels, metal objects and coins were created, many carrying imperial imagery.

Art in Roman society served all. Commissioned works reinforced the status of emperors and nobles, while more modest decorations were found in shops, homes and public spaces. Roman art reflected a vast cultural diversity, often blending local traditions with Classical ideals.

In a nutshell
Ambitious, realistic and political, Roman art fused ancient Greek aesthetics with innovation.

Why it matters
Shaped the course of Western art and architecture.

Key figures
Iaia of Cyzicus, 2nd century BCE
Gaius Fabius Pictor, 4th century BCE
Pacuvius, 220–130 BCE
Spurius Tadius (also known as Ludius or Studius), *fl.*late 1st century BCE – early 1st century CE

Make the connection
carving, p.61
trompe l'oeil/ verisimilitude, pp.106–7
mosaic, p.118

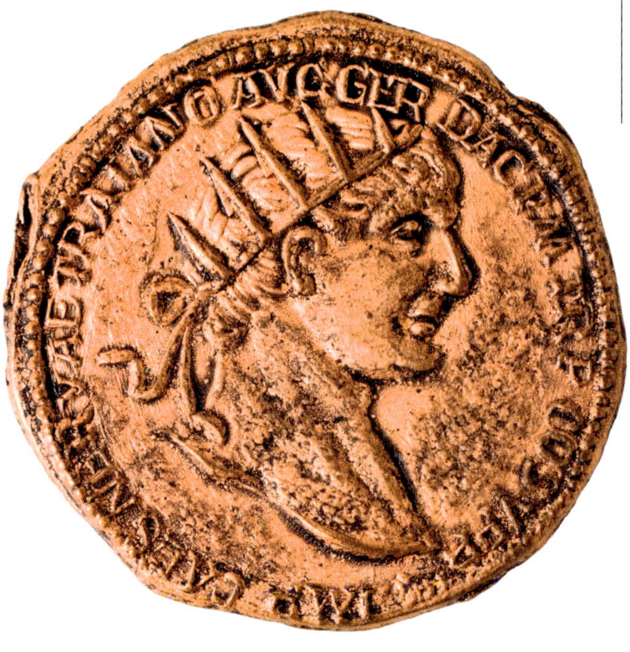

Ancient Roman coin from the rule of Emperor Trajan, 117 BCE

Romanesque art

During a period of religious revival, Romanesque art emerged in medieval Europe between approximately 1000 and 1150 CE. It mainly aimed to follow ancient Roman architectural principles, but was also influenced by Christian doctrine, feudalism and a growing sense of regional identity. The term 'Romanesque' primarily refers to architecture (see below), but sculpture, painting and decorative arts were also integral.

Thick stone walls, round arches, barrel vaults and small windows characterize Romanesque architecture. Churches were the dominant building type. These structures were fortress-like, emphasizing stability. Sculpture played an essential and symbolic role, frequently integrated into church façades. Figures were stylized rather than realistic, with elongated proportions and expressive gestures. Designed to teach and inspire an illiterate population, the works focused on themes such as salvation, the Last Judgement and saints. Painting, mostly in fresco and illuminated manuscripts, was similarly instructive. It featured bold colours, flat figures and strong outlines. Metalwork, embroidery (notably the Bayeux Tapestry), and reliquaries enriched religious spaces and rituals.

Romanesque art united diverse regions under shared Christian themes while allowing for local variation (much like the art of the Roman Empire).

In a nutshell
A precursor to the European Gothic style of the 12th century; architecture characterised by rounded arches, thick walls and large towers.

Why it matters
Unified Christian Europe visually and spiritually.

Key figures
Gislebertus, 12th century CE
Renier de Huy, 12th century CE
Master Mateo, active 1168–88 CE
Hugo d'Oignies, *c.*1187–1240 CE

Make the connection
Gothic, p.11
carving, p.61
fresco, p.64
embroidery, p.117

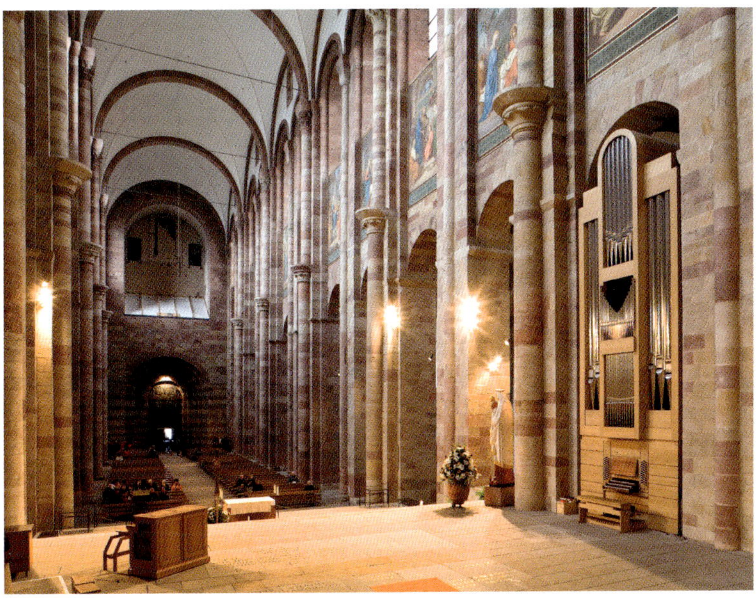

Interior view, Speyer Cathedral, founded 1030, rebuilt 1077

Byzantine

From the 4th to the 15th centuries CE, Byzantine art expressed the Eastern Roman Empire's spiritual and imperial identity, aiming to evoke a sense of divine presence and holiness. It prioritized symbolism over realism, with stylized figures conveying divine presence rather than earthly likenesses. Gold backgrounds, flattened imagery and expressionless faces were essential characteristics of the artwork, which was mainly created for worship.

Art was often commissioned by emperors and clergy, reinforcing the unity between the Church and state. Similarly, art was usually made as a spiritual offering rather than as personal expression. Adorning church interiors, shimmering mosaics with glass and gold tesserae evoked heavenly light. Central to devotional life, and seen as direct windows to the divine, were icons, or painted images of Christ, the Virgin Mary and saints. Frescoes and illuminated manuscripts were created for storytelling and ritual purposes. Architecturally, Byzantine churches, such as the Hagia Sophia of Istanbul (then Constantinople), blended ancient Roman engineering with spiritual symbolism; they featured innovative domes and centralized plans.

Even during periods of iconoclasm, when religious images were destroyed, Byzantine art continued to develop, taking in influences from neighbouring cultures and spreading its ideas across Eastern Europe, the Middle East and Russia. Its emphasis on spiritual presence and visual splendour inspired later movements, including the Italian Renaissance.

In a nutshell
Conveyed a divine presence, as evident in the use of gold, symmetry and stylized forms.

Why it matters
Profoundly shaped Orthodox Christian imagery, linking antiquity and medieval Europe; influenced the development of Renaissance and Islamic art.

Key figures
Manouil Panselinos
Theophanes the Greek *c.*1330/40–1405
Michael Astrapas and Eutychios Astrapas, *fl. c.*1295–1317

Make the connection
fresco, p.64
mosaic, p.118
encaustic, p.121

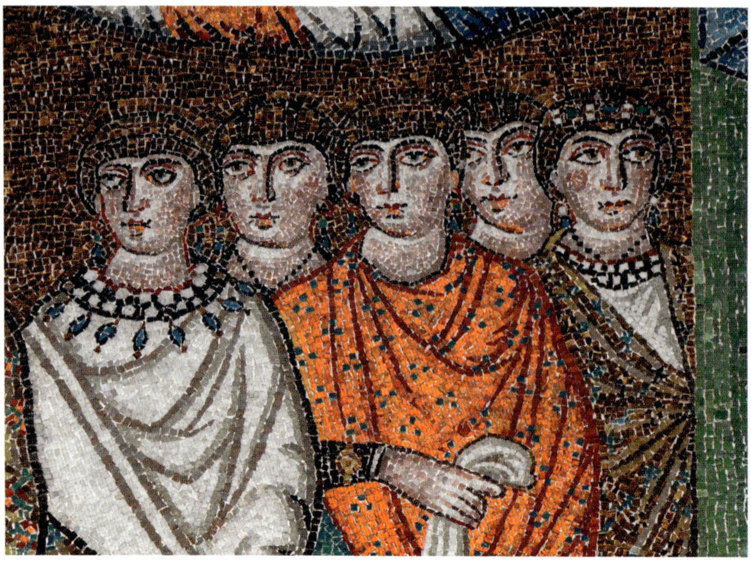

'Five ladies of the court of Theodora', detail of Byzantine mosaic in the apse of the Basilica di San Vitale at Ravenna, 6th century CE

Gothic

The innovations of Gothic architecture developed through the French abbot and statesman Abbot Suger (1081–1151 CE), who believed that churches should convey God's presence on earth. This area of spiritual art combined aspects of Byzantine and Romanesque styles, as well as borrowing from Islamic architecture.

It emerged in mid-12th-century France and proliferated across Europe until the 16th century. The Gothic movement was primarily associated with architecture, particularly soaring cathedrals, such as Notre-Dame de Paris, Chartres and Reims. Characterized by pointed arches, ribbed vaults and flying buttresses, these structures allowed for vast, dazzling stained-glass windows that bathed interiors in coloured light, symbolizing divine presence. Wealthy noblemen commissioned elaborate manuscript illuminations, and by the end of the Gothic era, sumptuous altarpieces and frescoes were becoming more common in churches and chapels.

In painting and sculpture, Gothic art emphasized naturalism (see p.6) and emotional expression. Figures exhibit graceful poses and tender gestures, moving away from the rigid stylization of Byzantine art. Biblical scenes, saints and the Virgin Mary were depicted with increasing realism. Sculpture adorned cathedral façades; artists paid close attention to anatomy, drapery and facial expressions. While Byzantine art emphasized spiritual symbolism and flat, otherworldly forms, Gothic art strived for naturalism, depth and emotional realism.

In a nutshell
A period when soaring cathedrals were built, with pointed arches, stained glass and expressive sculpture.

Why it matters
Revolutionized architecture and deepened emotional storytelling in religious art.

Key figures
Giotto, *c.*1267/76 –1337
Simone Martini, 1284–1344
Claus Sluter, 1340 – 1405/6
Abbot Suger, 1081–1151

Make the connection
Romanesque, p.9
carving, p.61
bas-relief, p.74

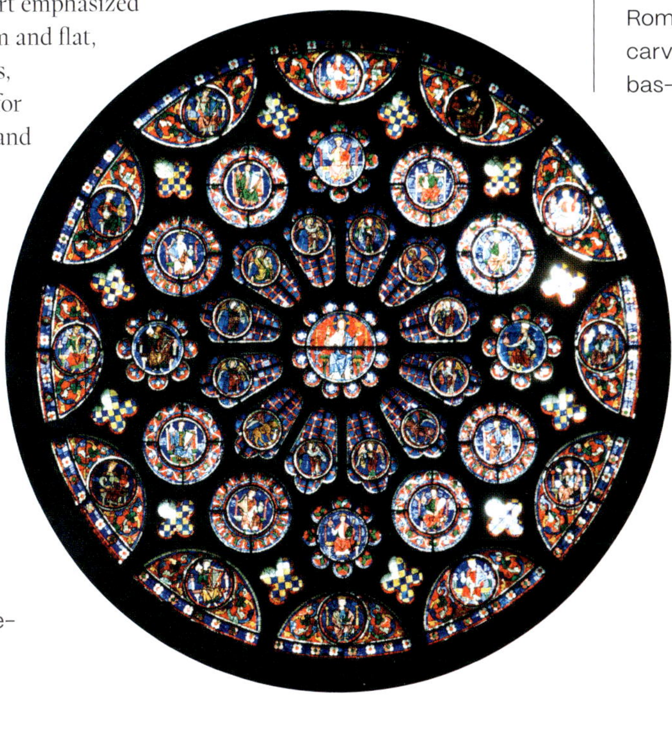

Stained-glass window in the Cathedral of Notre-Dame de Paris, 13th century CE

Tang Dynasty art

The Tang Dynasty (618–907 CE) was a golden age of cosmopolitan culture in China, marked by a flourishing of art that included bold colours, dynamic compositions, expressive brushwork and realistic figures, often illustrating court life and Buddhist themes, as well as exhibiting foreign influences. It was a time of great cultural exchange – facilitated by the Silk Road – during which new ideas, materials and artistic influences were introduced.

Buddhist art proliferated, with grand murals and sculptures adorning cave temples such as Longmen and those at Dunhuang. These artworks blended various artistic styles from across Asia, emphasizing spiritual grandeur and emotional resonance. Sculpture, made for these temples and tombs, followed Buddhist themes.

There was official support for artists and the establishment of schools such as the Hanlin Academy in Chang'an. The first history of Chinese art was written during the Tang Dynasty, and new techniques and styles emerged, such as *shanshui* (mountain-water painting), which emphasized the essence of nature over strict realism. Tang artists used refined, intricate ink-and-wash techniques to express nature's beauty and the elegance of court life.

Calligraphy played a central role, with artists cultivating their own individual styles and inventive techniques. Diverse and bold, Tang ceramics ranged from the lively *sancai* (three-colour) glazes adorning funerary works to the refined porcelain and celadon glaze innovations that were developed during the period.

In a nutshell
Reflecting the dynasty's wealth, beliefs, diversity and spirituality, Tang art was often extravagant, dynamic and varied.

Why it matters
Conveys imagination and craftsmanship, and influenced the visual language of East Asia.

Key figures
Han Gan, *c.*706–783
Wang Wei, 699–759
Wu Daozi, *c.*686–760
Yan Liben, *c.*600–673
Zhou Fang, *c.*730–800

Make the connection
mural, p.65
sculpture, p.82
watercolour, p.122

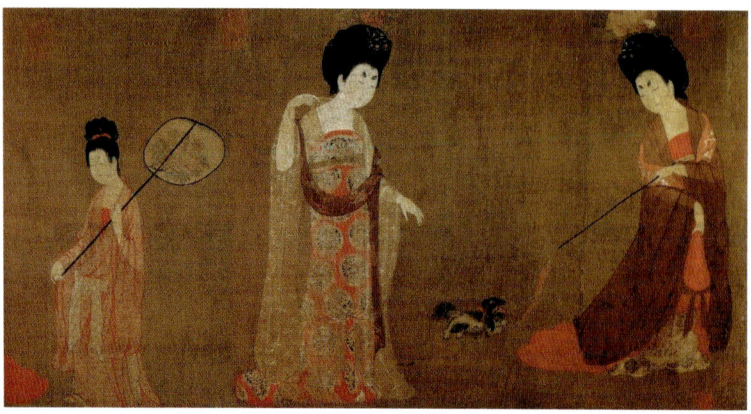

Zhou Fang, *Court Ladies Wearing Flowered Headdresses* (detail), 8th century
Liaoning Provincial Museum, Shenyang

Song Dynasty art

Following the Tang Dynasty, and the Five Dynasties and Ten Kingdoms period, the Song Dynasty (960–1279 CE) saw a flowering of art that was refined and original, characterized by restraint and introspection. While Tang Dynasty art emphasizes grandeur, colour and cosmopolitan elegance, Song Dynasty art values subtlety, naturalism (see p.6) and expression of the inner spirit.

Patronage was an essential aspect of Song Dynasty art, and many wealthy families commissioned their own private artworks. The imperial court also played a large role in promoting the arts. Emperor Huizong (r. 1100–1126) was an accomplished artist himself and established his own painting academy, the Hanlin Huayuan.

While the Tang Dynasty was influenced by Buddhism, the Song Dynasty saw the rise of Neo-Confucianism, often infused with Taoist ideas. To reflect Taoist and Neo-Confucian ideals about the magnificence of nature and the smallness of humanity, artists painted huge scrolls depicting misty mountains and meandering rivers. Painting styles varied by region and artist, but landscape, figures and bird-and-flower painting were common subjects.

The 'Literati' painting style evolved, with scholar-artists combining poetry, calligraphy and painting (collectively referred to as 'brush art') into unified expressions of personal philosophy, marking a shift towards more introspective art.

In a nutshell
Blended elegance and intellect, with lyrical paintings, fine ceramics, careful calligraphy and fluid brushwork.

Why it matters
Profoundly shaped Chinese aesthetics, elevating art as a form of scholarly expression.

Key figures
Fan Kuan, *c.*950–1032
Guo Xi, 1020–1090
Emperor Huizong, 1082–1135
Li Cheng, 919–967
Zhang Zeduan, 1085–1145

Make the connection
atmospheric perspective, p.78
asymmetry, p.109
watercolour, p.122

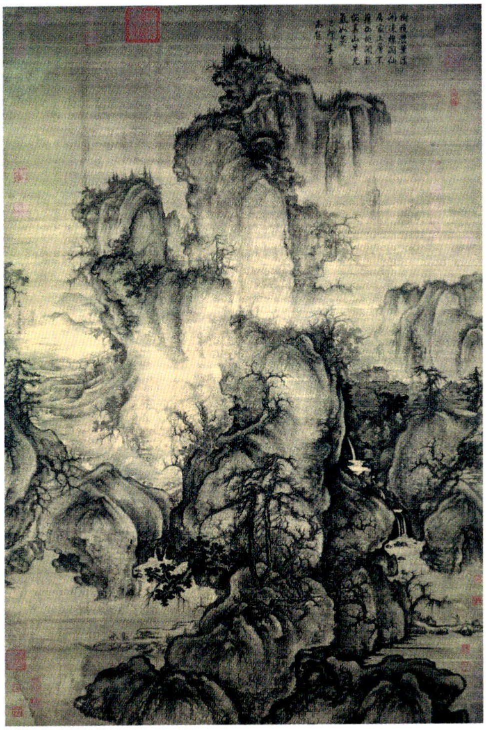

Guo Xi, *Early Spring*, 1072 CE
National Palace Museum, Taipei, China

Early Renaissance

Lasting approximately from 1400 to 1490, the Early Renaissance was a period of rebirth of the philosophies, literature, architecture and art of ancient Greece and Rome. Developments began in Florence and Siena, Italy, as artists, scientists and philosophers simultaneously rediscovered the past and found their individuality.

Early Renaissance artists emphasized realism, naturalism (p.6), proportion, perspective and individuality – ideas largely neglected during the medieval period. Notable figures include Filippo Brunelleschi, who revolutionized architecture with the dome of Florence Cathedral and pioneered linear perspective; Leon Battista Alberti, a polymath who laid theoretical foundations for Renaissance art; Masaccio, whose frescoes displayed astonishing realism; and Botticelli, who blended Classical myths with elegant lines. Donatello transformed sculpture by endowing biblical and mythological figures with genuine human presence.

This period saw the rise of humanism – a way of thinking that shifted attention to human experience and individuality, rather than focusing solely on the afterlife. The ideals of Christianity were not abandoned, but artists also explored secular subjects. Patronage from influential families enabled artists to experiment and flourish. This all laid the foundation for even more refined artistic achievements.

In a nutshell
Mainly in Florence, Italy, art was revived through Classical ideals, connecting medieval traditions with modern innovation.

Why it matters
It laid the intellectual and artistic foundations for Western modernity.

Key figures
Leon Battista Alberti, 1404–1472
Sandro Botticelli, *c.*1445–1510
Filippo Brunelleschi, 1377–1446
Donatello, 1386–1466
Masaccio, 1401–1428

Make the connection
carving, p.61
fresco, p.64
linear perspective, p.79
tempera, p.120

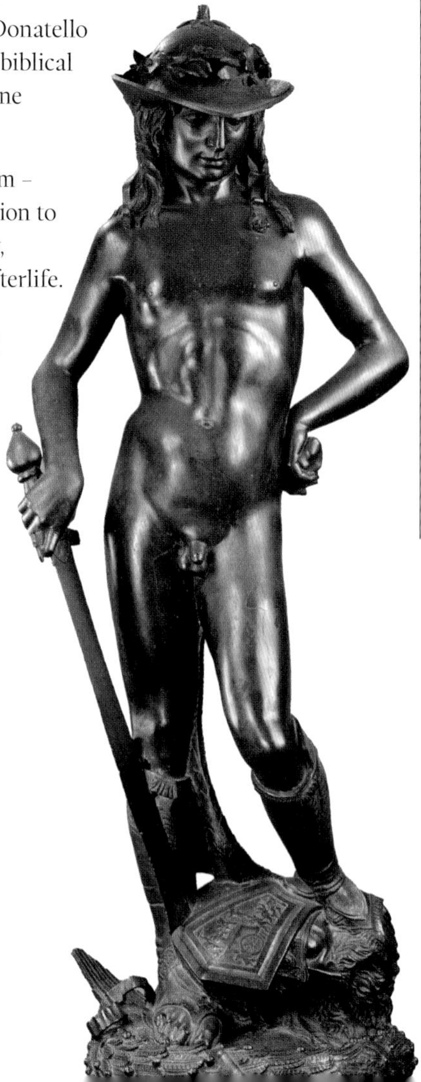

Donatello, *David*, *c.*1440
Museo Nazionale del Bargello, Florence

High Renaissance

The High Renaissance (*c.*1490–1527) represents a zenith of artistic expression. Mainly based in Rome, it built on the innovations of the Early Renaissance, integrating still greater technical mastery and philosophical depth. Painting and sculpture reached a peak of technical competence, with realistic interpretations, compositional balance and drama that matched or surpassed that seen in the works of ancient Greece and Rome. Many historians cite *The Last Supper* (1495–8) by Leonardo da Vinci as the start of the High Renaissance, coinciding with the shift of the cultural centre from Florence to Rome, where Pope Julius II commissioned much important art.

The study of anatomy was not new, but was considered sacrilegious. However, amid the intense interest in and growing demand for lifelike art, some artists risked studying the body through dissection, to create more accurate depictions. Two representations of the biblical David embody the differences between the Early and High Renaissance: Donatello's exhibits youthful realism and Classical form, while Michelangelo's *David* represents the High Renaissance ideal of perfected anatomy, heroic scale and spiritual grandeur.

The era concluded with increasing political turmoil, including the Sack of Rome in 1527, which led to the stylized Mannerist movement.

In a nutshell
Harmony, naturalism, realism and sophistication characterized the High Renaissance.

Why it matters
Defined and established the standard of artistic genius and humanist ideals.

Key figures
Leonardo da Vinci, 1452–1519
Albrecht Dürer, 1471–1528
Raphael, 1483–1520
Titian, d.1576

Make the connection
buon fresco, p.66
triptych/diptych, pp.68–9
bas-relief, p.74
verisimilitude, p.107

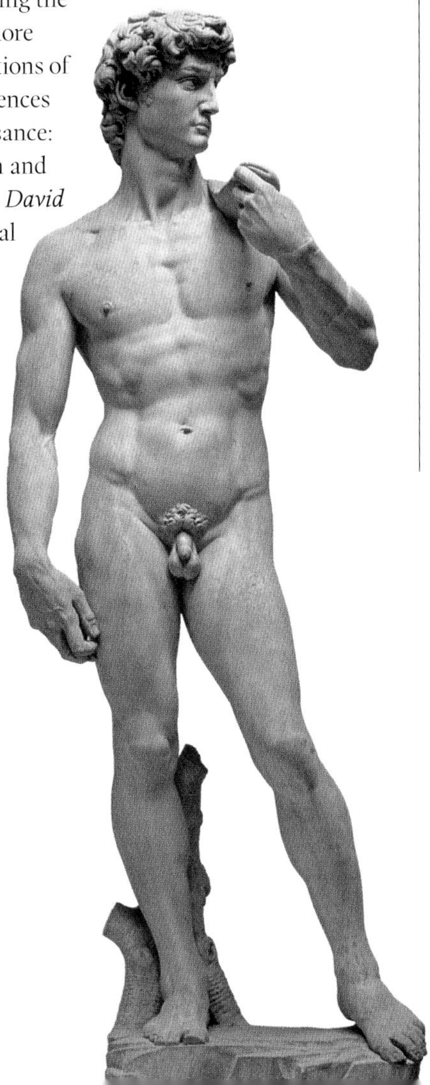

Michelangelo, *David*, 1501–04
Galleria dell'Accademia di Firenze

Renaissance

The term 'Renaissance', meaning 'rebirth', came to be used in the 19th century to describe a period in European history that lasted roughly from the 14th to the 17th centuries, marked by a profound cultural awakening that signalled the end of the medieval world and the dawn of the modern age. Originating in Italy, firstly in Florence, a renewed fascination with the Classical achievements of ancient Greece and Rome influenced all areas of human endeavour.

At the heart of the Renaissance was humanism: an attitude that attached importance to human rather than divine matters. This intellectual shift was supported by growing urban wealth and patronage. Renaissance artists aimed to be more realistic and to create images from a human viewpoint. They sought to create art that showed beauty, dignity, depth and meaning, in flowing, harmonious compositions. Both painting and sculpture were revolutionized: paintings such as *The Last Supper* and the Sistine Chapel ceiling exemplify a new mastery of anatomy, perspective and proportion; sculptors like Donatello and Michelangelo revived the Classical tradition of freestanding statues, portraying the human form with dramatic realism and emotional intensity. Architects such as Brunelleschi and Palladio also drew inspiration from ancient models, reviving symmetry and clarity in their designs.

The Renaissance was a period of revival and reinvention, reshaping European civilization by promoting creativity, intellectual freedom and a deeper understanding of the world.

In a nutshell
Balanced, realistic, human-centred art combining Classical ideals and scientific observation.

Why it matters
Revolutionized Western art, blending beauty, perspective and intellect.

Key figures
Filippo Brunelleschi, 1377–1446
Leonardo da Vinci, 1452–1519
Michelangelo, 1475–1564
Raphael, 1483–1520

Make the connection
buon fresco/fresco secco, pp.66–7
sfumato, p.71
bas-/high relief, pp.74–5
atmospheric/linear perspective, pp.78–9

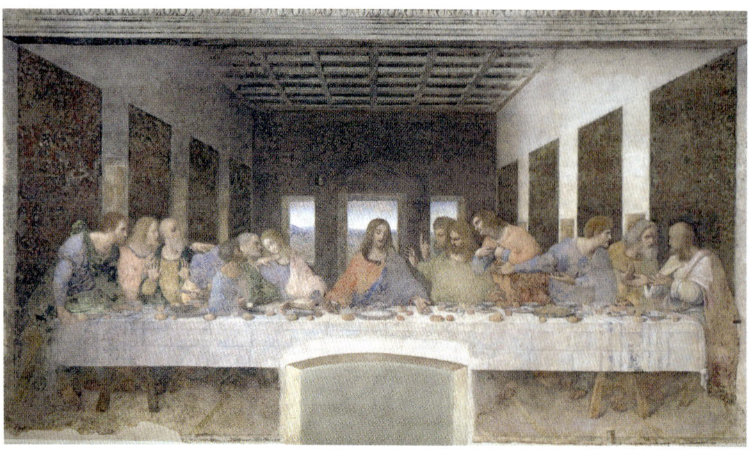

Leonardo da Vinci, *The Last Supper*, 1495–7
Cenacolo Vinciano e Museo, Santa Maria delle Grazie, Milan

Mannerism

Following the High Renaissance, Mannerism emerged in Italy around 1520 and lasted until the end of the 16th century. As a reaction to the harmonious ideals of the Renaissance, Mannerists deliberately moved away from balance, proportion and naturalism, instead exploring complexity, distortion and artifice. The movement developed during a period of political turmoil and religious upheaval, including the Sack of Rome in 1527 and the Protestant Reformation.

Mannerist compositions are emotionally charged or ambiguous, often featuring elongated figures, exaggerated poses and irrational spatial arrangements. Colours are frequently expressive and theatrical. Figures twist in unnatural poses – often the *figura serpentinata*, in which the lower limbs face in one direction and the torso turns the opposite way. *The Deposition from the Cross* (1528) by Jacopo Pontormo and *Madonna with the Long Neck* (below) by Parmigianino are two works that deliberately challenged traditional aesthetic norms. Mannerism spread from Italy across Europe, influencing artists in France (notably at the School of Fontainebleau), Spain and the Netherlands.

Though sometimes seen as decadent, it was highly experimental, introducing new approaches to story-telling, symbolism and artistic expression in an increasingly complex world.

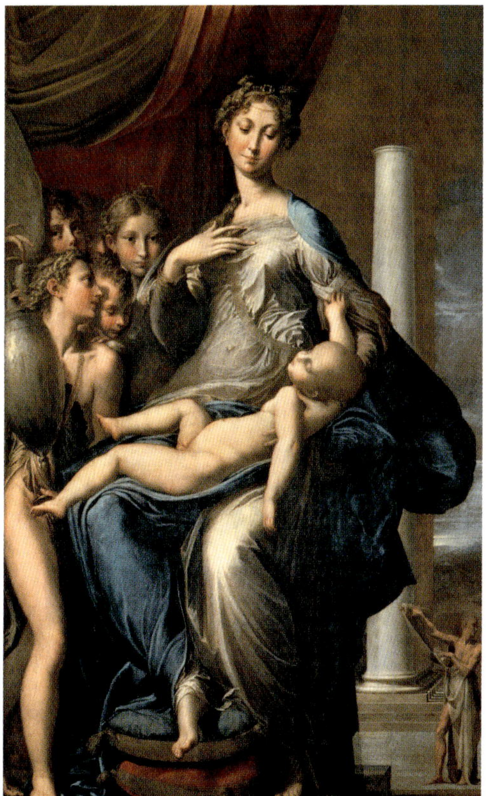

Parmigianino, *Madonna with the Long Neck*, 1534–40
Gallerie degli Uffizi, Florence

In a nutshell
Stylized, exaggerated art that distorted figures and objects for elegance, drama and complexity.

Why it matters
Marked a shift from conformity towards individual interpretation, paving the way for the Baroque.

Key figures
Bronzino, 1503–72
Parmigianino, 1503–40
Jacopo Pontormo, 1494–1556
Giulio Romano, 1499–1546

Make the connection
High Renaissance, p.15
distortion/foreshortening, pp.84–5
asymmetry, p.109

Baroque

Against a backdrop of religious upheaval, Baroque art lasted from around 1600 until approximately 1750, helping to reassert the Roman Catholic Church's image. Monarchs, aristocrats and clergy used artworks to display authority, while variations of the style also appeared in Protestant regions – more restrained but still expressive.

A possible origin of the term is the Portuguese word *barroco* (Spanish: *barrueco*), used to describe an irregularly shaped pearl. The word 'Baroque' came to describe art that appeared irregular or that departed from established standards and proportions. This art is characterized by its dramatic intensity, rich colour palettes and strong contrasts of light and dark, often achieved through chiaroscuro or tenebrism. A sense of grandeur and emotional immediacy is central, with attention-grabbing compositions and figures in dynamic poses, their faces animated by strong feeling.

In painting, some artists pioneered the use of stark lighting and heightened realism to intensify the scene. Others brought vibrant colour, energetic form and sensuality to religious and mythological subjects, or explored psychological depth through portraits and biblical scenes. In sculpture, Gian Lorenzo Bernini combined spiritual fervour with movement and luxurious detail in works like the *Ecstasy of Saint Teresa* (below). With sweeping curves, gilding and elaborate ornamentation, architecture also embraced the Baroque aesthetic.

In a nutshell
Uniting spirituality and sensation, Baroque art dazzled with drama, grandeur and movement.

Why it matters
Reshaped visual storytelling, echoing religious fervour and political power across Europe.

Key figures
Gian Lorenzo Bernini, 1598–1680
Caravaggio, 1571–1610
Rembrandt, 1606–69
Peter Paul Rubens, 1577–1640

Make the connection
shadow/tone, pp.62–3
chiaroscuro, p.70
underpainting, p.81
foreshortening, p.85

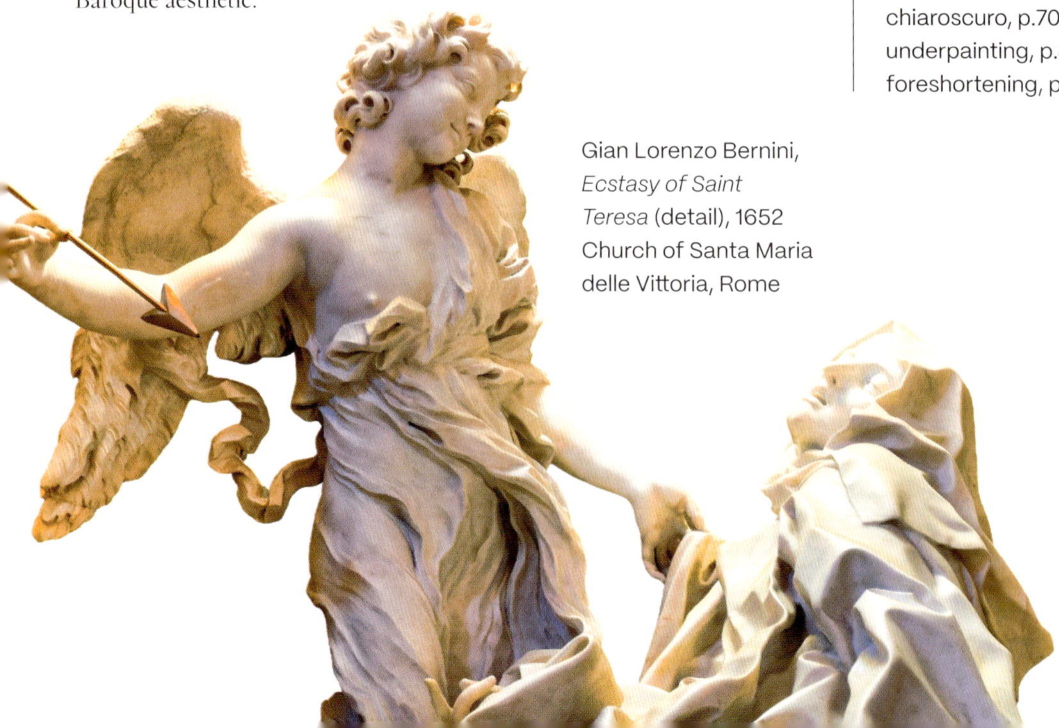

Gian Lorenzo Bernini, *Ecstasy of Saint Teresa* (detail), 1652
Church of Santa Maria delle Vittoria, Rome

Rococo

Baroque and Rococo are sometimes confused, because both are ornate and dramatic, but while the Baroque emphasizes grandeur, tension and power, Rococo (which lasted from approximately 1720 to 1780) favours lightness, grace and decorative whimsy.

Initially called 'the French style', Rococo art and design developed from the ostentation of Louis XIV's magnificent palace at Versailles – the home of the French court from 1682 – conveying the idea that art should adorn rather than inform. Louis XIV's successor, Louis XV, was influenced by his mistress Madame de Pompadour, who favoured lighter styles. The focus on light, fun and adornment became the Rococo style, where themes of romance, mythology, fantasy and everyday life were preferred over historical or religious subjects. Pastel colours, asymmetrical forms and curling lines appeared in scenes of idyllic love and leisurely garden parties. Rococo interiors feature mirrors, cherubs, stucco flourishes and shell motifs ('rococo' comes from the French word *rocaille*, meaning rock- or shell-work).

The late 17th and 18th centuries in Europe are often referred to as the Age of Enlightenment. Printing had made knowledge widely available, enabling the new urban middle classes to develop well-informed independence of thought. This inspired optimism for the future, and the Rococo style was its visual manifestation. Eventually, however, the Rococo came to be seen as superficial and frivolous, often associated with aristocratic excesses.

In a nutshell
Favouring pastel colours, curved forms and romantic themes, Rococo – intended to delight – marked a moment of escapism and charm.

Why it matters
Reflects 18th-century aristocratic taste, offering insight into pre-Revolutionary social culture and aesthetics.

Key figures
François Boucher, 1703–70
Jean-Honoré Fragonard, 1732–1806
Élisabeth Vigée Le Brun, 1755–1842
Antoine Watteau, 1684–1721

Make the connection
fresco, p.64
atmospheric perspective, p.78
symmetry, p.108
history painting, p.136

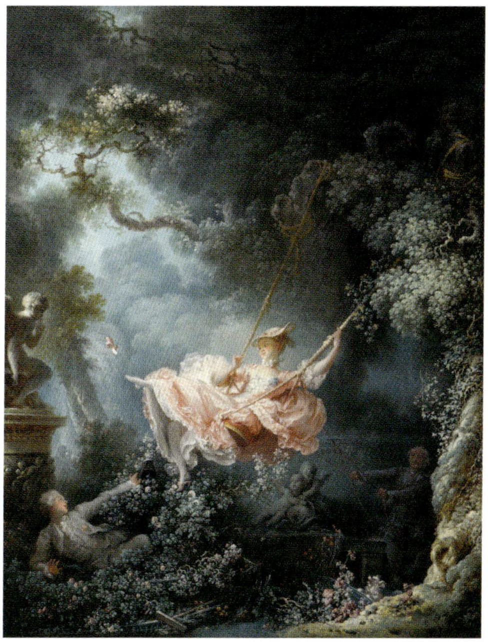

Jean-Honoré Fragonard, *The Swing*, 1767
Wallace Collection, London

Romanticism

Romanticism, with a capital 'R', was a sweeping artistic and intellectual movement that emphasized emotion, imagination and the sublime (see p.152). Flourishing from the late 18th to the mid-19th century, it challenged 18th-century rationalism; both Romanticism and the more ordered, structured Neoclassicism, a revival of Classical styles in art, reflect the revolutionary spirit of their times – the scientific and industrial innovations and political upheaval that saw the erosion of some traditions. While Neoclassicists embraced it all, Romanticists expressed concern about the rapid pace of change.

Romantic artists such as Eugène Delacroix, Francisco Goya and Caspar David Friedrich painted with intensity and emotion, communicating using skilful brushwork and bright palettes. Delacroix's *Liberty Leading the People* (1830) expressed the spirit of revolution, while Friedrich's *Wanderer Above the Sea of Fog* (below) induced contemplation and conveys the overwhelming scale of the natural world. Romantic landscapes often depict nature as overpowering, emphasizing the fragility of humanity in contrast.

Romanticists created emotionally charged scenes that evoked wonder or longing. They aimed to stir awe, contemplation or passion, and rather than copy external appearances, reveal internal truths.

In a nutshell
Opposing rationalism, restraint and cool Classicism, Romanticism conveyed emotion and the grandeur of nature.

Why it matters
Expanded the acceptance and exploration of emotion and drama in art.

Key figures
Eugène Delacroix, 1798–1863
Caspar David Friedrich, 1774–1840
Francisco Goya, 1746–1828
J. M. W. Turner, 1775–1851

Make the connection
chiaroscuro, p.70
picturesque, p.146
scumbling, p.86

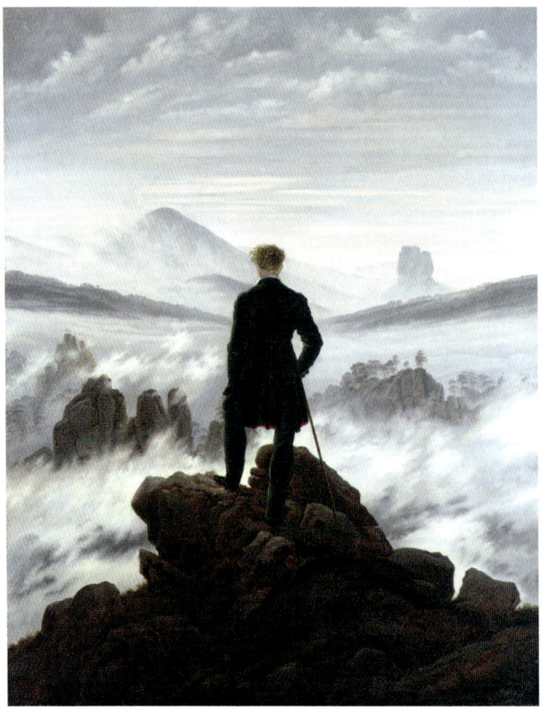

Caspar David Friedrich, *The Wanderer above the Sea of Fog*, 1818
Hamburger Kunsthalle

Realism

Realism broke away from the emotional approaches of Romanticism in favour of depicting the real world truthfully. The 1848 revolution in France and the rise of industrialization were contributing factors to this break, as were new scientific and technical discoveries, including the invention of photography, which challenged artists to reconsider the role of painting. At the same time, the rise of investigative journalism and sociology encouraged a more analytical view of society.

Realists portrayed the world as they saw it, with unadorned honesty. They focused on ordinary people, including labourers and workers, as they went about their daily tasks. This was in contrast with the mythological, heroic, aristocratic and religious themes that had dominated European art for centuries. One of the leading Realist painters, Gustave Courbet, declared, 'I cannot paint an angel because I have never seen one.'[1] In painting commonplace subjects and themes, they were also championing human rights. Pioneers like Courbet, Jean-François Millet and Honoré Daumier portrayed the poor – for example, in *A Burial at Ornans* (1849–50) and *The Gleaners* (below) – imbuing them with as much importance as earlier artists had bestowed on the rich.

By asserting that authenticity was more important than beauty or tradition, Realism influenced later movements, such as Naturalism and Impressionism, and became the basis for Modernism.

In a nutshell
Rejecting idealized or romanticized subjects or approaches, Realism portrayed ordinary life with raw honesty.

Why it matters
By focusing on everyday people and authentic experiences, Realism democratized art.

Key figures
Rosa Bonheur, 1822–99
Gustave Courbet, 1819–77
Honoré Daumier, 1808–79
Jean-François Millet, 1814–75

Make the connection
Impressionism, p.22
tone, p.63
observation, p.94
chalk pastel, p.114

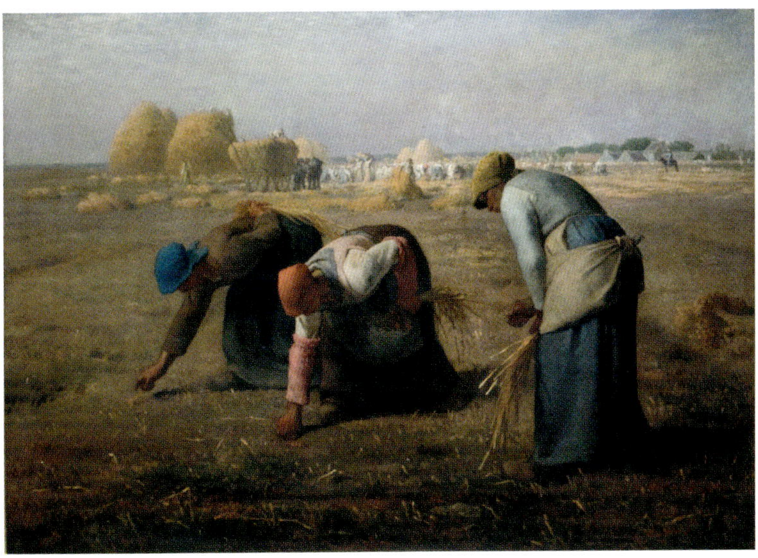

Jean-François Millet, *The Gleaners*, 1857
Musée d'Orsay, Paris

Impressionism

The term 'Impressionism' originated from a critical response to Claude Monet's *Impression, Sunrise* (below), a painting that exemplified the movement's loose brushwork and emphasis on sensory experience. Most of the artists involved shared a commitment to painting *en plein air* (outdoors) and a desire to depict the transient qualities of light and colour. Innovations in paint technology and the development of portable tin paint tubes enabled artists to work more spontaneously outside the studio.

Emerging in France in the 1860s and 1870s, Impressionism rejected the rigid academic standards of art at the time. The artists aimed to capture the fleeting moments of modern life, depicting everyday scenes with quick brushstrokes and vibrant, often unmixed colours (not black – many Impressionists, instead, made their darkest tones from mixtures of colours). Rather than focusing on details, they sought to convey an impression of a moment. When the official Salon rejected them, the Impressionists organized several independent exhibitions, from 1874 until 1886. Each artist had a distinct style, but they shared a commitment to visual immediacy and a rejection of the polished finish and historical or mythological themes favoured by the Académie des Beaux-Arts.

Within a few years, hostility towards Impressionism abated. Ultimately, it changed both the execution and the perception of art.

In a nutshell
Rejected academic tradition; captured fleeting moments with loose brushwork, bright colours and a focus on light.

Why it matters
Prioritized personal perception and everyday subjects over historical or idealized themes.

Key figures
Edgar Degas, 1834–1917
Claude Monet, 1840–1926
Camille Pissarro, 1830–1903
Pierre-Auguste Renoir, 1841–1919

Make the connection
mark, p.57
sketching, p.58
plein-air painting, p.104
warm/cool colours, pp.148–9

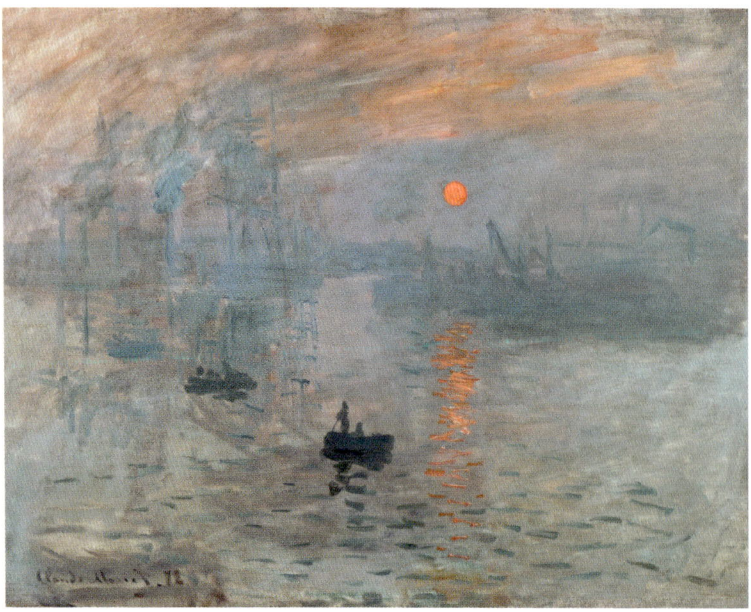

Claude Monet, *Impression, Sunrise*, 1872
Musée Marmottan Monet, Paris

Post-Impressionism

While the Impressionists focused on capturing visual impressions of light and movement, most Post-Impressionists moved beyond naturalistic representation as, from the 1880s, they sought to add structure, emotion and symbolic meaning to their work.

The Post-Impressionists did not form a cohesive group, and many pursued divergent goals. The term 'Post-Impressionism' was first used by art critic Roger Fry in London in 1910 to describe a group of artists, including Paul Cézanne, Paul Gauguin, Vincent van Gogh and Georges Seurat, all of whom had died by then. Each had a distinctive style and vision. Cézanne aimed to reduce natural forms to their structural essentials. Van Gogh used bold colours and dynamic brushstrokes to express psychological intensity. Gauguin drew on non-Western influences and symbolic imagery to evoke spiritual themes. Seurat developed pointillism (see p.96). They all shared a desire to push beyond Impressionism's emphasis on surface and explore deeper psychological, formal or spiritual content.

While most Post-Impressionists continued the bright colours and loose brushwork of Impressionism, they often employed more deliberate compositions and a stronger sense of form. These innovations marked a crucial transition from 19th-century naturalism to the abstract and conceptual tendencies of 20th-century Modern art, in which individual artistic exploration became central.

In a nutshell
Added structure, symbolism and emotional depth to Impressionism's colour and brushwork.

Why it matters
Vivid colours, bold forms and symbolic content conveyed emotion and structure, moving beyond the focus on fleeting visual impressions.

Key figures
Paul Cézanne, 1839–1906
Paul Gauguin, 1848–1903
Georges Seurat, 1859–91
Vincent van Gogh, 1853–90

Make the connection
impasto, p.100
pigment, p.111
symbolism, p.134
still life, p.138

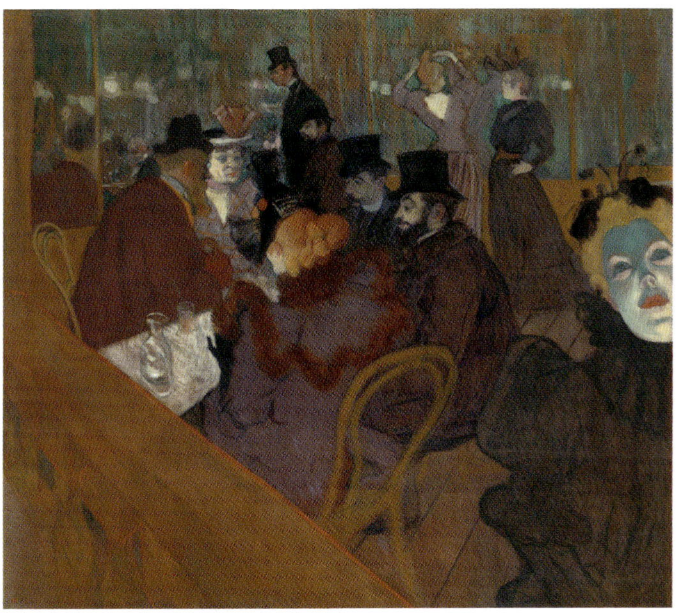

Henri de Toulouse-Lautrec, *At the Moulin Rouge*, 1892/95
Art Institute of Chicago

Primitive art

The term 'primitive' originally signified early forms of artistic expression, including tribal and Indigenous art from Africa, Oceania and the Americas, which were admired in the West for their raw stylizations. The term, however, implies a hierarchy that places Western art at the pinnacle of sophistication, often overlooking the rich traditions and meanings in these non-Western works.

'Primitivism' is a term used to describe the controversial tendency among Western artists, particularly in the late 19th and early 20th centuries, to draw inspiration from the visual cultures of non-Western societies. This was not a unified movement but a common rejection of the perceived artificiality and decadence of modern European life in favour of the elemental qualities of 'primitive' art. This fascination coincided with increased colonial expansion and the influx of African, Oceanic and Native American artefacts into European museums. Artists such as Paul Gauguin, Henri Matisse and Pablo Picasso were influenced by these objects and incorporated simplified forms, bold colours and symbolic motifs into their own work, emphasizing expression over realism. For example, African masks helped inspire Picasso's *Les Demoiselles d'Avignon* (below).

Primitivism developed through Western artists' dissatisfaction with their own cultures and a romanticization of others. Although unique to each artist, Primitivism perpetuated stereotypes and colonial attitudes; the term 'primitive' reflects a Eurocentric hierarchy.

In a nutshell
Aspects of early non-Western art reinterpreted in simplified, symbolic ways by Western artists.

Why it matters
Challenged Western aesthetics, inspiring some modern movements and raising questions about cultural appropriation.

Key figures
Marc Chagall, 1887–1985
Paul Gauguin, 1848–1903

Make the connection
Modernism, p.34
Cubism/Futurism, pp.36–7
contrast, p.92

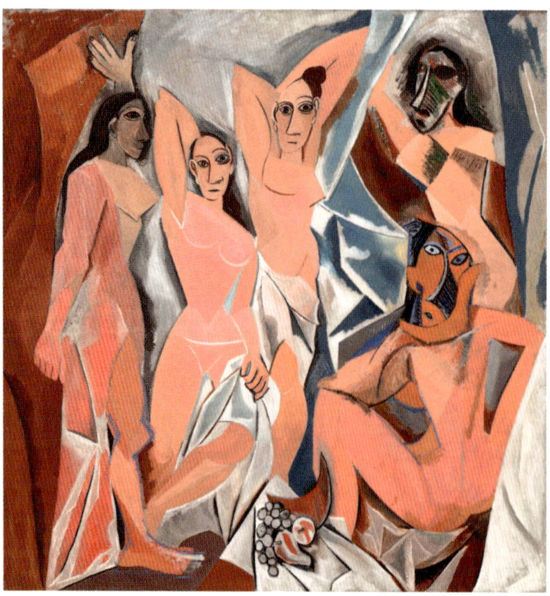

Pablo Picasso, *Les Demoiselles d'Avignon*, 1907
Museum of Modern Art (MoMA), New York

Naïve art

Unpretentious and unsophisticated, Naïve art is produced by self-taught artists with little or no formal training, in contrast to the academically trained figures often highlighted in mainstream art history. Naïve artworks are typically characterized by simplified forms, bright colours, flattened space and a disregard for conventional rules of perspective, proportion and composition.

Importantly, Naïve art is not a discrete historical movement, but a descriptive term applied to work made outside established academic traditions. While Primitivism refers to late 19th- and early 20th-century Western artists who deliberately adopted simplified forms inspired by non-Western or prehistoric art to challenge academic conventions, Naïve art emerges organically from the artists themselves. Its visual language emerges through individual intuition and imagination.

Naïve art gained wider recognition in the early 20th century, as collectors and modern artists increasingly valued unfiltered expression over academic polish. The most celebrated Naïve artist is Henri Rousseau, whose dreamlike scenes depict imagined jungles he had never encountered (below).

Closely related, Art Brut ('Raw Art') emerged in mid-20th-century France to describe self-taught artists working outside the art establishment. While both emphasize spontaneity, Art Brut often conveys greater intensity than Naïve art.

In a nutshell
Created by the untrained, Naïve art often features flat shapes, simplified perspectives and bright colours.

Why it matters
Influencing several Modernist movements, Naïve art respected honesty and challenged academic traditions.

Key figures
Séraphine Louis, 1864–1942
Grandma Moses, 1860–1961
Henri Rousseau, 1844–1910
Alfred Wallis, 1855–1942

Make the connection
line, p.56
imagination, p.95
warm/cool colours, pp.148–9

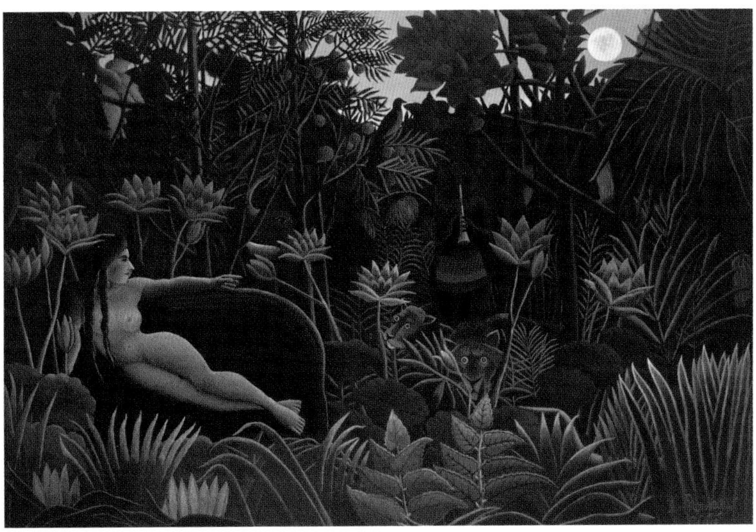

Henri Rousseau, *The Dream*, 1910
Museum of Modern Art (MoMA), New York

Ukiyo-e

Translating as 'Pictures of the Floating World', Ukiyo-e is a genre of Japanese art that primarily comprises paintings and woodblock prints. The 'floating world' (ukiyo) refers to the transient and pleasure-seeking culture of Edo-period Japan (1603–1868), also known as the Tokugawa period, characterized by its vibrant urban lifestyle and beautiful landscapes. 'E' means pictures.

Ukiyo-e prints, which depict actors, courtesans, sumo wrestlers, landscapes and the seasons, were mass-produced and affordable, in comparison to elite ink painting. The newly affluent yet socially low-ranking merchant class of cities like Edo (modern-day Tokyo) enthusiastically bought this accessible art form. The production of a single print was a collaborative effort; the *eshi* (artist) designed the image, the *horishi* (carver) chiselled the woodblocks, the *surishi* (printer) applied ink and pressed the paper, and the *hanmoto* (publisher) financed and distributed the work. Early prints were monochrome, but by the mid-18th century, full-colour *nishiki-e* ('brocade prints') became more common.

Ukiyo-e artists blended realism with stylization – flattened perspective, bold outlines, asymmetrical composition and bright colour. Images by Katsushika Hokusai and Utagawa Hiroshige – including 'Under the Wave off Kanagawa' (below) – are particularly renowned. Although Ukiyo-e declined after the Meiji Restoration (1868), which restored imperial rule in Japan, it profoundly influenced Impressionism, Art Nouveau and Post-Impressionism.

In a nutshell
A Japanese art style of woodblock prints that capture fleeting urban pleasures, landscapes and legends.

Why it matters
It shaped Japanese visual culture and profoundly influenced Western Modern art.

Key figures
Utagawa Hiroshige, 1797–1858
Katsushika Hokusai, 1760–1849
Tōshūsai Sharaku, *fl.*1794/95
Kitagawa Utamaro, d.1806

Make the connection
line, p.56
woodcut, p.72
unity, p.93
asymmetry, p.109

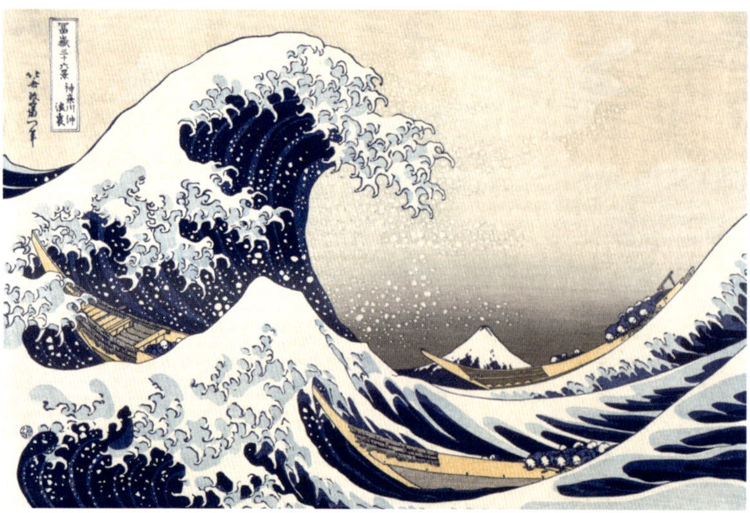

Katsushika Hokusai, 'Under the Wave off Kanagawa', or 'The Great Wave', from the series *36 Views of Mt Fuji*, *c.*1830–31
Private collection

Cloisonnism

Mainly developed by French artists Émile Bernard and Louis Anquetin, and later embraced by Paul Gauguin, Cloisonnism emerged in the late 19th century. The name was coined in 1888 by art critic Édouard Dujardin, from the decorative metalwork technique of cloisonné, which creates compartments (cloisons) filled with coloured enamel. Both Ukiyo-e and Cloisonnism used bold outlines and flat areas of colour, but Ukiyo-e occurred in Japanese painting and woodblock prints, while Cloisonnism was a Western Post-Impressionist style that emphasized decorative abstraction.

Cloisonnists painted solid, flat areas of colour rather than using tonal contrasts to define forms, which gave their work a bold, graphic quality. Dark outlines surrounded figures and objects, evocative of stained-glass windows or Japanese woodblock prints, both of which strongly influenced the movement. Rather than striving for realism, Cloisonnism emphasized symbolic representation and emotional resonance. By flattening perspective and simplifying colour, artists could evoke mood and meaning more directly. Although this was not a major movement, it helped to prepare the way for later Modernist movements, including Synthetism and Neo-plasticism.

The Yellow Christ (below) by Paul Gauguin, Émile Bernard's *Breton Women in the Meadow* (1888) and Louis Anquetin's *Avenue de Clichy: Five O'Clock in the Evening* (1887) all convey the spiritual intensity and stylistic innovation of Cloisonnism.

In a nutshell
Uses flat colour fields bounded by dark outlines to create symbolic, decorative imagery.

Why it matters
It broke from realism, influencing Symbolism and early Modernist movements.

Key figures
Louis Anquetin, 1861–1932
Émile Bernard, 1868–1941
Paul Gauguin, 1848–1903

Make the connection
Impressionism/ Post-Impressionism, pp.22–3
Japonisme, p.28
line, p.56

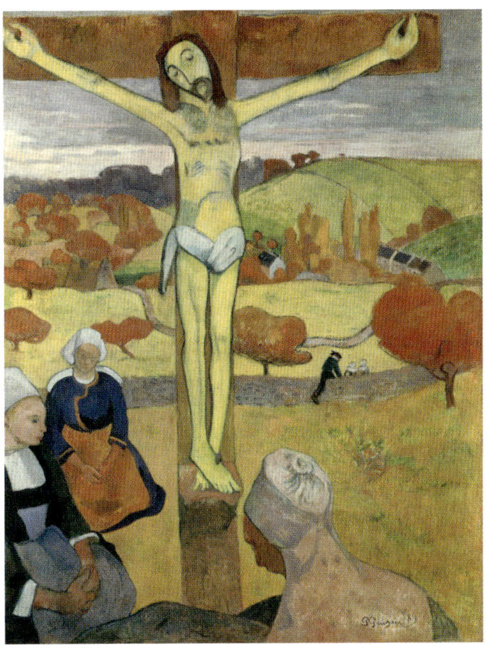

Paul Gauguin, *The Yellow Christ*, 1889
Albright Knox Art Gallery, Buffalo

Japonisme

The term 'Japonisme' was devised by French critic Philippe Burty in 1872, 18 years after Japan reopened to international trade following centuries of isolation. The arrival of Japanese prints, ceramics, textiles and other decorative arts in Europe sparked a wave of fascination. Japonisme refers, then, to the influence of Japanese art on the West, particularly in France and Britain, from 1858 onwards.

Ukiyo-e art (see p.26), especially the woodblock prints, was especially influential, with artists such as Hokusai and Hiroshige inspiring European painters with their flattened perspectives, bright colours, asymmetrical compositions and bold outlines. These features contrasted with traditional academic realism and linear perspective. Artists associated with Impressionism and Post-Impressionism were particularly inspired. Among others, Claude Monet, James McNeill Whistler, Edgar Degas and Vincent van Gogh collected Japanese prints and reinterpreted their sense of light, space and colour, as well as their reduced, asymmetrical compositions.

Japonisme also influenced design, appearing in movements such as Art Nouveau and the Aesthetic Movement, with designers such as Christopher Dresser and the architect Edward William Godwin. The impact of Japonisme provoked a broader rethinking of composition in general and the role of ornament in art.

Japonisme has a powerful legacy, as one of the first significant artistic exchanges between the East and West in the modern era.

In a nutshell
Western fascination with Japanese art and design, particularly Ukiyo-e prints, influenced 19th-century European aesthetics.

Why it matters
Transformed composition, perspective and decoration in modern Western art.

Key figures
Mary Cassatt, 1844–1926
Edgar Degas, 1834–1917
Claude Monet, 1840–1926
Vincent van Gogh, 1853–90

Make the connection
Impressionism/Post-Impressionism, pp.22–3
Art Nouveau , p.32
line , p.56
asymmetry, p.109

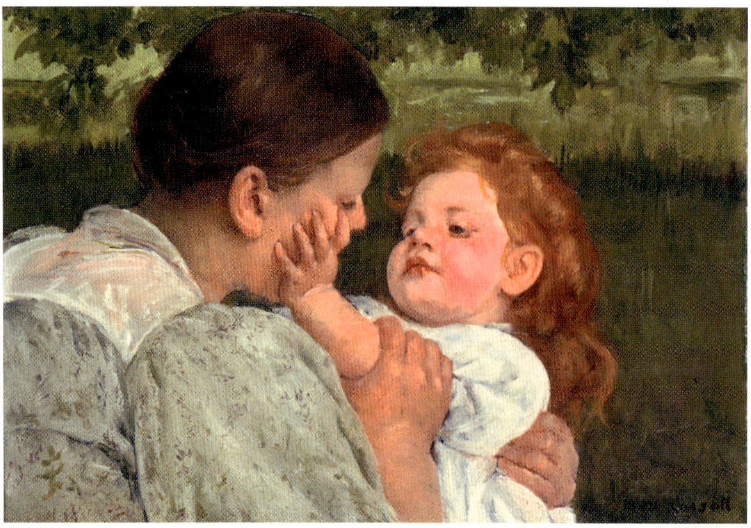

Mary Cassatt, *Maternal Caress*, *c.*1896
Philadelphia Museum of Art

Orientalism

Referring to the depiction of the Middle East, North Africa and parts of Asia by Western artists during the 19th century, Orientalism was fuelled by colonial expansion, archaeological discovery and increased travel. It reflected a general, growing European fascination with what was perceived as exotic, sensual and culturally different. Orientalists portrayed light, colour and texture, but reinforced colonial beliefs and ideologies in their depictions of Eastern cultures.

Orientalism was a trend, not a formal school, across painting, literature and the decorative arts. Artists portrayed scenes of deserts, bustling markets, religious rituals and grand architecture, often with romanticized or imagined details. Rarely accurate representations, these project European stereotypes about Eastern life.

French artists were particularly prominent in Orientalism. Jean-Léon Gérôme, for example, painted meticulously detailed scenes of Islamic architecture, slave markets and bathhouses. Eugène Delacroix, inspired by his 1832 trip to Morocco and Algeria, infused his works with dramatic colour and movement. British artists such as John Frederick Lewis also contributed.

In the 20th century, Edward Said's book *Orientalism* (1978) declared that such depictions were part of a broad system of cultural domination. Nowadays, the technical accomplishments of the art continue to be admired, but the focus and content are generally reconsidered and reassessed.

In a nutshell
Western artists' depictions of aspects of the Middle East, North Africa and Asia; reflected colonial viewpoints.

Why it matters
For years, Orientalist art shaped European perceptions of the 'East' and reflected colonial attitudes.

Key figures
Adolphe Aze, 1823–84
Henriette Browne, 1829–1901
Jean-Léon Gérôme, 1824–1904
John Frederick Lewis, 1804–86

Make the connection
Romanticism, p.21
verisimilitude, p.107

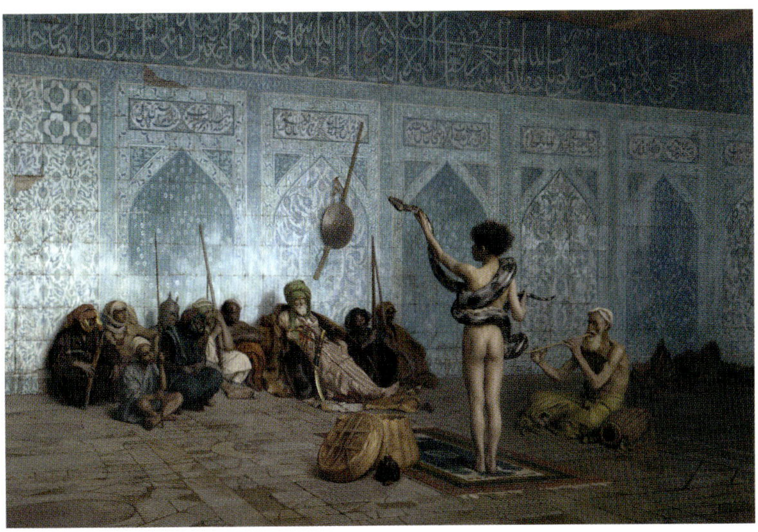

Jean-Léon Gérôme, *The Snake Charmer*, c.1879
Sterling and Francine Clark Art Institute, Williamstown

Expressionism

Developing in the early 20th century, chiefly in Germany, partly as a reaction against Realism (see p.21) and Impressionism, and building on Post-Impressionist ideas, Expressionism rejected the objective depiction of the external world. Instead, Expressionists sought to convey their emotional and psychological experiences and evoke intense feelings, such as anxiety, despair or alienation. They worked with distorted forms, exaggerated colours and dynamic brushwork.

Expressionist art emerged roughly concurrently across Germany, reflecting a society that felt increasingly uncomfortable and anxious about the modern world. More than outer realities, the art emphasized the artists' inner worlds. It was deeply personal to each artist and yet reflected the social tensions and existential crises of the time, especially in the years leading up to and following the First World War. Using bold, unnatural colour and exaggerations, Expressionists emphasized mood over realism, exploring themes such as isolation, urban chaos, spiritual conflict and societal damage; they painted angular, contorted figures and other objects.

Two major Expressionist groups were Die Brücke (The Bridge), founded in Dresden in 1905, which included Ernst Ludwig Kirchner and Emil Nolde, and Der Blaue Reiter (The Blue Rider), formed in Munich in 1911, led by Wassily Kandinsky and Franz Marc.

Expressionism strongly influenced art movements that aimed to express subjective feeling rather than objective appearances.

In a nutshell
An early 20th-century German movement that departed from the objective depiction of the external world in search of internal truth.

Why it matters
Rejected traditional lifelike or 'comfortable' aesthetics in favour of raw, visceral expression.

Key figures
Wassily Kandinsky, 1866–1944
Ernst Ludwig Kirchner, 1880–1938
Franz Marc, 1880–1916
Edvard Munch, 1863–1944

Make the connection
Impressionism/Post-Impressionism, pp.22–3
line/mark, pp.56–7
warm/cool colours, pp.148–9

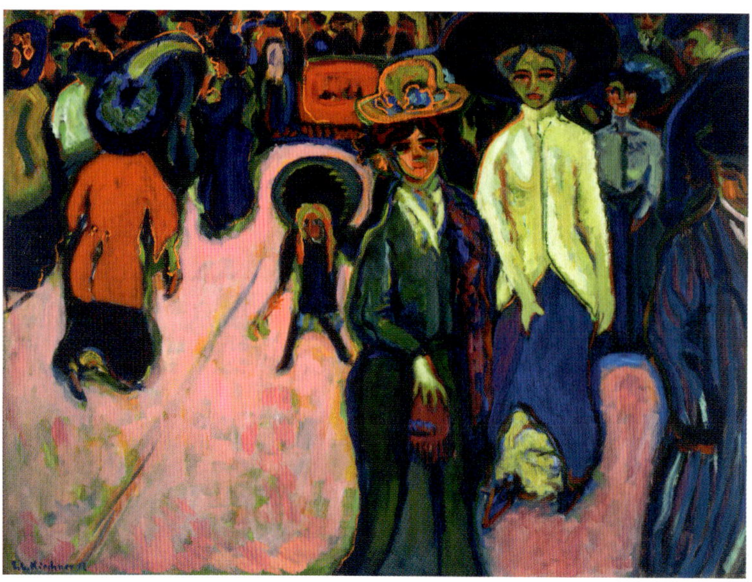

Ernst Ludwig Kirchner, *Rue, Dresden* (Germany), 1908
Museum of Modern Art (MoMA), New York

Abstract Expressionism

From 1941, when America entered the Second World War, shocking images and descriptions of the atrocities that were occurring in Europe were seen by the American public. By the mid-1940s, several artists working in and around New York had decided to express their feelings about the state of the world. They employed abstraction to explore both these feelings and the human condition – in this respect, the origins of their art were similar to those of German Expressionism. In general, both movements prioritized emotional intensity and individual expression, but Expressionists often depicted recognizable subjects distorted for effect, while Abstract Expressionists abandoned figurative forms entirely.

The Abstract Expressionists were a small group of loosely associated artists. The painters often used dynamic, sweeping brushstrokes to convey their energy and emotions, and sculptors shared that emotional intensity and experimental spirit, often using industrial or found materials. The art was frequently large and imposing, designed to evoke awe or introspection. Several Abstract Expressionists practised automatism, a method of creating art without conscious thought.

Influenced by European movements including Surrealism (see p.43) and Cubism (p.36), Abstract Expressionism became America's first significant international art movement, making the US the centre of avant-garde art. The movement is often divided into two stylistic camps: Action Painting and Colour Field painting (pp.44–5).

In a nutshell
An American abstract art movement that emerged during the 1940s and 1950s, characterized by emotional intensity.

Why it matters
It was the first American artistic movement to achieve international influence, transferring the centre of art from Europe (specifically Paris) to New York.

Key figures
Helen Frankenthaler, 1928–2011
Willem de Kooning, 1904–97
Jackson Pollock, 1912–56
Mark Rothko, 1903–70

Make the connection
impasto, p.100
abstract, p.128

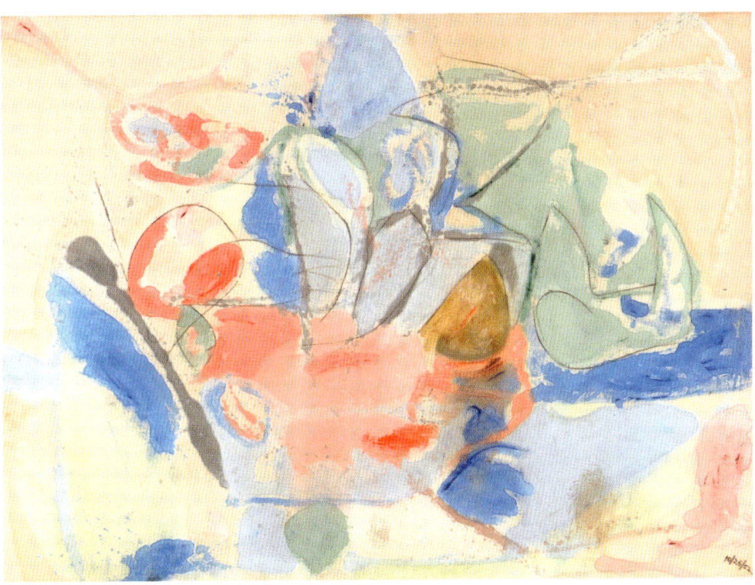

Helen Frankenthaler, *Mountains and Sea*, 1952
National Gallery of Art, Washington D.C.

Art Nouveau

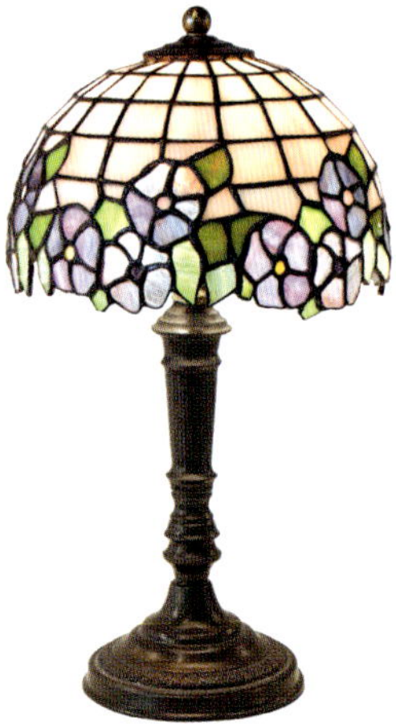

In many ways a response to the Industrial Revolution, Art Nouveau was an international art and design movement that peaked between 1890 and 1910. Emphasizing organic forms, flowing lines and decorative elegance, it aimed to break down the traditional hierarchy between fine and applied arts.

Art Nouveau practitioners employed a diverse range of materials, including iron, glass, pewter, bronze and silver. Influenced by Symbolism, as well as by Celtic and Japanese art, the style was characterized by sinuous and asymmetrical shapes and soft colours, frequently inspired by natural forms such as the curves of plants, flowers, insects and the female form. Artists and designers sought to create total works of art, or *Gesamtkunstwerk*, in which buildings, interiors and furnishings were harmoniously unified.

The name 'Art Nouveau' derives from the Maison de l'Art Nouveau, an interior design shop that opened in Paris in 1896, specifically to promote Modern art. Art Nouveau, meaning 'New Art' in French, reflects the movement's intention to create a contemporary aesthetic for the new century. Initially, it was known in different countries by various names. In Germany, it was *Jugendstil*, derived from a magazine of the same name. In Italy, it was *Stile Liberty*, after the London store owned by Arthur Lasenby Liberty. In Spain, it was Modernista; in France, Modern Style (or *Style Nouvelle* – new style); and in Austria it was *Sezessionstil*, or Vienna Succession.

In a nutshell
A decorative style marked by flowing lines, floral motifs and organic forms, aiming to unify art and design.

Why it matters
The first movement to give equal weight to fine art and design; paved the way for Modernist movements such as Art Deco and Bauhaus.

Key figures
Antoni Gaudí, 1852–1926
Victor Horta, 1861–1947
Alphonse Mucha, 1860–1939

Make the connection
Japonisme, p.28
art/design, pp.54–5
line, p.56
asymmetry, p.109
cool colours, p.149

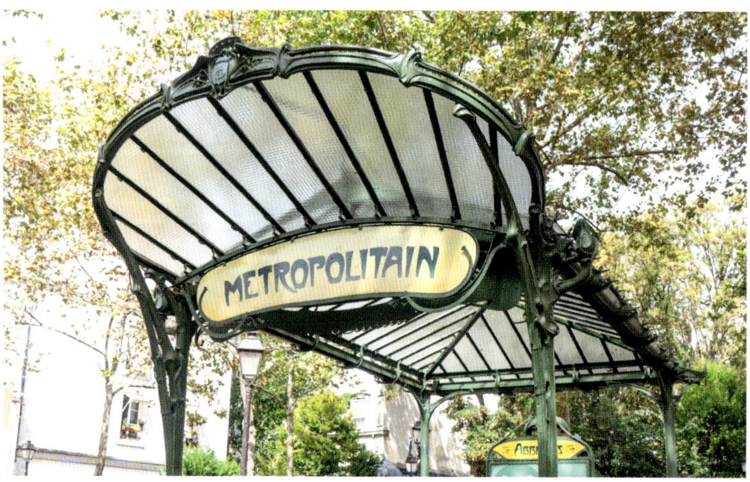

Above: Tiffany-style table lamp

Left: Entrance to the Paris Métro, Abbesses station, designed by Hector Guimard, opened 1913

Art Deco

A glamorous design style that emerged in the early 20th century, Art Deco influenced everything from architecture and fashion to furniture and graphic design. Using sleek materials, Art Deco designs often featured sunbursts, zigzags and symmetry (in contrast to the soft sinews of Art Nouveau). It was all about modernity, luxury and progress. Designs featured modern materials such as chrome, reinforced concrete, steel, glass and marble.

Beginning in France before the First World War, Art Deco evolved from earlier movements, including Art Nouveau and the Vienna Secession, and was influenced by Cubism, Fauvism, Futurism and the Ballets Russes. It also drew inspiration from ancient Egypt, following the discovery of Tutankhamun's tomb by Howard Carter in 1922. Initially, it was not perceived as one homogenous style and was referred to by various names, including *Style Moderne* and *Style Contemporain*.

The style gained international attention at the Exposition Internationale des Arts Décoratifs et Industriels Modernes in Paris in 1925, where new decorative arts were displayed that encapsulated the machine age, featuring speed, power and innovation. It gave the movement its name: Art Deco, short for Arts Décoratifs. Art Deco became synonymous with the optimism and glamour of the era. However, it was not until 1966 that the term Art Deco was officially adopted to describe the movement retrospectively.

In a nutshell
A sleek, geometric design style that blended luxury with modernity, expressed in art, design and architecture.

Why it matters
Lasting until the 1940s, Art Deco symbolized progress, elegance and industrial innovation.

Key figures
René Lalique, 1860–1945
Tamara de Lempicka, 1894–1980
Émile-Jacques Ruhlmann, 1879–1933

Make the connection
Cubism/Futurism, pp.36–7
line, p.56
tone, p.63

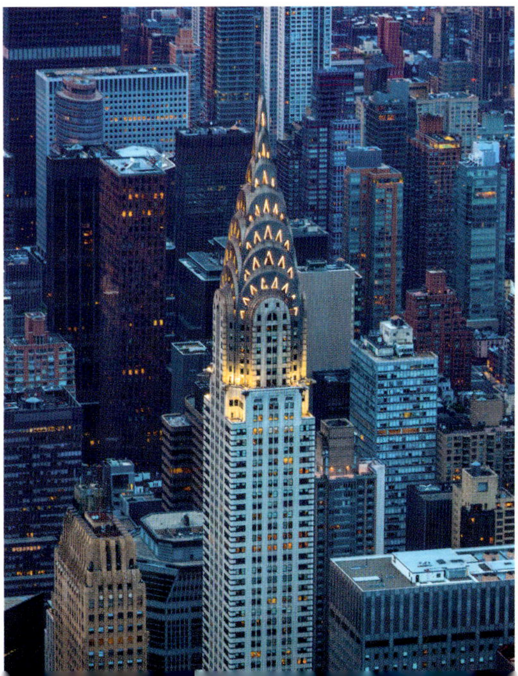

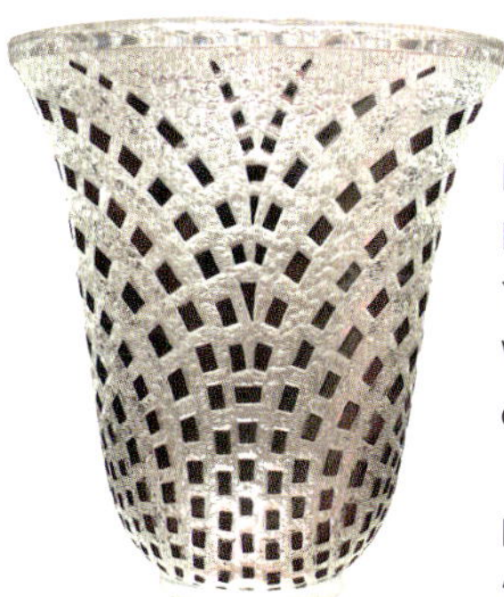

Far left: Chrysler Building, New York, designed by William Van Alen, completed 1930

Left: René Lalique, 'Damiers' vase, 1935

Modernism

A broad cultural, artistic and intellectual movement that emerged in the late 19th century, Modernism reached its peak in the 1930s and essentially came to an end by 1950. Driven by the observation that the world was changing at an unprecedented pace, Modernists decided that art, design and literature needed to reflect these transformations coherently.

Challenging traditional ideas about art, Modernist artists such as Pablo Picasso, Wassily Kandinsky and Henri Matisse embraced abstraction and experimentation. They used bold colours, simplified shapes and distorted forms to express inner experiences. Movements like Cubism, Futurism and Surrealism are all Modernist art, each offering a different interpretation of how to break from the past.

In design, Modernism focused on simplicity, functionality and the idea that 'form follows function'. Designers shifted away from decorative excess to embrace clean lines, geometric shapes and an efficient use of materials. The Bauhaus school in Germany epitomized this approach, with figures such as Walter Gropius and Marcel Breuer uniting art, craft and industrial design. Charlotte Perriand and Le Corbusier designed Modernist buildings and interiors, emphasizing clean lines, light, comfort and simplicity.

Modernism was exemplified by artists and designers who challenged conventions. It was about innovation, progress and paring down, with a shared belief in reducing excess and fuss.

In a nutshell
An early-20th-century cultural movement concerned with reshaping artistic expression to reflect the modern era.

Why it matters
Reflecting the rapidly changing world, Modernism reshaped generations of art and design traditions.

Key figures
Marcel Duchamp, 1887–1968
Henri Matisse, 1869–1954
Piet Mondrian, 1872–1944
Pablo Picasso, 1881–1973

Make the connection
Cubism/Futurism, pp.36–7
Surrealism , p.43
innovation, p.133

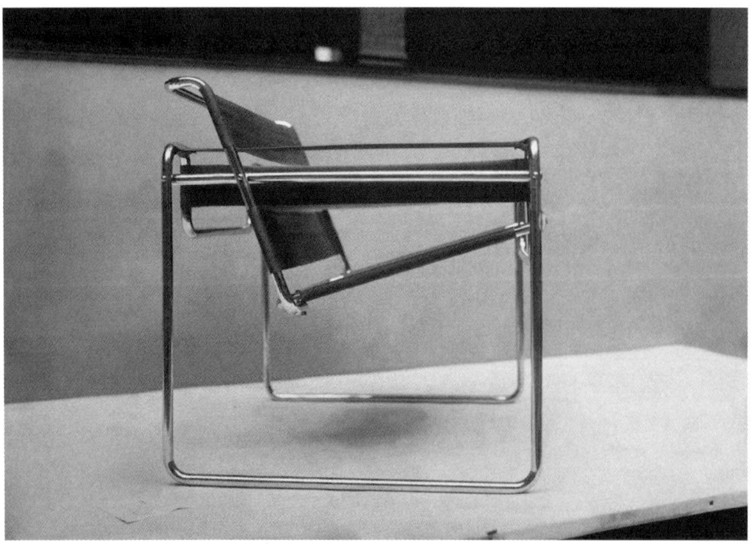

Marcel Breuer, Wassily Chair, B3, designed 1925–6

Postmodernism

After the horrors of the Second World War, people began questioning Modernism's exaltation of progress, rationality and objective truth. Postmodernism was a reaction that developed from the late 1940s to the early 1950s, resisting the notion of a single approach, and it became more broadly recognized in the 1960s and 1970s. Peaking in the 1970s and 1980s, it remained popular until the early 2000s, when it was succeeded by other movements, including Metamodernism, Digimodernism and Post-Postmodernism.

Like Modernism, Postmodernism appeared in art, design, architecture and literature, but there the similarities ended: Postmodern practitioners explored eclectic, colourful styles, featuring playful contradictions and provocations. Postmodernists embraced pop culture, irony and media saturation, blurring the boundaries between 'high' and 'low' art. Civil rights, feminist, LGBTQ+ and anti-colonial movements had destabilized older power structures, encouraging more pluralistic worldviews.

Eventually, however, the constant irony, mix of styles and deconstruction was pushed aside. The internet age and social media required new approaches and concepts.

Artists working under the Postmodern 'umbrella' included Jean-Michel Basquiat, with his graffiti-inspired Neo-Expressionism; Barbara Kruger, with her text-based feminist art; Cindy Sherman, with her photographic self-portraits that challenge identity and representation; and Jenny Holzer, with the provocative messages of her LED-based text art. In architecture, notable figures included Robert Venturi, who championed the theory of 'Less is a bore' and Frank Gehry (below) who pioneered Deconstructivist forms.

In a nutshell
A rejection of Modernism's ideals, instead embracing irony and pluralism.

Why it matters
Questioned objectivity and authority.

Key figures
Jean-Michel Basquiat, 1960–88
Barbara Kruger, b.1945
Robert Rauschenberg, 1925–2008

Make the connection
Pop art, p.46
contrast, p.92
imagination, p.95
assemblage, p.102

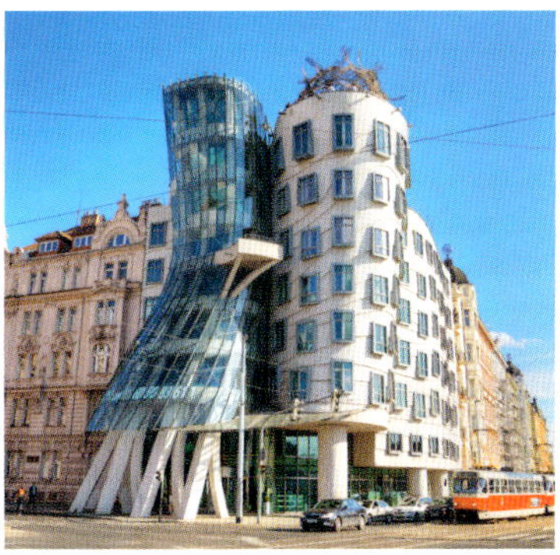

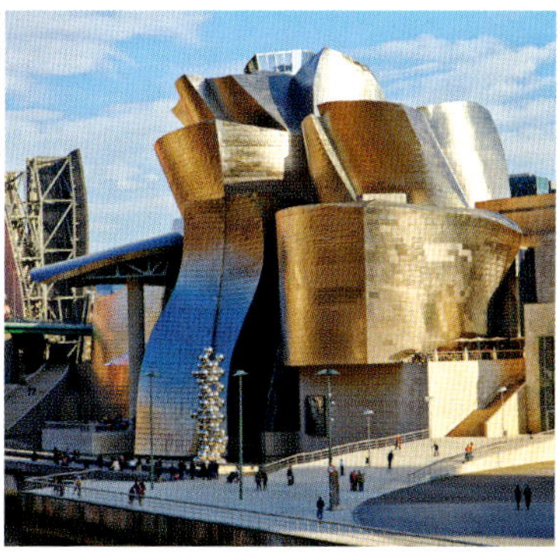

Below left: 'Dancing House' (Nationale-Nederlanden building), Prague, designed by Vlado Milunić and Frank Gehry, completed 1996; right: Guggenheim Museum Bilbao, designed by Frank Gehry, 1993–7

Cubism

By rejecting linear perspective (see p.79), realistic modelling and the illusion of depth, Cubists sought to represent objects from multiple viewpoints simultaneously. Anything represented looked like it was made up of geometric shapes. This approach was intended to show more of a subject, but it actually made images difficult to interpret.

Cubism began in Paris in 1907. Pablo Picasso and Georges Braque pioneered it after seeing Paul Cézanne's retrospective exhibition at the Salon d'Automne that year. Cézanne's exploration of multiple perspectives and his method of breaking natural forms into geometric shapes helped to inspire Cubism's radical departure from traditional representation. Cubism was also influenced by African tribal art, which simplified shapes to their essence.

In Picasso and Braque's Cubism, there were two main phases: Analytical Cubism (1909–12) was characterized by muted colour palettes and intricate deconstructions. Synthetic Cubism (1912 onwards) introduced brighter colours, simpler shapes and collage elements. Juan Gris developed a more systematic and crisply structured variant that emphasized clarity.

Cubism's radical rethinking of visual representation influenced later movements, including Futurism (p.37), Rayonism, Orphism, Suprematism, Constructivism and Abstract Expressionism (p.31).

In a nutshell
Aiming to be more representative than traditional imagery, Cubism depicted objects from multiple viewpoints simultaneously.

Why it matters
Revolutionized the way visual artists thought, paving the way for abstraction and Modernist experimentation.

Key figures
Georges Braque, 1882–1963
Juan Gris, 1887–1927
Fernand Léger, 1881–1955
Pablo Picasso, 1881–1973

Make the connection
Suprematism/Constructivism, pp.38–9
observation, p.94
still life, p.138

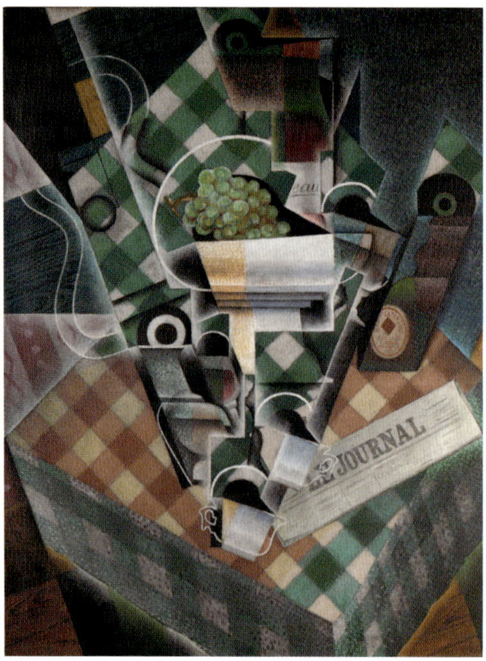

Juan Gris, *Still Life with Checked Tablecloth*, 1915
The Metropolitan Museum of Art, New York

Futurism

While the Cubists were working in France, an avant-garde art movement was launched in Italy with the publication of *The Futurist Manifesto* (1909) by poet Filippo Tommaso Marinetti. Like the Cubists, Futurists shrugged off artistic traditions and conventional realism; in their place, they celebrated the modern world, including machines, violence and the energy of urban life.

Rejecting the past, Futurists called for the destruction of museums and libraries; they were obsessed with speed, aggression and technological prowess. They captured a sense of movement through fragmented forms, bold lines and vibrant colours. Their works depict cities under construction, cars racing and figures in motion.

As many Futurists believed that war would cleanse the world and instigate cultural renewal, they looked forward to the impending global conflict. Politically, some Futurists aligned with nationalism and later with Fascism, which has complicated the movement's legacy. By 1916, after several of the main protagonists died during the First World War, it had lost its momentum. However, Futurist ideas appeared in later movements such as Constructivism and Dada (p.42), as well as in aspects of modern graphic design.

Futurism was a sweeping demand to discard the past and embrace the industrialized future, with all its contradictions, explosive energy and, as it turned out, danger.

In a nutshell
Rejected the past and tradition, but celebrated speed, technology and modernity.

Why it matters
Fascination with technology and dynamic movement radically reshaped visual language and inspired later avant-garde movements.

Key figures
Giacomo Balla, 1871–1958
Umberto Boccioni, 1882–1916
Filippo Tommaso Marinetti, 1876–1944
Gino Severini, 1883–1966

Make the connection
Suprematism/Constructivism, pp.38–9
line, p.56
modelling, p.60
warm colours, p.148

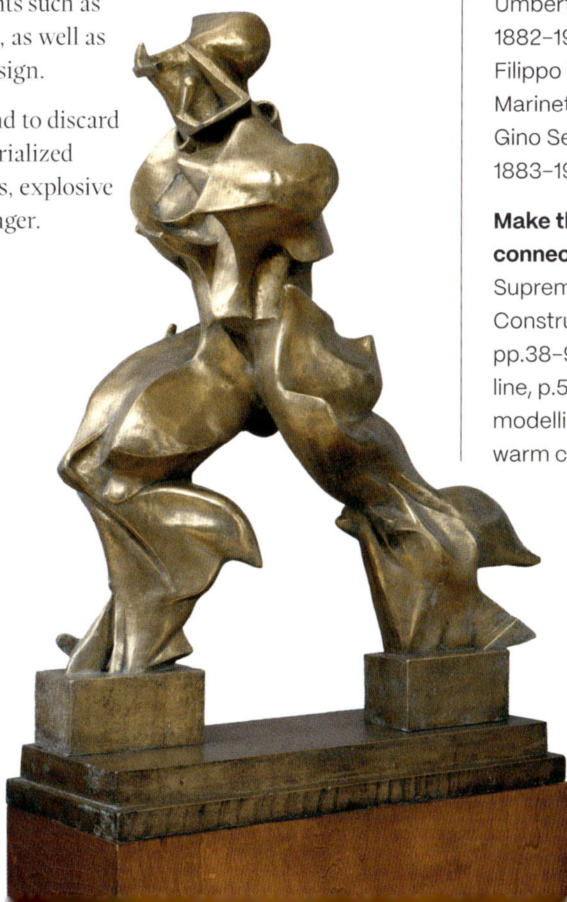

Umberto Boccioni, *Unique Forms of Continuity in Space*, 1913
Metropolitan Museum of Art, New York

Suprematism

Deriving directly from Cubism and Futurism, Suprematism was invented in Russia by Ukrainian-born artist Kazimir Malevich. His aim, he said, was 'to free art from the ballast of objectivity'.[2] Suprematists eliminated any evocative, symbolic or narrative content, condensing all elements to their simplest, purest forms.

In December 1915 in Petrograd (now St Petersburg), Malevich showed his work at *0,10 the Last Futurist Exhibition*. His paintings consisted solely of rectangles, circles, triangles and crosses, with flat, smooth paint and no attempt at tonal gradation or lifelike representations. His shapes, lines and colours appeared to float on his canvases. To accompany the exhibition, he wrote a leaflet titled *From Cubism and Futurism to Suprematism: The New Realism in Painting*, describing the progression of avant-garde art movements since through the 20th century. Malevich was also influenced by primitive art, but unlike those earlier art styles, his images contained no references to the surrounding world. Mathematics, philosophy and theories about the 'fourth dimension' were among his other preoccupations.

Almost coinciding with the Russian Revolution of 1917, the Suprematist movement was based on idealistic principles. Members believed that they were helping to shape a new society in which acquisitiveness would be replaced with spiritual freedom. Although not religious, Malevich believed his approach to art was spiritual.

In a nutshell
A Russian abstract art movement emphasizing pure geometric forms and emotional expression over realism.

Why it matters
Pioneered non-objective art, influencing Bauhaus, De Stijl and modern design.

Key figures
El Lissitzky, 1890–1941
Kazimir Malevich, 1879–1935
Lyubov Popova, 1889–1924

Make the connection
Cubism/Futurism, pp.36–7
De Stijl/Bauhaus, pp.40–1

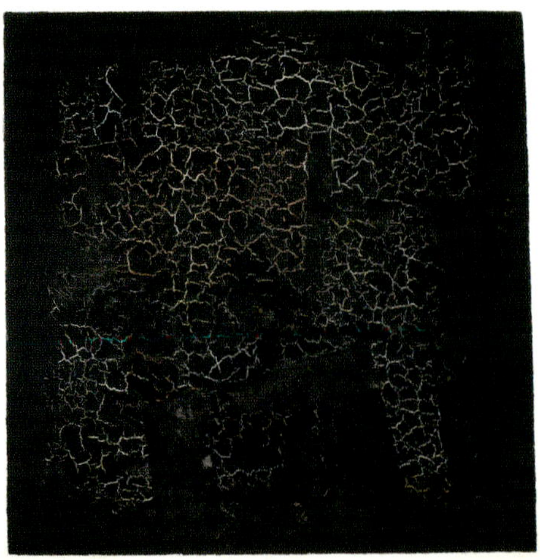

Kazimir Malevich, *Black Square*, 1915
Tretyakov Gallery, Moscow

Constructivism

Like Suprematism, Constructivism was inspired by Cubism and Futurism. In 1913, Vladimir Tatlin travelled from Russia to Paris, where he visited Picasso and saw his experiments with three-dimensional collage constructions. On his return to Russia, Tatlin began creating abstract constructions using industrial and scrap materials. He said that the space around and between them – the negative space – was as important as the structures themselves.

Whereas the Suprematists sought pure artistic expression independent of practical or political function, Constructivists believed that their art would instigate social change and progress. From 1915, Tatlin worked with Alexander Rodchenko to produce purely abstract designs, using industrial materials, geometric shapes and utilitarian design, that aligned with the ideals of the new Soviet society. The movement emphasized *faktura* (material properties) and *tektonika* (spatial presence), aiming to integrate art into everyday life.

Immediately following the 1917 Russian Revolution, more artists returned to Russia from Europe, including the brothers Naum Gabo and Antoine Pevsner, as well as Wassily Kandinsky. Pevsner named the movement 'Constructivism', declaring that its artists were concerned with modernizing art, design and architecture. The movement ended during the 1930s, though its philosophy had a lasting influence on Western movements such as the Bauhaus and De Stijl (overleaf).

In a nutshell
A 20th-century Russian art movement focused on geometric abstraction, functional design and industrial materials.

Why it matters
It redefined art as a tool for societal change and influenced global Modernist design.

Key figures
Naum Gabo, 1890–1977
El Lissitzky, 1890–1941
Alexander Rodchenko, 1891–1956
Vladimir Tatlin, 1885–1953

Make the connection
design, p.55
installation, p.83
unity, p.93
negative space, p.140

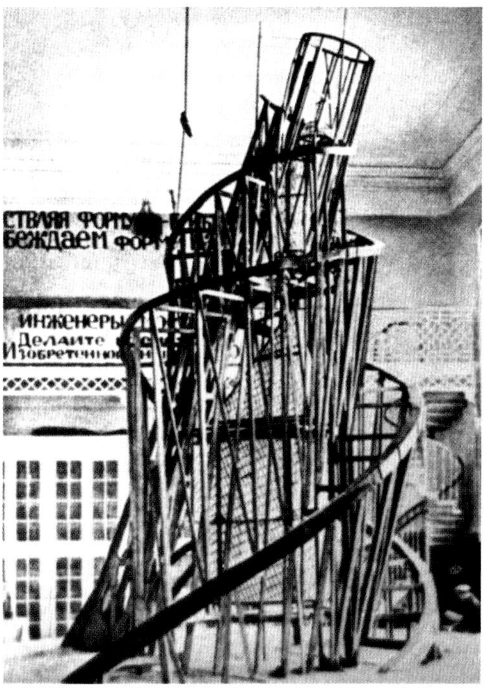

Vladimir Tatlin, *The Monument to the Third International (Tatlin's Tower)* (model), 1920

De Stijl

Characterized by geometric forms – particularly rectangles and squares, and horizontal and vertical lines – and a palette limited to primary colours, along with black, white and grey, De Stijl disregarded naturalistic representation (see p.6). The artists instead focused on expressing what they felt to be the essence of the universe, as well as exploring balance and asymmetry.

Founded in 1917 by painter and theorist Theo van Doesburg, with key contributions from Piet Mondrian, a pioneer of abstract art, De Stijl (Dutch for 'The Style') was an influential Dutch art and design movement. The artists and designers involved sought to create a new, harmonious and ordered visual language, rejecting individualism and ornamental excess in favour of pure abstraction and simplicity. One of De Stijl's central principles was 'Neo-plasticism', a term invented by Mondrian from the Dutch term *Nieuwe Beelding*, meaning 'new form' or 'new plastic art'. Mondrian's philosophy was that art should express pure reality and universal harmony, aiming to reflect a spiritual, universal order.

The artists and designers involved believed that Cubism had not been sufficiently extreme in its development of abstraction and that Expressionism (p.30) was too subjective. Russian Suprematism and Constructivism also influenced them. De Stijl was seen by those involved as a means to transform society through art and design. The group formally dissolved in the early 1930s following van Doesburg's death.

In a nutshell
Dutch art movement using geometric abstraction and primary colours to achieve universal harmony.

Why it matters
Focus on clarity and reduction influenced movements including the Bauhaus, Minimalism and Modernist architecture.

Key figures
Theo van Doesburg, 1883–1931
Bart van der Leck, 1876–1958
Piet Mondrian, 1872–1944
Gerrit Rietveld, 1888–1964

Make the connection
Cubism, p.36
Suprematism/Constructivism, pp.38–9

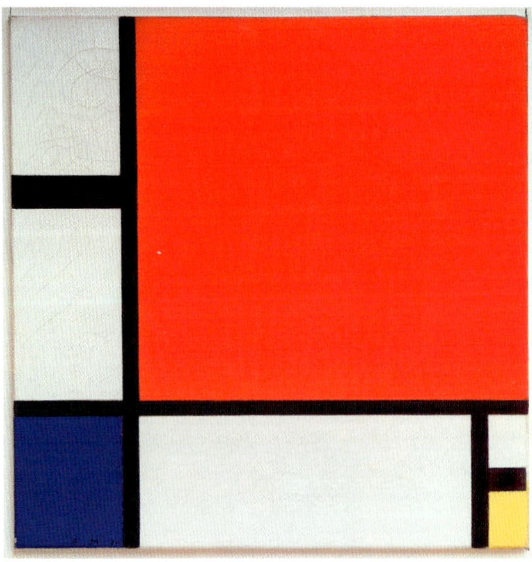

Piet Mondrian, *Composition with Red, Blue and Yellow*, 1930
Kunsthaus, Zurich

Bauhaus

Founded in 1919 in Weimar by architect Walter Gropius, the Bauhaus was a revolutionary German art and design school that sought to unite art, craft and technology. Eliminating traditional boundaries between fine and applied arts – the application of artistic designs and aesthetics to everyday objects – it treated all creative disciplines as parts of a modern, functional whole. Unlike De Stijl, which emphasized geometric abstraction and spiritual harmony through strict order and primary colours, the Bauhaus focused on practicality, material innovation and the integration of art into everyday life.

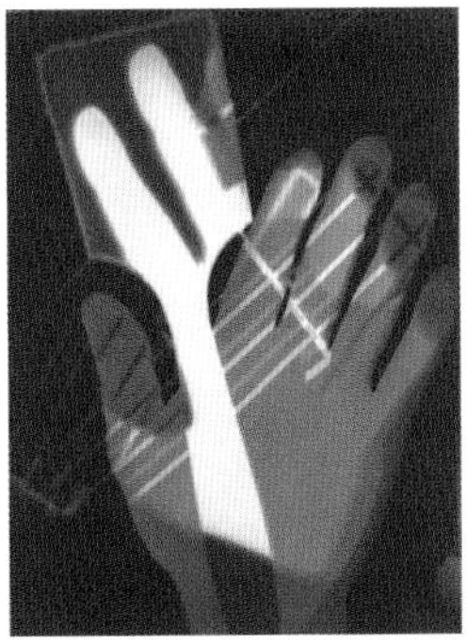

László Moholy-Nagy, photogram, 1926

Artists and designers created works that were attractive, useful, affordable and suitable for mass production. The school's guiding principle was 'form follows function', resulting in an aesthetic characterized by geometric forms and minimal ornamentation. It attracted leading artists and thinkers including Paul Klee, Wassily Kandinsky, Marianne Brandt, and Josef and Anni Albers. Designed by Gropius in 1925, the purpose-built Bauhaus building in Dessau (below) became a symbol of Modernist architecture.

Although the Bauhaus school was closed by the Nazis in 1933, its ideas spread globally as many of its members fled Germany. It had a profound influence on 20th-century Modernism.

In a nutshell
The Bauhaus was a German art and design school that unified art, craft and technology.

Why it matters
The philosophies of the Bauhaus – its focus on functional modern output – continue to influence many aspects of applied design.

Key figures
Anni Albers, 1899–1994
Walter Gropius, 1883–1969
Paul Klee, 1879–1940
László Moholy-Nagy, 1895–1946

Make the connection
Modernism, p.34
Constructivism, p.39
design, p.55
unity, p.93

Bauhaus school, Dessau, designed by Walter Gropius, 1926

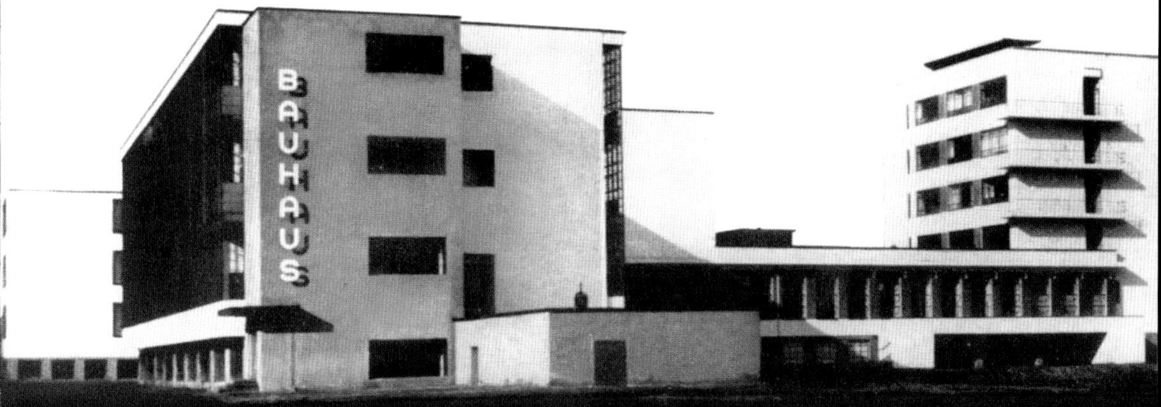

Dada

A response to the horrors of the First World War, Dada began in 1916 in neutral Switzerland. Those involved called it an 'anti-art' movement. They were writers, artists and musicians who reacted against the values of a society that had allowed such atrocities to take place.

The founders – including the writer Hugo Ball, the artist and poet Jean (Hans) Arp, and the Romanian poet Tristan Tzara – met at the Cabaret Voltaire in Zurich while war was still raging to discuss the abominations of the conflict and its repercussions. They allegedly chose the name 'Dada' for the movement at random from the dictionary. In French it means 'hobby horse' and in several Slavic languages, it means 'Yes, yes'. Overall, it meant little.

Dadaists declared that because of 'man's inhumanity to man', art and culture were hypocritical, and they attempted to mock what had gone before. Dada was intentionally irrational, aiming to reject all previously established artistic standards. It deliberately provoked strong reactions in many viewers because, as well as being anti-art, Dada was also anti-war and anti-capitalist.

Ball said: 'For us, art is not an end in itself, but it is an opportunity for the true perception and criticism of the times we live in.'[3] Soon, as well as in Zurich, Dadaists appeared in Paris, Berlin, Cologne and New York City.

In a nutshell
Arising from disillusionment and horror over the First World War, Dada embraced absurdity, chance and protest against traditional values.

Why it matters
It challenged artistic norms, paving the way for Surrealism, Conceptual and Performance art.

Key figures
Hugo Ball, 1886–1927
Marcel Duchamp, 1887–1968
Hannah Höch, 1888–1978
Tristan Tzara, 1896–1963

Make the connection
photomontage, p.91
contrast, p.92
assemblage/collage, pp.102–3

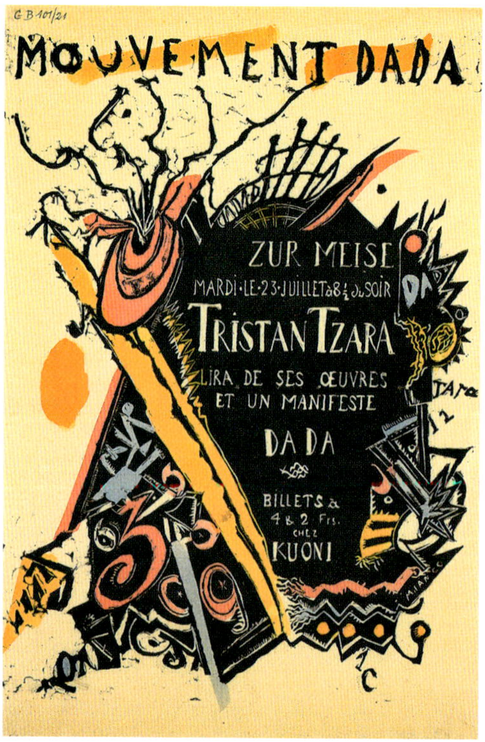

Marcel Janco, poster advertising 'Mouvement Dada', 1918. The text, in French, announces that Tristan Tzara will read from his writings.

Surrealism

After the First World War, Surrealism emerged in Paris as a development of Dada. It began as a literary movement, defined by three writers in a 1924 publication, *The Surrealist Manifesto*. In 1917, the poet Guillaume Apollinaire had invented the term 'Surrealism' to describe a reality beyond the ordinary, and writers later used it to emphasize the unconscious and irrational aspects of the mind. The manifesto explained that Surrealism sought to free our conscious thought processes from reason and logic.

The theories of Sigmund Freud, the founder of psychoanalysis, strongly influenced Surrealism. In late 1899, Freud published *The Interpretation of Dreams*, in which he identified the unconscious, a part of the human mind where memories and fundamental instincts are stored. Freud believed that accessing the unconscious allowed us to understand ourselves and the world more fully.

The Surrealists explored dreams, fantasies and irrational thoughts. Salvador Dalí and Yves Tanguy, for example, depicted these imaginings in paintings and, in Dalí's case, films and sculptures. Another of the methods used – taken from Freud – was 'free association', or 'automatism'. In this method, writers and artists stopped thinking and made marks unconsciously. They believed this would uncover underlying feelings and emotions.

In a nutshell
Aiming to unlock deeper truths through art and writing, Surrealism explored dreams, the unconscious and irrationality.

Why it matters
Changed ideas about creativity, influencing modern art, literature and psychology.

Key figures
André Breton, 1896–1966
Salvador Dalí, 1904–89
Max Ernst, 1891–1976
René Magritte, 1898–1967

Make the connection
Realism, p.21
Abstract Expressionism, p.31
imagination, p.95
symbolism, p.134

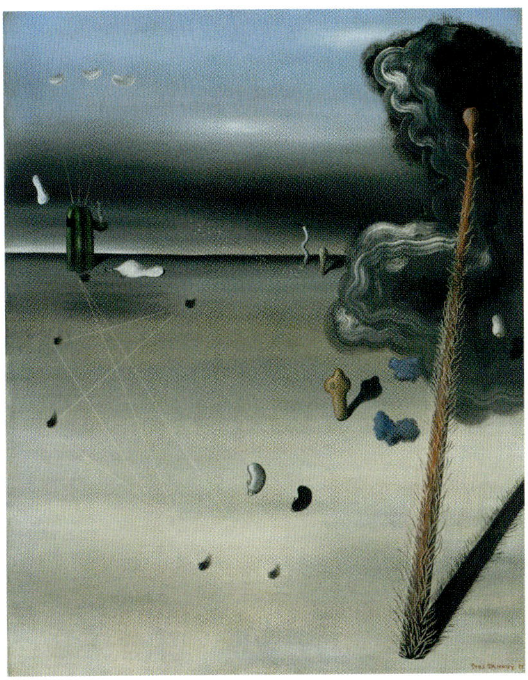

Yves Tanguy, *Mama, Papa is Wounded!*, 1927
Museum of Modern Art (MoMA), New York

Action Painting

A dynamic style of abstract art that emerged in the mid-20th century as part of Abstract Expressionism, Action Painting emphasized the physical act of painting. The term was first used in 1952 by the art critic Harold Rosenberg, who declared that painting was not just about representation, but also about performance and gesture.

Rather than carefully planning their compositions, Action Painters worked intuitively, employing spontaneous techniques such as dripping, splashing, throwing and smearing paint. The approach, alternatively called Gestural Abstraction, involved the artist's emotions and was influenced by Surrealist automatism (see p.43), which encouraged unconscious creativity. Jackson Pollock produced the first artworks to be called Action Painting, placing large canvases on the floor and pouring, flinging and smearing paint across them.

Action Painting moved the focus of art away from the finished image. It was a way of questioning conventional ideas about what art could be, and from it developed movements like Performance and Conceptual art. It also resonated with the post-war atmosphere, where the act of painting came to represent personal struggle and a search for freedom. By the early 1960s, however, a growing number of artists prioritized meaning over gesture. Some, including those who would become Pop artists (see p.46), criticized Action Painting as overly self-indulgent.

In a nutshell
A form of Abstract Expressionism defined by vigorous, expressive brushwork used to channel intense emotion.

Why it matters
Focused on the process of painting – the artist's procedure – even more than the result.

Key figures
Willem de Kooning, 1904–97
Franz Kline, 1910–62
Lee Krasner, 1908–84
Joan Mitchell, 1925–92
Jackson Pollock, 1912–56

Make the connection
Abstract Expressionism, p.31
impasto, p.100

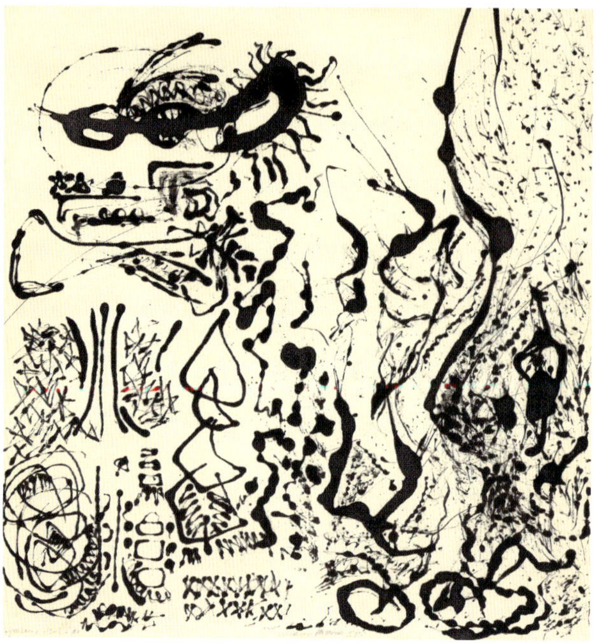

Jackson Pollock, *Number 5 'Elegant Lady'*, 1951
Private collection

Colour Field

Emerging in the late 1940s and 1950s in the United States, Colour Field painting is characterized by large areas of solid colour. These flat, expansive surfaces are intended to evoke emotional or contemplative responses. Like Action Painting, Colour Field is part of Abstract Expressionism, but unlike that energetic, gestural style, it emphasizes subtlety, stillness and the power of colour itself.

Colour Field artists sought to move away from representational content – which aims to depict objects, figures or scenes as they appear in the natural world – and even personal expression, aiming instead for a more universal language that explored pure visual experience. Mark Rothko was the best-known Colour Field painter, applying swathes of colour to large canvases to evoke emotions in the viewer. Another Colour Field innovation was Helen Frankenthaler's soak-stain technique, where she poured thinned oil paint onto unprimed canvas, allowing it to create fluid fields of colour.

By the 1960s, Colour Field painting had gained prominence in American art. However, it was followed by movements such as Minimalism, Pop art (see p.46), Conceptual art and Performance art, which intentionally distanced themselves from spiritual themes. At the same time, developments including the rise of the civil rights movement, feminism and opposition to the Vietnam War prompted artists and viewers to gravitate to art that addressed political issues.

In a nutshell
Broad, unbroken areas of colour that aimed to inspire emotional response, Colour Field paintings were vast and uncomplicated.

Why it matters
Treated colour itself as the central subject, with a lasting impact on post-war Modernist movements.

Key figures
Helen Frankenthaler, 1928–2011
Morris Louis, 1912–62
Barnett Newman, 1905–70
Mark Rothko, 1903–70
Clyfford Still, 1904–80

Make the connection
Abstract Expressionism, p.31
acrylic paint, p.124

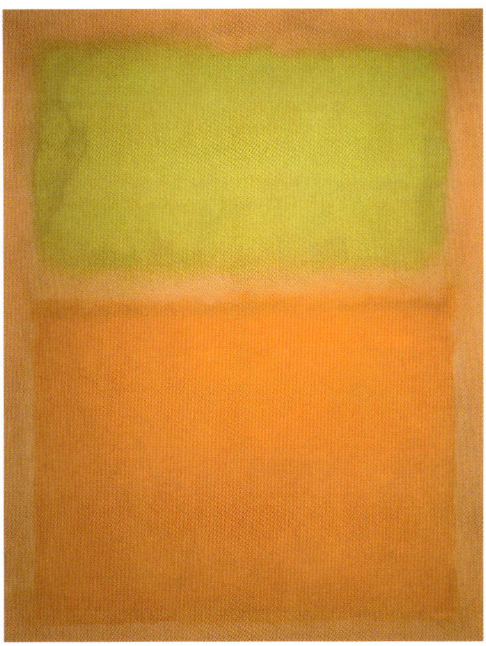

Mark Rothko, *Orange and Yellow*, 1956
Albright-Knox Art Gallery, Buffalo

Pop art

After the rationing and austerity of the Second World War, mass production and mass media proliferated across much of Europe and America. Consumerism had arrived, and some artists in London and New York chose to explore it. Based on popular culture – advertising, comic books, consumer goods and celebrities – their creations became known as Pop art, the antithesis of Abstract Expressionism (see p.31).

Pop art originated in London in 1956 with the exhibition *This Is Tomorrow*. Exhibiting artists from the Independent Group included Richard Hamilton and Eduardo Paolozzi. Hamilton's collage *Just What Is It That Makes Today's Homes So Different, So Appealing?* (1956) is often cited as the first true Pop artwork.

Soon after, Pop art emerged in New York, with artists such as Andy Warhol and Roy Lichtenstein directly engaging with mass media, celebrity culture and consumerism. Warhol's *Campbell's Soup Cans* and Lichtenstein's comic-inspired paintings exemplify this approach. The art was at once ironic and detached, celebratory of commercialism and consumption, yet cynical about it.

In attempts to brighten the post-war world and make art more accessible, Pop artists sought to embrace commercial culture and its methods, while dismissing attitudes that had contributed to two world wars. In doing so, they challenged traditional notions of fine art.

In a nutshell
A bold, colourful movement that drew on popular culture in both subject matter and technique.

Why it matters
Challenged traditional fine art by celebrating everyday imagery and demonstrating that art is relevant to everyone.

Key figures
Peter Blake, b.1932
Richard Hamilton, 1922–2011
Roy Lichtenstein, 1923–97
Eduardo Paolozzi, 1924–2005
Andy Warhol, 1928–87

Make the connection
design, p.55
woodcut, p.72
collage, p.103
acrylic paint, p.124

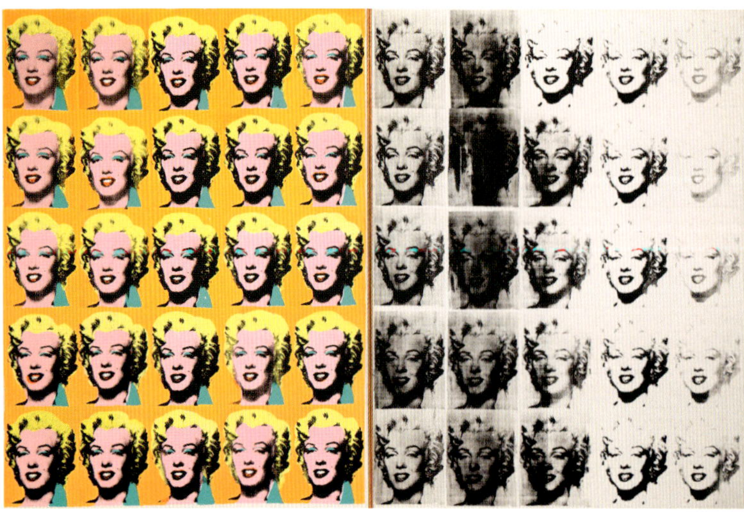

Andy Warhol, *Marilyn Diptych*, 1962
Tate

Op art

Op (short for 'Optical') art describes a style of visual art that emerged in the 1960s, characterized by the use of optical illusions. Op artists created works that give the viewer the impression of movement, flashing, vibrating patterns, or warping and swelling surfaces. These effects are achieved through precise arrangements of shapes, colours and lines, often in black and white or in bold contrasting colours.

Op art was named in *Time* magazine in 1964. It was also sometimes referred to as Retinal art. Its evolution can be traced back to earlier movements, such as Suprematism, Constructivism, Bauhaus and Futurism, which also explored abstraction, geometry and perception. However, Op art focused overtly on visual perception and how the eye interprets visual information. In 1965, the movement was brought to the attention of the American public with an exhibition at New York's Museum of Modern Art, titled *The Responsive Eye*. This established Op art as a significant movement.

Although Op art developed alongside Pop art and shared its fascination with modern visual culture and perception, it departed from Pop's focus on consumer imagery and mass media, turning instead towards pure abstraction and optical experience. Its popularity began to wane in the 1970s, but it helped shape later developments in kinetic and digital art.

In a nutshell
Relies on geometry and colour contrast to produce visual illusions that challenge the eye.

Why it matters
Pushed boundaries in how we understand sight and perception, leaving a legacy that spans art, design and psychological studies.

Key figures
Bridget Riley, b.1931
Jesús Rafael Soto, 1923–2005
Victor Vasarely, 1906–97

Make the connection
Futurism, p.37
Suprematism/Constructivism, pp.38–9
Bauhaus, p.41

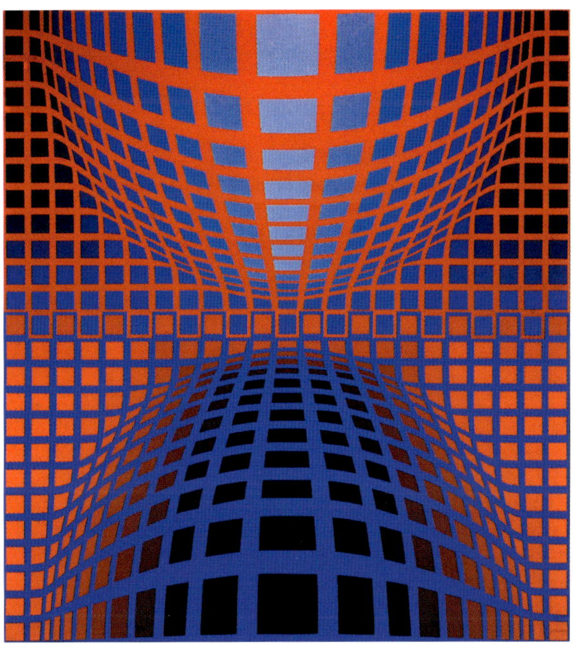

Victor Vasarely, *Opus III*, 1970–74
Musée d'Art Moderne de la Ville de Paris (MAM)

graffiti

Have you ever despaired at the sight of a spray-painted tag on a train or building? Maybe it's time to look more closely at this much-maligned art form. Graffiti art originated as a subcultural movement, particularly in urban areas such as New York City during the 1970s. Initially associated with 'tagging', it evolved into a more elaborate artistic practice, featuring complex lettering, characters and vibrant compositions.

Graffiti is often regarded as one of the four foundational elements of hip-hop culture, along with DJing, MCing (also known as rapping) and breakdancing. Early practitioners used it as a voice for marginalized communities, asserting their presence and commenting publicly on social and political issues. Yet, due to its association with vandalism and illegality, graffiti is often controversial. The distinction between 'graffiti' and Graffiti art, according to some, lies in the complexity, intent and skill of the work.

Notable graffiti artists include Dondi White, Lady Pink and Seen, who helped push the boundaries of graffiti as an art form. Many contemporary artists, including Banksy, began with graffiti before moving into broader street art practices. Over time, some graffiti art has gained some acceptance in galleries and museums, and it continues to influence graphic design, fashion and Contemporary art. Yet it still sparks debates about public space, ownership, skill and creative freedom.

In a nutshell
Involves stylized lettering or imagery, often spray-painted on public surfaces.

Why it matters
It challenges norms, voices rebellion and reclaims urban space.

Key figures
Jean-Michel Basquiat, 1960–88
Keith Haring, 1958–90
TAKI 183, b.1953

Make the connection
Dada, p.42
creativity, p.130
acrylic paint, p.124
positive shapes, p.141

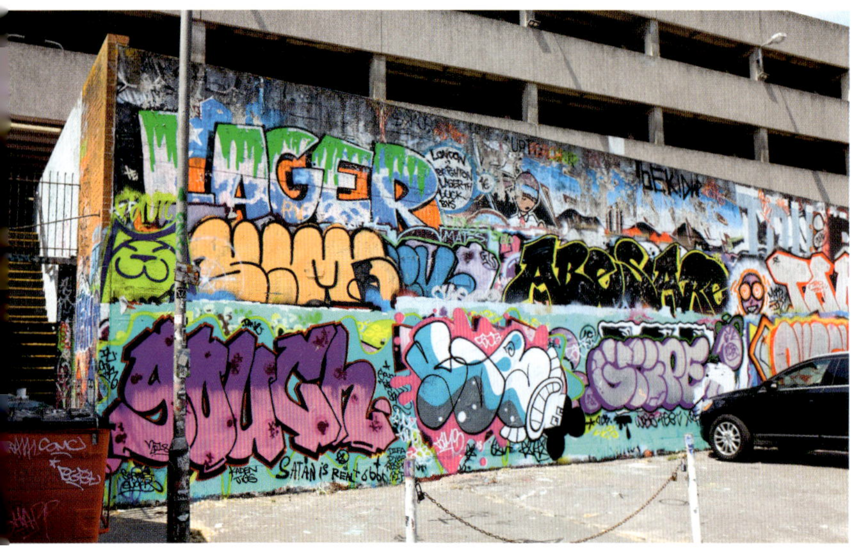

Colourful graffiti, 2009

street art

A broad category of visual art created in public locations, usually outside traditional art venues, Street art emerged in the late 20th century. It incorporates a range of media and techniques, including stencilling, 'wheat-pasting' (posting paper art using flour-based glue), murals, stickers (portable graffiti), installations and digital projections. Unlike graffiti, which often focuses on stylized lettering or tags, street art is usually image-based.

Often challenging established authority, street art is intended to engage the public directly. While graffiti emphasizes an artist's identity and territorial presence, street art may be humorous, poetic, subversive or confrontational; it can blur the line between art and activism. Significant artists include Banksy, who works anonymously with politically-charged stencils, and JR, who creates large-scale photographic installations. Shepard Fairey is another prominent artist whose work merges propaganda aesthetics with activism.

Berlin, London and São Paulo are among the cities that have gained a reputation for their lively street art scenes. In some places, artists are even given legal walls for their work. Southend-on-Sea in the UK hosts the annual Southend City Jam, which brings together artists to transform the streets into a vibrant outdoor gallery. Despite this growing legitimacy, street art generally remains transient and vulnerable to removal or destruction.

In a nutshell
Often large in scale and thought-provoking, street art encompasses murals, stencils and installations in public spaces.

Why it matters
It democratizes art, sparks dialogue and brightens urban spaces.

Key figures
Banksy, b.1974
Cornbread, b.1953
Shepard Fairey, b.1970
JR, b.1983

Make the connection
mural, p.65
installation, p.83
theme, p.127

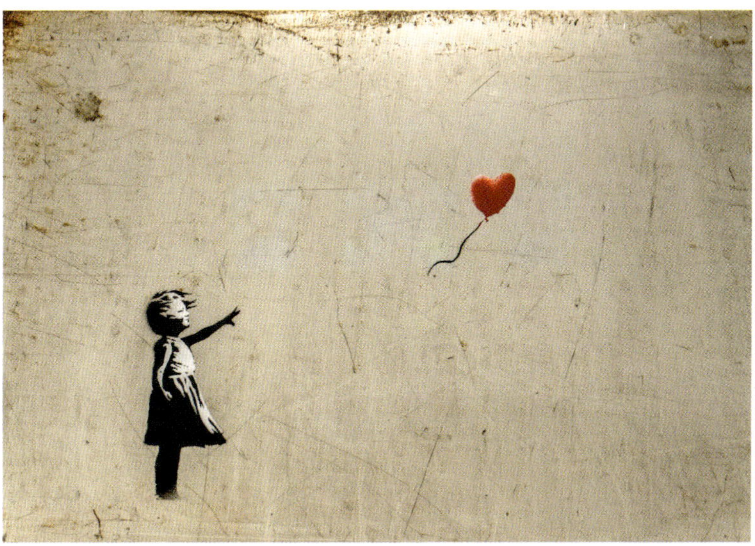

Banksy, *Girl with Balloon*, 2003
Moco Museum, Amsterdam

Photorealism

The term 'Photorealism' was coined by art dealer Louis K. Meisel in 1969 to describe artworks that replicate photographs with exacting precision. Using photographs as their primary source material, artists such as Chuck Close, Richard Estes, Audrey Flack and Ralph Goings were pioneers of the genre, which emerged in the United States during the late 1960s and early 1970s.

The paintings of Photorealists appeared as sharply realistic as photographs. Often using mechanical techniques, such as projecting images onto canvases to ensure accuracy, Photorealists did not seek to 'fool the eye' as trompe l'oeil paintings do (see p.106), but to create images that appear to be taken from photographic imagery while maintaining painterly integrity. The movement emphasized meticulous planning and technical skill, the revival of traditional academic methods, contrasting with many Modernist styles.

Subjects ranged from urban scenes – streets, shops, vehicles and cafés – to still lifes, often reflecting (mainly American) consumer culture. While some artists denied any social commentary, the choice of subject matter often invoked themes of mass production and modern urbanism. Audrey Flack, for example, infused her work with emotional depth and symbolic references to time and mortality.

Photorealism challenged the boundaries between photography and painting, raising questions about perception, reality and skill. It was in contrast with the more concept-based movements of recent history.

In a nutshell
A painting style that mimics high-resolution photography with meticulous detail.

Why it matters
It refocused painting skills and blurred the boundaries between photography and painting.

Key figures
Chuck Close, 1940–2021
Richard Estes, b.1932
Audrey Flack, 1931–2024
Ralph Goings, 1928–2016

Make the connection
Realism, p.21
observation, p.94
Fibonacci sequence, p.130
life drawing, p.139

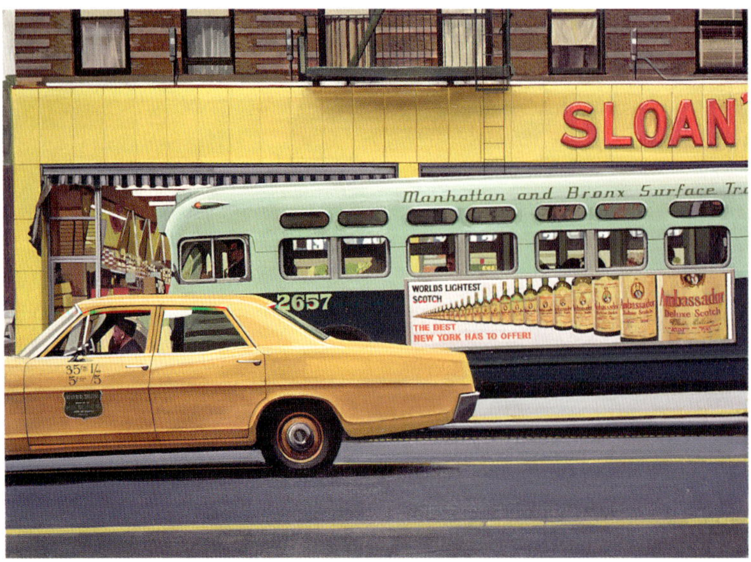

Richard Estes, *Sloan's*, 1999
Private collection

Hyperrealism

Evolving from Photorealism in the early 1970s, Hyperrealism was named by Belgian art dealer Isy Brachot during the 1973 exhibition *L'Hyperréalisme*. While Photorealism aimed to replicate photographs with technical fidelity, Hyperrealism goes further, with artists creating artworks that appear more real than reality itself.

Hyperrealism also built on the writings of French sociologist and philosopher Jean Baudrillard, who explored the (blurry, he argued) distinction between reality and representation. Hyperrealist artists like Carole Feuerman, Duane Hanson, Ron Mueck and Gottfried Helnwein often use photography, but they enhance images with emotional, narrative or symbolic elements. Their paintings and sculptures often feature exaggerated textures, lighting effects and details that exceed what the human eye would naturally perceive.

Unlike Photorealism, which tends to be neutral or detached, Hyperrealism engages with subjective themes such as identity and mortality. Hanson's life-sized sculptures of everyday people confront viewers with uncomfortable truths about society, while Simon Monk, who always paints from life, plays with illusion, making the viewer question perception, and often evokes nostalgic feelings.

While both Photorealism and Hyperrealism are built upon the imitation of photographic detail, Hyperrealism goes beyond replication, transforming photographic precision into a more subjective and expressive art form.

In a nutshell
Incredibly realistic illusions in two and three dimensions that arouse emotional responses.

Why it matters
Pushes realism to extremes to explore the complexities of perception, emotion, and the human condition.

Key figures
Duane Hanson, 1925–96
Gottfried Helnwein, b.1948
Ron Mueck, b.1958
Denis Peterson, b.1944

Make the connection
observation, p.94
verisimilitude, p.107

Tjalf Sparnaay,
Foodscape, 2014
Moveo Art Collection

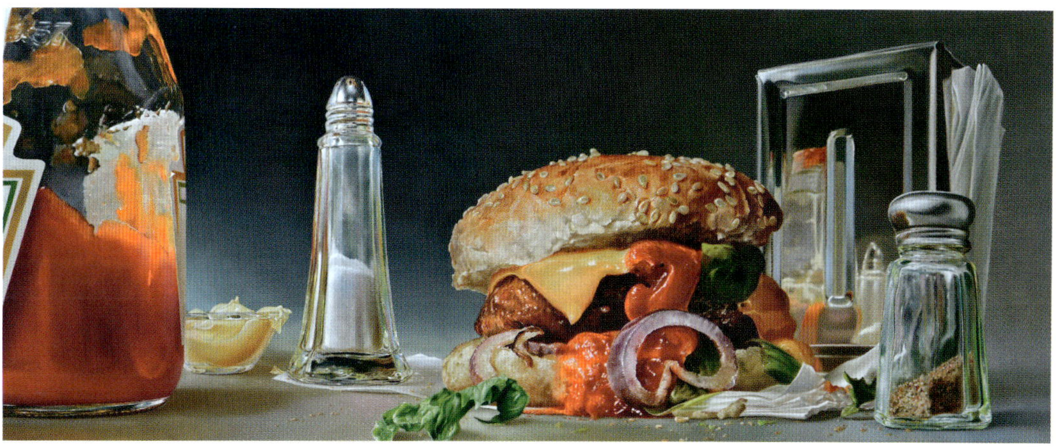

Modern art

Modern art refers to Western art produced approximately between the 1860s and the 1970s, a period marked by radical innovation and departures from traditional forms of representation. This era also coincided with rapid industrialization, urbanization, scientific development and socio-political change, which led many artists to seek new ways to express the complexities of modern life.

Modern art, therefore, is an umbrella term encompassing several art movements. It began with Impressionism (see p.22). It progressed through numerous avant-garde movements, including Post-Impressionism, Expressionism, Cubism, Fauvism, Futurism, Dada (p.42) and Abstract Expressionism. Key figures such as Pablo Picasso, Henri Matisse, Marcel Duchamp, Frida Kahlo and Sonia Delaunay were significant in redefining the boundaries of art.

Characterized by its focus on experimentation, innovation and artists' internal visions, Modern art incorporated abstract forms, fragmented perspectives and symbolic content. Artists challenged traditional notions of beauty, often prioritizing expression or idea over naturalistic representation. Crucially, Modern art moved towards artistic autonomy, or the belief that art need not serve religious, political or moral functions. Modern artists sought universal truths or utopian ideals while reflecting disillusionment with modernity, especially during and after the two world wars.

In a nutshell
A break from tradition, embracing abstraction, experimentation and new perspectives.

Why it matters
Revolutionized artistic expression and questioned cultural norms.

Key figures
Paul Cézanne, 1839–1906
Marcel Duchamp, 1887–1968
Henri Matisse, 1869–1954
Pablo Picasso, 1881–1973

Make the connection
Expressionism, p.30
Cubism/Futurism, pp.36–7
imagination, p.95
creativity/innovation, pp.132–3

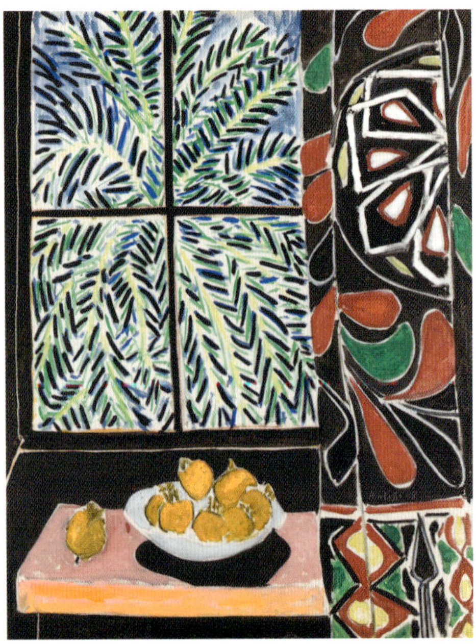

Henri Matisse, *Interior with Egyptian Curtain*, 1948
The Phillips Collection, Washington, D.C.

Contemporary art

Art produced from the late 20th century to the present day is commonly referred to as Contemporary art. It overlaps slightly with Modern art and is more diverse, with fewer defined movements. As artistic practices continue to evolve, new categories may emerge as the terms 'modern' and 'contemporary' become less useful. For now, Contemporary art reflects the rapidly changing world in which it is created, exploring cultural identity, technology and globalization.

Contemporary artists work across a wide variety of media – including digital technology, video, performance, installation and conceptual art – often blurring boundaries between disciplines. Artworks are frequently interactive, immersive or participatory. Artists such as Gerhard Richter, Cindy Sherman, Kara Walker and Olafur Eliasson produce works that question cultural narratives, power structures and the nature of art itself.

There is no dominant Contemporary art movement or single unifying aesthetic. Instead, it embraces multiplicity, inclusivity and critical dialogue. This openness enables artists from diverse cultural backgrounds and social positions to contribute to the global art scene through new platforms and institutions, including biennials, art fairs, online exhibitions and interdisciplinary collaborations.

While Modern art sought to break free from tradition, Contemporary art continuously redefines itself, asking questions about the world around us and how it functions.

In a nutshell
Art made since the late 1960s, reflecting diverse media and globalization.

Why it matters
It engages with society, identity and technology in real time.

Key figures
Olafur Eliasson, b.1967
Tracey Emin, b.1963
Gerhard Richter, b.1932
Cindy Sherman, b.1954
Kara Walker, b.1969

Make the connection
installation, p.83
imagination, p.95
acrylic paint, p.124
innovation, p.133

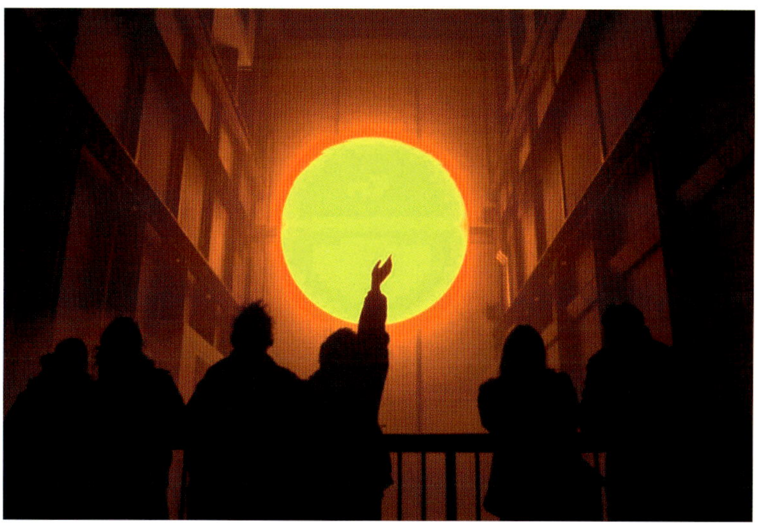

Olafur Eliasson, *The weather project*, 2003
Installation view, Tate Modern, London, 2003

art

What is art? Many have tried to define it. Broadly, it is a form of human expression that communicates ideas, emotions and experiences through various visual media, such as painting, sculpture, performance and installation. It originates from creativity and personal vision.

Throughout history, art has served many roles, including spiritual, political, personal and cultural. From prehistoric cave paintings to contemporary digital works, it has evolved – in style, materials and purpose – but has always remained deeply tied to the human condition. Artists usually engage subjectively with their work, exploring themes beyond the tangible and often delving into the philosophical, emotional and abstract. The meaning of a work is not always fixed, leaving room for interpretation and emotional responses from the viewer. Historically, art focused on aesthetic appeal, though that changed in the early 20th century.

Art exists on a spectrum, from representational to abstract, from traditional to avant-garde. It may be seen in galleries or museums, or outside conventional 'art' venues, and it can be commissioned, commodified or created on a whim. It can be produced by artists who seek to resonate with their viewers, and it often invites contemplation and encourages dialogue. Reflecting the complexities of identity and the imagination, its value lies in its ability to convey what cannot always be expressed in other ways.

In a nutshell
A visual language that conveys emotion, thought and experience, art often expresses more than words.

Why it matters
Art influences the viewer, often changing how we think. It records and expresses views on the world.

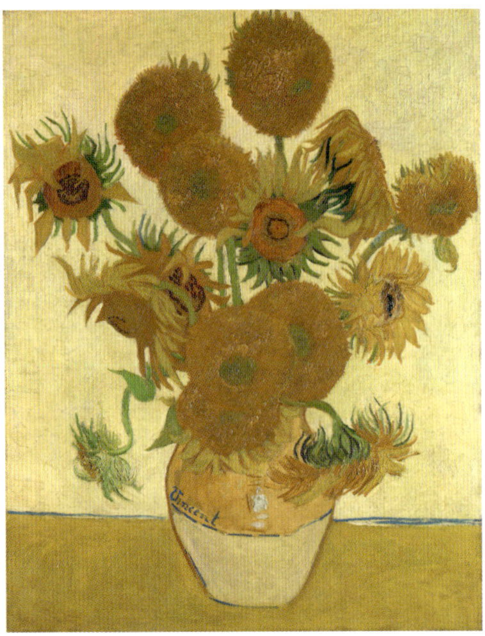

Vincent van Gogh, *Sunflowers*, 1888
National Gallery, London

design

Design is the intentional arrangement of elements to solve problems, convey ideas or improve functionality. It spans disciplines such as graphic and industrial design, architecture and fashion, and is often defined by its need to be functional or practical. Whether it is a chair, a website, a toothbrush or a map, design is judged by how effectively it meets its goals, balancing aesthetics with utility.

Art, by contrast, is typically driven by expression, emotion or technical skill. Usually, art does not need to solve a problem; nor does it fulfil a function. A painting might provoke thought, stir feeling or challenge perception, but it is not necessarily 'useful' in a conventional sense. It often invites interpretation rather than prescribing a solution.

Despite these differences, design and art share common ground. Both rely on the visual principles of composition, colour, form and balance, and both are creative. The boundary between them is fluid; for example, a poster can be both a design and an artwork. Designers often draw inspiration from art to infuse their work with greater aesthetic appeal, while some artists incorporate design elements into their compositions.

Design is creativity at work. It blends artistic expression with purpose. Along with visual appeal, it responds to needs and challenges, and most designers aim to solve problems, answer questions and improve everyday life.

In a nutshell
The process of crafting solutions that balance how things work, look and feel.

Why it matters
It influences how we interact with the world around us — from the tools we use to the spaces in which we live.

iMac, presented at Apple Expo 1998, Paris

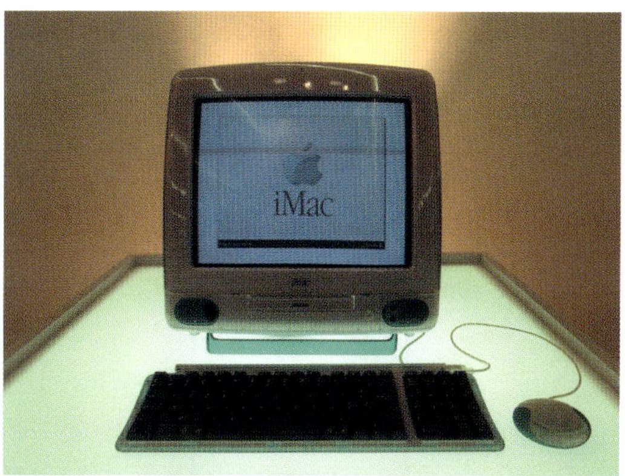

Braun table radiogram, model SK5, *c.*1962

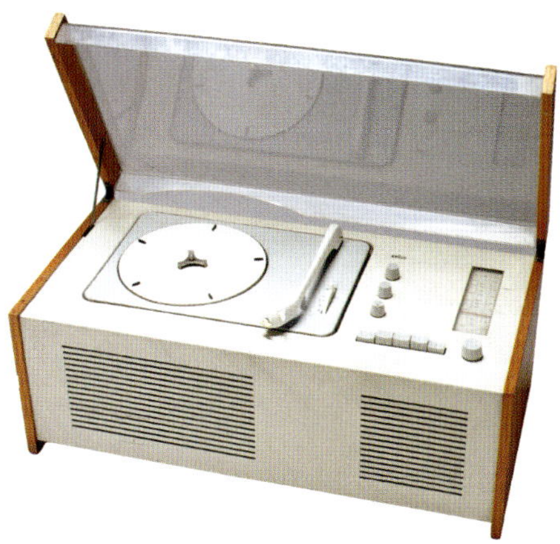

line

One of the most fundamental elements of art, line is a continuous path traced by a moving point. A line can vary in width, direction, length and texture, and is used to define shapes, suggest movement, create space and convey emotion.

Lines can be contour lines, which outline shapes and forms; gestural lines, which express energy or movement; or implied lines, where the eye connects points to form a line. Lines can be horizontal, creating a sense of calmness or stability, vertical (strong or formal), diagonal (dynamic or tense), or curved (graceful and soft).

In drawing, the line is often the primary means of representation, as in pencil sketches or the inkwork of East Asian scrolls. In works such as *El Jaleo* (below), John Singer Sargent used dynamic lines to convey movement and rhythm, guiding the viewer's eye through the interplay of the dancer's pose, flowing drapery and flickering light. In abstract art, artists such as Paul Klee treated line as an independent visual language. Similarly, in Minimalist or Conceptual art, the line may become the subject itself. A line can guide or direct the viewer's eye, or suggest depth and distance, as in linear perspective (see p.79).

Ultimately, from prehistoric to Contemporary art, drawing to sculpture, line is a practical tool and a powerful expressive device.

In a nutshell
A fundamental element in art, used to define shape, suggest movement and convey emotion.

Why it matters
Line guides the viewer's eye, builds structure and expresses mood or energy.

Key figures
Katsushika Hokusai, 1760–1849
Michelangelo, 1475–1564
Georgia O'Keeffe, 1887–1986
Egon Schiele, 1890–1918

Make the connection
Realism, p.21
Art Nouveau, p.32
pencil, p.113

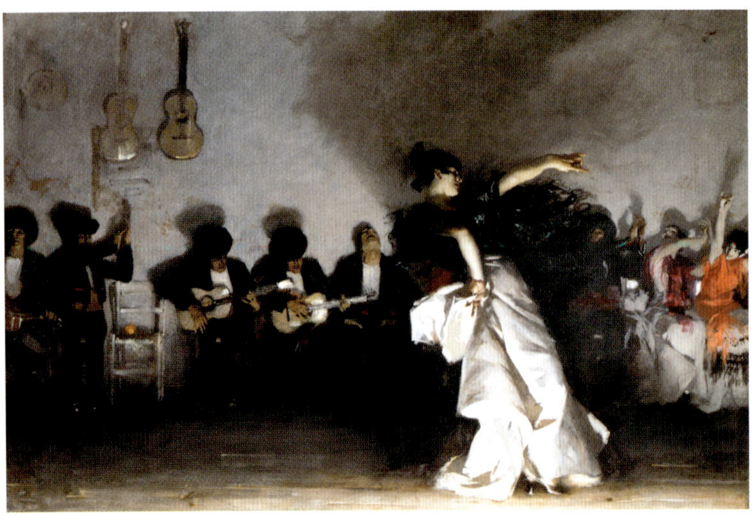

John Singer Sargent, *El Jaleo*, 1882
Isabella Stewart Gardner Museum, Boston

mark

Any deliberate sign made by an artist on a surface – a brushstroke, a pencil scratch, a smear, a fingerprint or even a digital glitch – is a mark. Marks are the physical record of an artist's action, and they can suggest texture, emotion, rhythm or intention. Unlike the more defined concept of line, a mark is about gesture. Lines are also marks, but marks can be more than lines.

Marks are often used by artists to create atmosphere, movement or emotional tone. For instance, the expressive brushwork of Vincent van Gogh or the energetic splatters of Jackson Pollock are central to the artworks' meanings. Always unique and individual, marks are an artist's 'language'. They appear in almost any material an artist works with, from paint to bronze or pastels.

In Contemporary art, mark-making is frequently linked with identity and process. Artists like Cy Twombly transformed marks into a kind of visual handwriting. Marks can also be political or conceptual. Graffiti and street art, for example, involve acts of public mark-making that assert identity or resistance. In Minimalism or Conceptual art, even the absence of marks can carry meaning.

Ultimately, marks – including lines – record the thoughts, feelings, intentions, mistakes and actions of artists. Whether bold or subtle, deliberate or accidental, marks are essential elements of nearly all artworks.

In a nutshell
The lines, patterns, textures and gestures artists use to express emotion, movement or form.

Why it matters
Marks reveal an artist's style, intent and individuality.

Key figures
Jean-Michel Basquiat, 1960–88
Joan Mitchell, 1925–92
Camille Pissarro, 1830–1903
Cy Twombly, 1928–2011

Make the connection
Post-Impressionism, p.23
Expressionism, p.30
paint, p.110
charcoal, p.112

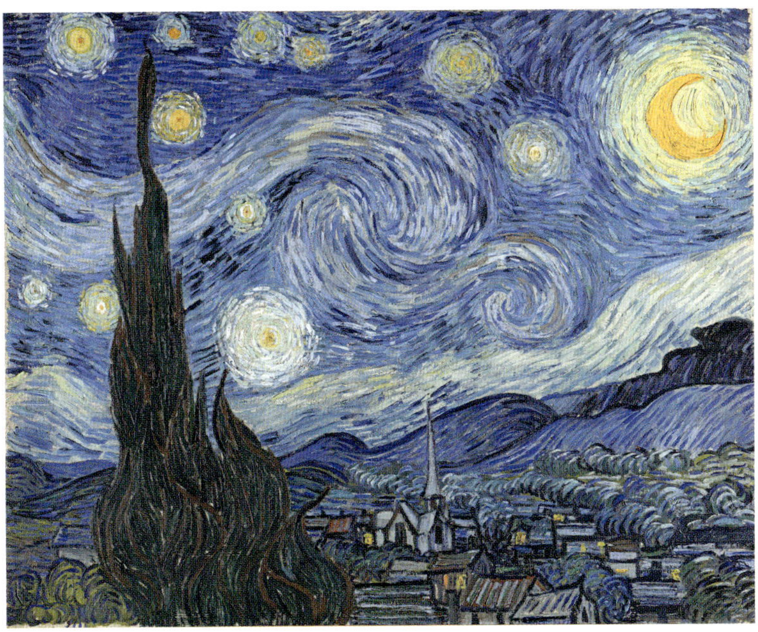

Vincent van Gogh, *The Starry Night*, 1889
Museum of Modern Art, New York

sketching

Often the first step in the creative process, sketching is the act of making freehand drawings that capture the essence of a subject without particular neatness or detail. It is a way for artists to explore ideas, experiment with composition and record observations. Sketches can be spontaneous or studied, but are always part of the artist's thought processes.

Artists have always sketched. In ancient Greece and Rome, artists sketched on wax tablets and papyrus, and during the Renaissance, sketching as a preparatory step became essential. For example, in his *Studies for the Libyan Sibyl* (*c*.1510–11), Michelangelo was working out poses, anatomy and gestures. Some parts of the sheet are rough and gestural, especially the hands and feet.

By the 18th and 19th centuries, various inventions made it easier for artists to sketch outdoors with graphite pencils, charcoal, watercolours and oil paints, leading to the popularity of plein-air sketching. John Constable, J. M. W. Turner, Claude Monet and John Singer Sargent, among other painters of the period, filled their sketchbooks with studies that served as aides-memoire for their planned paintings.

Artists sketch for many reasons, including idea development, testing out concepts and sharpening their observational skills. Sketches can serve as visual notes, or, sometimes, as finished works in their own right, valued for their immediacy and raw emotion.

In a nutshell
Sketching is the act of drawing loosely to capture ideas and observations.

Why it matters
Fosters creativity, sharpens observation and lays the foundation for finished artworks or designs.

Key figures
David Hockney, b.1937
Rembrandt, 1606–69
J. M. W. Turner, 1775–1851
Vincent van Gogh, 1853–90

Make the connection
Realism, p.21
observation, p.94
plein-air painting, p.104
pencil, p.113

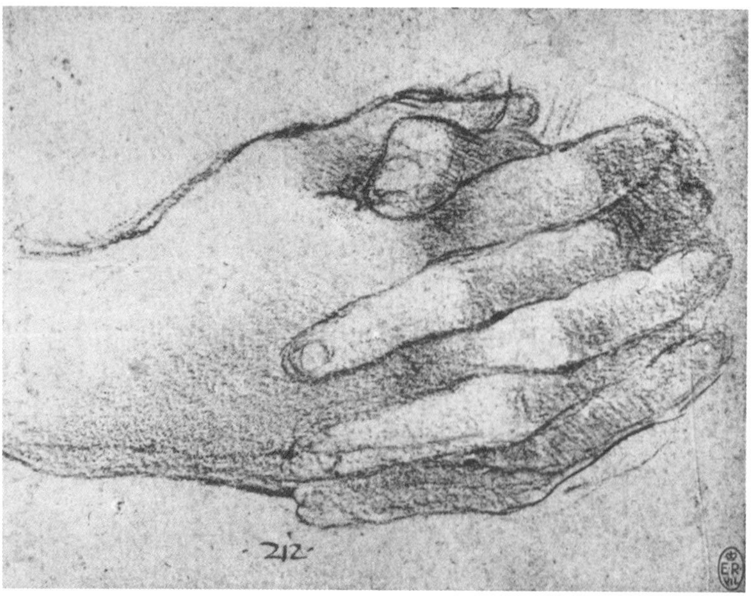

Leonardo da Vinci, *The hands of St John in the Last Supper*, *c*.1495
Royal Collection Trust, London

drawing

The art of making marks on a surface using tools like pencils, charcoal, ink or digital styluses, drawing is a visual language, used to express ideas, emotions and observations. Drawing can be representational (see p.45) or abstract, detailed or minimal. Unlike sketching, which is typically quick and exploratory, drawing is usually more considered and refined. Drawings are often finished artworks or formal studies in their own right.

Drawing has been a central component of artistic practice since prehistoric times. In ancient Egypt and Greece, for example, drawing was used to design temples, record myths and decorate tombs. During the Renaissance, drawing became an essential aspect of an artist's education. By the 17th and 18th centuries, drawing had evolved even further, with artists such as Rembrandt, Peter Paul Rubens and Jean-Auguste-Dominique Ingres producing drawings to explore light, texture and the human form. Academic institutions included life drawing (for men only) as an essential aspect of an artist's training. In the 19th century, artists such as Edgar Degas, Georges Seurat and Vincent van Gogh produced hundreds of drawings. Today, drawing encompasses digital artwork as well.

Artists draw for many reasons, including experimenting with composition and technique. While sketching is often quick and loose, drawing typically involves more deliberate planning, leading to more carefully developed visual expression.

In a nutshell
Drawing is both the act of making careful marks and the resulting image.

Why it matters
Drawing is the basis of visual thinking, and a drawing can serve as both a planning tool and a finished artwork.

Key figures
John Constable, 1776–1837
Georges Seurat, 1859–91
Vincent van Gogh, 1853–90
Leonardo da Vinci, 1452–1519

Make the connection
Bauhaus, p.41
design, p.55
observation, p.94
charcoal/pencil, pp.112–13

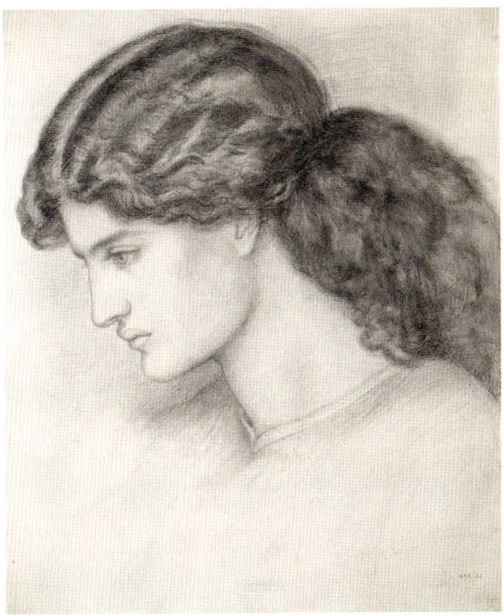

Dante Gabriel Rossetti, *Profile of a Lady (Jane Morris)*, 1861
Victoria and Albert Museum, London

modelling

A sculptural technique in which a pliable material is shaped to create a three-dimensional form, modelling encompasses a range of techniques, from the manipulation of materials – clay, plaster and wax – to the implementation of digital tools. With the development of computer graphics in the late 20th century, digital modelling became a powerful tool for artists and designers, used in everything from video games to Computer-Aided Design and Manufacture.

In the traditional sense of modelling for sculpture, artists manipulate their materials with their hands or tools, and they generally work intuitively, adding small amounts of material or removing and reapplying it to achieve their desired effects – this is known as the additive process. Artists build their modelled forms gradually. The malleable substances used, unlike rigid materials such as stone, bone or wood (which are usually carved), can retain impressions, finger marks and mistakes. Also, fine details can be constantly altered until the artist is satisfied.

Sculptural modelling is often used to make preparatory studies or maquettes before executing a final artwork in a more permanent medium (although modelling is also used to create many finished works). Once the model is complete, it may be fired (as in ceramics), cast (for example, in bronze), or preserved as is.

Modelling is a three-dimensional art that allows for flexibility, expression and experimentation.

In a nutshell
Shaping pliable materials like clay or wax to build form.

Why it matters
Allows artists to create volume, texture, lifelike details and to shape future finished sculptures.

Key figures
Gian Lorenzo Bernini, 1598–1680
Camille Claudel, 1864–1943
Alberto Giacometti, 1901–66
Auguste Rodin, 1840–1917

Make the connection
ancient Roman art, p.8
Renaissance, p.16
design, p.55
observation, p.94

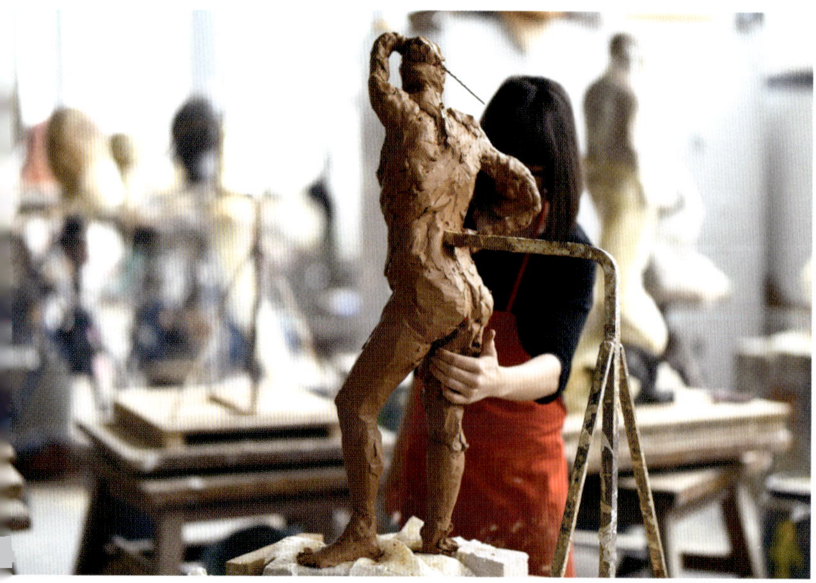

Young sculptor working in her studio, 2018

carving

An artist carves by removing excess material from a solid block – usually stone, wood or bone – and gradually refining it into a three-dimensional work of art (also known as a carving). Artists use chisels, mallets, scrapers and blades to cut, chip or whittle hard surfaces when carving; the process is physical, direct and immediate. Because each incision is permanent, mistakes are difficult or impossible to reverse. Planning, skill and confidence are required, with preliminary sketches and models used to guide the process.

Remains of sculpted stone artefacts and tools have been found from the New Stone Age (*c.*10,000–2,000 BCE). Ancient Egyptian artists created huge carved sculptures depicting gods and pharaohs, while the ancient Greeks carved statues and reliefs that emphasized realism and idealism. Wood carving played a significant role in the Māori culture from approximately 1100.

Wood carving was a significant aspect of religious art in Europe during the Middle Ages. Stone carving was revived during the Renaissance, with artists such as Donatello, Michelangelo and Gian Lorenzo Bernini producing lifelike, detailed sculptures. Unlike modelling, which is an additive process where pliable materials are shaped, carving is subtractive: the artist removes material to reveal the form. Carving, especially in materials like stone or marble, has often been given greater prestige than modelling, as it demands technical precision.

In a nutshell
Describes both the process of sculpting a hard material and the finished artwork that results from it.

Why it matters
Due to the need for precision, carving is often employed for monumental or sacred art.

Key figures
Gian Lorenzo Bernini, 1598–1680
Donatello, *c.*1386–1466
Michelangelo, 1475–1564
Auguste Rodin, 1840–1917

Make the connection
Romanesque, p.9
Early/High Renaissance, pp.14–15
Baroque, p.18

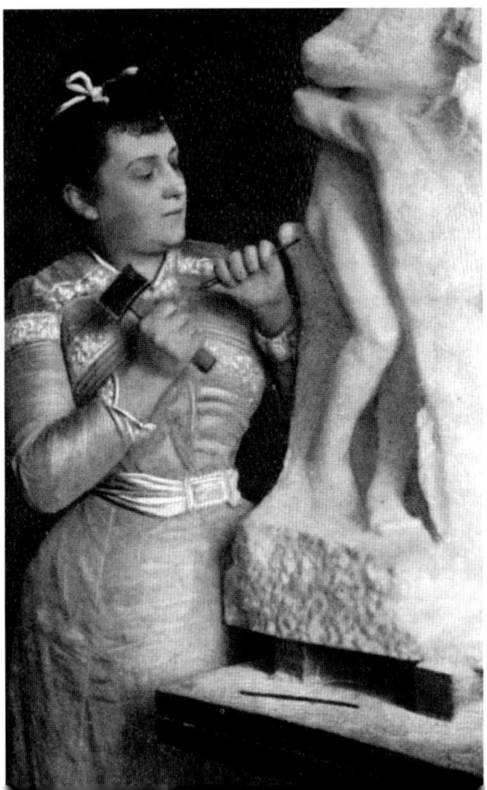

Camille Claudel carving her marble statue *Vertumnus and Pomona* (detail), *c.*1903

shadow

Artists depict shadows to add depth and volume to a drawing or painting. Shadows allow artists to create illusions that make objects appear further away or closer. Depending on their placement, intensity and colour, shadows can reveal the time of day or the direction of light.

There are two main types of shadows. Cast shadows are projected onto surrounding surfaces when an object blocks the light. They are influenced by the direction, angle and intensity of the light, as well as the shape of the object blocking the light, the surrounding environment and the colours. Form shadows appear on an object itself, usually as subtle shifts in tone that define the object's shape. The hand of the man in black and red in Rembrandt's *Night Watch* (below) is cast onto the man beside him in white. Understanding how light behaves when it interacts with different surfaces and is reflected or cast enables artists to depict believable shadows.

Depictions of shadows can enhance a story. Twentieth-century American artist Edward Hopper often used shadows to convey isolation and stillness in his paintings, while Italian Surrealist Giorgio de Chirico employed them to evoke mystery or psychological depth. Shadows have sometimes become the subject themselves: for example, in the installations of Kumi Yamashita, or in *Cold Dark Matter: An Exploded View* by Cornelia Parker (p.83).

In a nutshell
Shadow in art reveals depth, form and atmosphere through light's absence.

Why it matters
Evokes emotion, guides focus and enhances realism or abstraction.

Key figures
Giorgio de Chirico, 1888–1978
Edward Hopper, 1888–1967
René Magritte, 1898–1967
Cornelia Parker, b.1956
Rembrandt, 1606–69

Make the connection
Baroque, p.18
Romanticism, p.20
Surrealism, p.43
charcoal, p.112

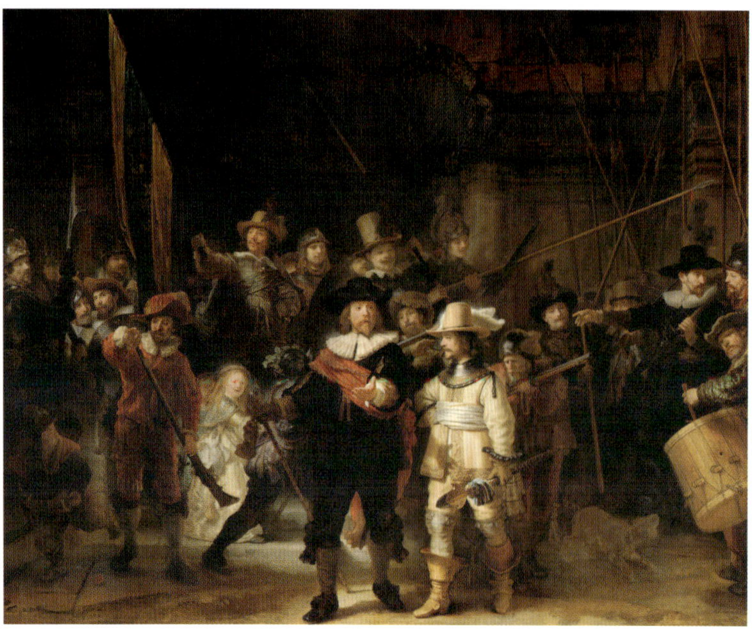

Rembrandt, *The Nightwatch*, 1642
Rijksmuseum, Amsterdam

tone

Unlike shadow, which is the physical blocking of light, tone is about relative values. Another word for tone is value, and sometimes the phrases 'tonal value' or 'tonal contrasts' are used. These essentially refer to lightness or darkness. Artists use tone in drawings and paintings to create contrast, mood and form. Whether in coloured or monochrome works, tonal contrasts can convey volume, weight, distance, dimension and atmosphere. Careful control of tone allows for subtle transitions or bold visual impact.

In any light, three-dimensional objects have tones, created by the way light falls on them. Artists create an impression of form and depth through gradations of tone, using techniques such as shading, blending and hatching. Rembrandt's tonal contrasts, for example, guide the viewer's eye through his paintings, while the subtle tonal gradations in Jan Vermeer's works (below) create luminosity, depth and a sense of cohesion. Caravaggio and Artemisia Gentileschi are known for their dramatic use of chiaroscuro (see p.70), which emphasizes strong contrasts between light and dark tones to create intense scenes with emotional impact. Francisco Goya evoked psychological tension through bold tonal contrasts, while James McNeill Whistler painted restrained, subtle tonal harmonies.

Shadow often conveys depth, drama or mystery, while 'tone' refers to the overall gradation of light and dark that shapes form and mood.

In a nutshell
Refers to the lightness or darkness of a colour or object.

Why it matters
In all art, whether figurative or abstract, tone defines form and can create atmosphere.

Key figures
Caravaggio, 1571–1610
Artemisia Gentileschi, 1593–1654
Rembrandt, 1606–69
Johannes Vermeer, 1632–75

Make the connection
High Renaissance, p.15
Baroque, p.18
Post-Impressionism, p.23
chalk pastel, p.114

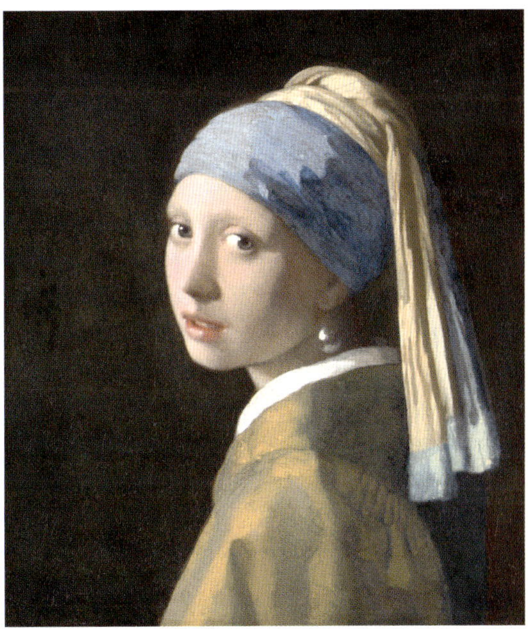

Johannes Vermeer, *Girl with a Pearl Earring*, c.1665–6
Mauritshuis, The Hague

fresco

A method of decorating walls and ceilings, used since antiquity, in which artists paint water-based pigments directly onto freshly laid lime plaster; the term 'fresco' originates from the Italian word *affresco*, meaning 'fresh'.

There are three types of fresco. Dry fresco, or fresco secco (see p.67), is painted onto dry plaster; semi-wet fresco, or mezzo fresco, is painted onto damp plaster; and true fresco, or buon fresco (see p.66), is painted onto wet plaster. As buon fresco dries, the pigments soak into the plaster and become part of the wall or ceiling, giving the result durability and longevity. In all three methods, artists must work quickly, but especially in buon fresco, the most popular and enduring method, as they must work before the plaster sets.

As mistakes are difficult to correct, artists producing frescoes have to plan and be precise. Despite its technical demands, fresco is admired for its luminous quality, historical significance and ability to harmonize with architectural space.

Fresco flourished during the Renaissance to Rococo periods, especially in Italy, with artists such as Michelangelo creating many monumental works, including, famously, the ceilings and altarpiece of the Sistine Chapel. The capacity to create detail, with countless colours and tones, and the works' durability, have meant that many frescoes around the world continue to be admired centuries after they were completed.

In a nutshell
A form of mural painting, frescoes are made with water-based pigments on fresh plaster.

Why it matters
As frescoes are so durable, ensuring generations can enjoy them and learn about the art of the past

Key figures
Piero della Francesca, *c.*1415/20–1492
Giotto, *c.*1267/76– 1337
Michelangelo, 1475–1564
Raphael, 1483–1520

Make the connection
Renaissance, p.16
Rococo, p.19
tempera, p.120

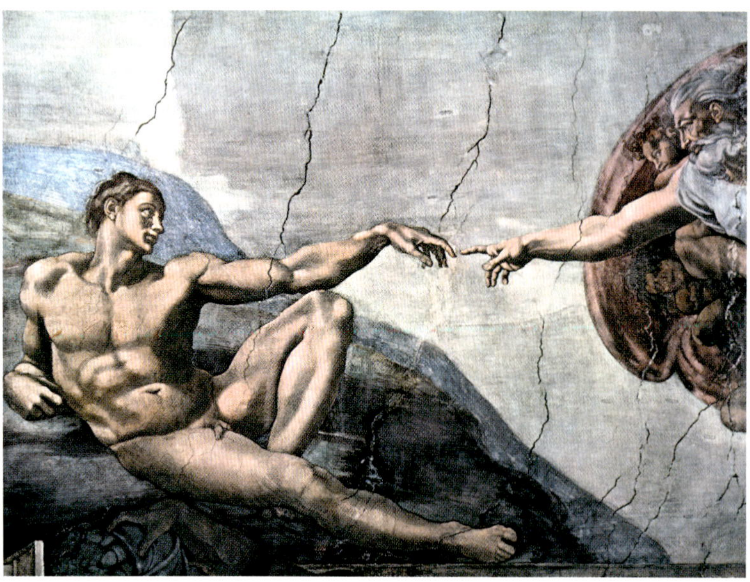

Michelangelo, *The Creation of Adam*, 1508–11 Sistine Chapel ceiling, Vatican City

mural

Usually large in scale and created on walls, ceilings or other relatively permanent, large surfaces, murals are site-specific works designed to complement or transform their surroundings. They can be made using a wide range of materials and techniques, including acrylics, oils, spray paint, mosaic and digital projection. A fresco is a specific type of mural, created by painting on to wet plaster.

Murals may be located on the inside or outside of buildings, often responding to or incorporating the architecture of the space. Mural artists frequently use grids, projectors or stencils to transfer their designs accurately onto the surface.

Some of the earliest examples of mural painting are in prehistoric cave sites such as Chauvet and Lascaux in France. In ancient civilizations, including those of Egypt, Rome and India, murals depicted religious, mythological and everyday scenes. Notable examples include Egyptian tomb paintings (from *c.*3150 BCE), Minoan palace wall paintings (*c.*1700–1600 BCE) and Roman villa decorations (1st century BCE to 1st century CE). In the 1920s, the Mexican Muralist movement emerged, promoting national identity following the Mexican Revolution. Artists such as Diego Rivera, José Clemente Orozco and David Alfaro Siqueiros created vivid public murals that communicated Mexico's history and social ideals to a wide audience.

Unlike fresco, mural is a broad term, encompassing many materials, methods and styles.

In a nutshell
A large-scale artwork painted directly on a wall or ceiling, often in public spaces.

Why it matters
Murals reflect cultural identities, provoke thought and enhance environments.

Key figures
Judy Baca, b.1946
Keith Haring, 1958–90
José Clemente Orozco, 1883–1949
Diego Rivera, 1886–1957
David Siqueiros, 1896–1974

Make the connection
street art, p.49
art/design, pp.54–5
subject, p.126

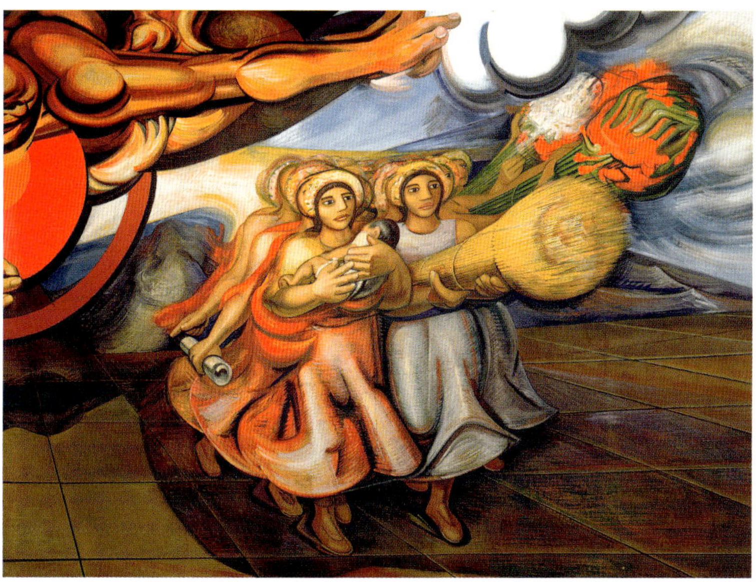

José Clemente Orozco, 'Mexican women, with their children and the products of their labour, marching to demand their rights', from the cycle *The Mexican People Call for Social Security*, 1930s

buon fresco

Water-based pigments applied to freshly plastered walls or ceilings are known as buon fresco, meaning 'true fresco'.

The process begins with a rough layer of plaster called *arriccio*, followed by a smooth top layer called *intonaco*. Pigments are applied directly to the wet lime plaster of the top layer. As the surface dries, a chemical reaction called carbonation occurs whereby the lime (calcium hydroxide) reacts with carbon dioxide in the air to form calcium carbonate. This reaction binds with the pigment, rather than leaving it as a separate layer on the surface. The result is a durable image that becomes an integral part of the architectural structure, resistant to flaking and fading over time.

The creation of buon fresco demands meticulous preparation and rapid execution. Artists typically start with a full-scale preparatory drawing, known as a cartoon, which is transferred onto the wall using methods such as pouncing (see p.112) or incising. Work is undertaken in sections, with each day's plaster application known as a *giornata* (Italian for 'a day's work'). Each section has to be painted while the plaster is still wet, as once it dries, no further changes can be made. The palette is also limited, as only certain pigments are compatible with lime.

Buon fresco was a dominant technique in mural painting from antiquity to the Baroque and Rococo periods.

In a nutshell
Water-based pigments are applied to wet plaster, chemically bonding the image to the wall as it dries.

Why it matters
Buon fresco creates durable, long-lasting artworks integral to architectural surfaces.

Key figures
Fra Angelico, 1395–1455
Giotto di Bondone, d.1337
Masaccio, 1401–28
Michelangelo, 1475–1564
Raphael, 1483–1520

Make the connection
Early/High Renaissance, pp.14–15
drawing, p.59
observation, p.94

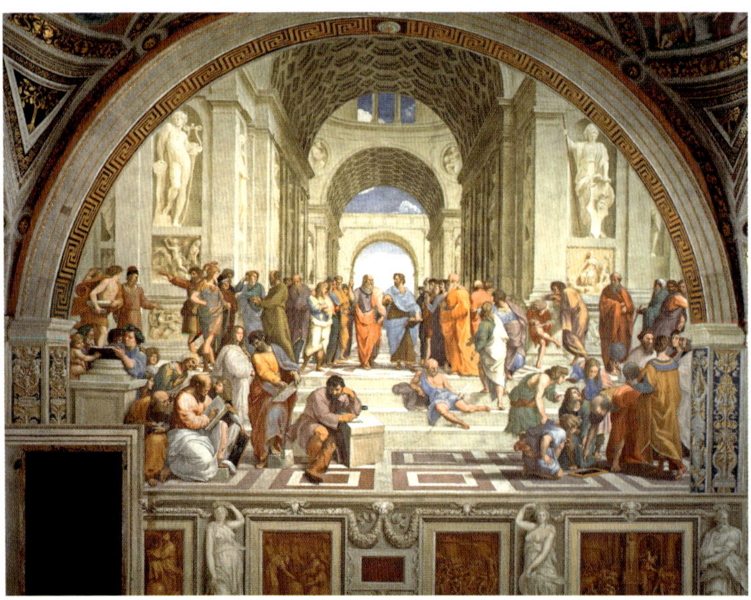

Raphael, *The School of Athens*, 1510–11
Stanze di Raffaello, Apostolic Palace, Vatican City

fresco secco

Fresco secco, or 'dry fresco', is a mural technique in which pigments are applied to dry plaster using a binding agent such as egg, glue, oil or limewater. The pigment does not chemically bind with the wall surface, as in buon fresco, but instead adheres mechanically through the binder. This allows for greater flexibility in application and a broader palette, including pigments that do not withstand the alkaline environment of wet plaster.

Artists can work more slowly with fresco secco than buon fresco, making it ideal for detailing or corrections and additions on existing frescoes. It is also well-suited to humid or variable climates, as it does not require precise drying times. The technique was commonly used in ancient Egyptian, Indian and Buddhist mural traditions.

However, fresco secco is less durable than buon fresco. As the pigment sits on a surface, it is more susceptible to flaking, peeling and moisture damage over time. It also tends to fade more quickly, especially if exposed to environmental stress.

Fresco secco offers greater control and finish than buon fresco, but its reliance on binders and surface adhesion means results can vary depending on materials and conditions. For this reason, it is often used in combination with buon fresco.

In a nutshell
A mural technique; pigments are applied to dry plaster, often using a binding agent such as egg, glue, or casein.

Why it matters
Allows for greater detail and a wider colour range than buon fresco.

Key figures
Ajanta cave painters, India, 2nd century BCE – 6th century CE
Leonardo da Vinci, 1452–1519

Make the connection
Byzantine, p.10
High Renaissance, p.15
drawing, p.59
golden ratio, p.131

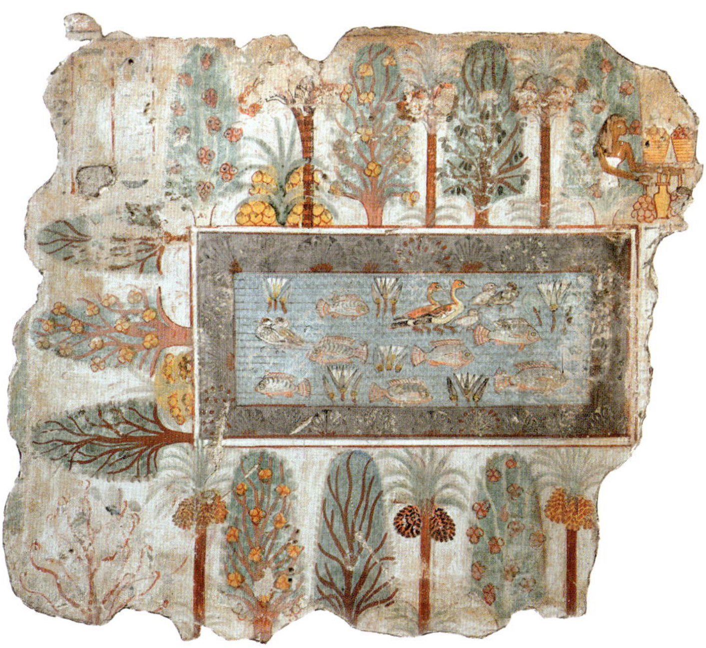

Wall painting from the Tomb of Nebamun, Thebes, New Kingdom, *c.*1350 BCE British Museum, London

triptych

A triptych is most commonly a painting or relief sculpture, divided into three panels. Traditionally, the central panel is the largest and flanked by two smaller side panels (called wings) that may be hinged, allowing them to close over the central image. Triptychs were popular in Christian art of the Middle Ages and the Renaissance, where they were commonly used as altarpieces.

The triptych's structure allowed layered storytelling or theological symbolism. They were usually painted to encourage meditative reflection and to teach worshippers about Christianity. The central panel typically contained the most significant scene – often the Virgin Mary, Christ or a major biblical event – while the side panels presented complementary narratives, saints, donors or symbolic motifs. The reverse sides of the wings were often painted in grisaille (see p.80) or monotone, for use in church services during Lent or times of mourning.

Artists such as Hieronymus Bosch, Rogier van der Weyden, Robert Campin, Matthias Grünewald and Hans Memling created triptychs filled with detail and complex iconography, such as *The Garden of Earthly Delights*, painted by Hieronymus Bosch (below). The format was also practical for the transport, storage and protection of these artworks. Over time, the triptych form was adopted in secular art: for example, in *Three Studies for Figures at the Base of a Crucifixion*, painted by Francis Bacon in 1944.

In a nutshell
A three-panel artwork, often hinged, with a central image flanked by related side scenes.

Why it matters
Enables layered, symbolic storytelling and practical display, especially in religious contexts.

Key figures
Hieronymus Bosch, d.1516
Robert Campin, 1378/9–1444
Matthias Grünewald, 1470–1528
Rogier van der Weyden, *c.*1399–1464

Make the connection
Early Renaissance, p.14
subject/theme, pp.126–7

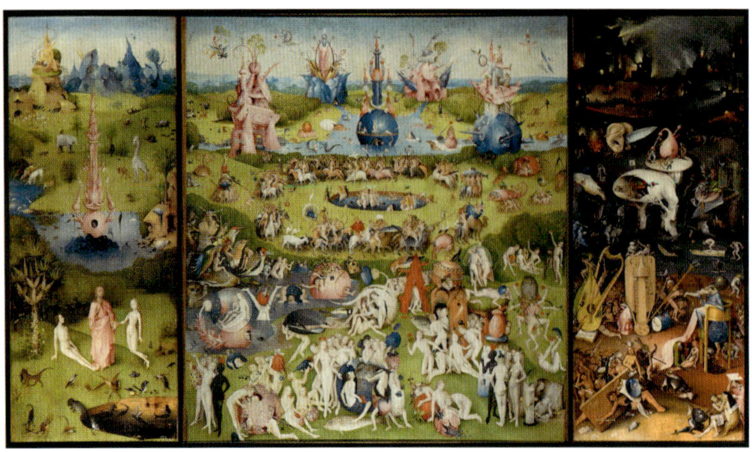

Hieronymus Bosch, *The Garden of Earthly Delights*, 1490–1500 Museo del Prado, Madrid

diptych

Dating back to ancient Roman wax tablets and Byzantine devotional objects, and flourishing in the Christian era, the diptych is a two-panelled artwork, typically hinged so that the panels can be closed like a book. While triptychs were common in churches as large altarpieces, diptychs, equally effective in large and intimate settings, were used for both public and private devotion.

Artists often exploited the dual nature of diptychs, pairing saints who complemented each other, double portraits, donor portraits with sacred figures, or related religious scenes. In the Northern Renaissance, painters frequently created diptychs that combined devotional imagery with lifelike donor portraits. The balance of the diptych lends itself to comparison and juxtaposition: life and death, sin and redemption, saints and sinners, husband and wife, parent and child, or the divine and earthly. By presenting two related yet distinct images adjacently, the format encourages a more reflective mode of viewing.

In *c.*1473–5, Piero della Francesca painted a diptych of the Duke of Urbino, Federico da Montefeltro, and his wife, Battista Sforza, in profile (below). Among other celebrated examples are the Wilton Diptych, showing King Richard II presented to the Virgin and Child by English saints, by an unknown English artist (*c.*1395–99), and Rogier van der Weyden's *Crucifixion Diptych* (*c.*1460), depicting Christ on the Cross and the grieving Virgin Mary.

In a nutshell
An artwork composed of two panels, often hinged, that form a unified whole.

Why it matters
They were crucial in religious art and later inspired storytelling in modern visual art.

Key figures
Francis Bacon, 1909–92
Hans Memling, 1430–94
Jan van Eyck, 1390–1441
Rogier van der Weyden, *c.*1399–1464

Make the connection
Early Renaissance, p.14
woodcut, p.72
tempera, p.120
creativity/innovation, pp.132–3

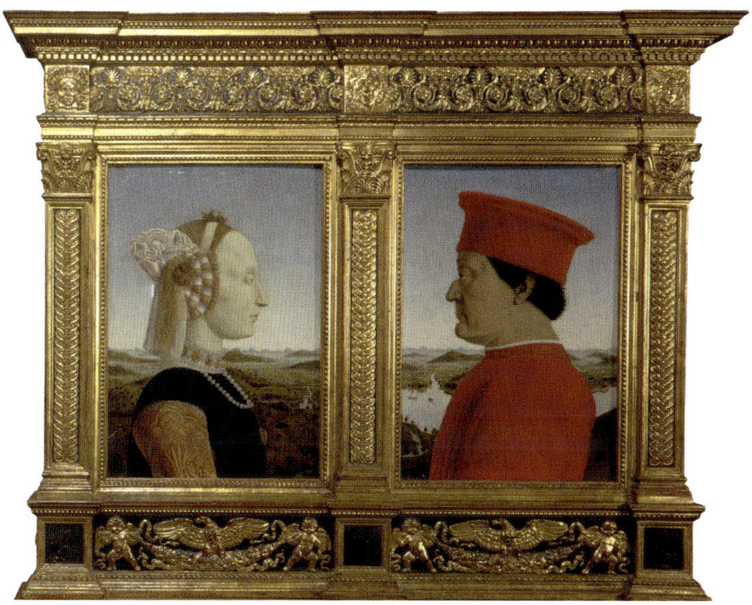

Piero della Francesca, *Portraits of Duke Federico da Montefeltro and Battista Sforza*, *c.*1473–5
Gallerie degli Uffizi, Florence

chiaroscuro

This term originates from the Italian words *chiaro* (meaning 'light') and *oscuro* (meaning 'dark'), and the technique features strong contrasts between light and dark to create a sense of volume, depth, three-dimensionality and drama. In essence, it describes the dramatic use of lighting to create an illusion of form. The use of chiaroscuro became especially prominent during the Renaissance and Baroque periods, when artists sought to make their figures and scenes more lifelike and emotionally intense.

The technique works by simulating how light falls across a subject, creating highlights where light strikes directly and deep shadows in areas that are blocked from light. In paintings or drawings, chiaroscuro can be subtle or highly dramatic, depending on the desired effect. Caravaggio is one of the most renowned masters of chiaroscuro, utilizing it to draw attention to key figures while plunging backgrounds into darkness, to theatrical effect. When the drama of chiaroscuro is heightened and exaggerated, the technique is called tenebrism, widely used in the Baroque period.

Chiaroscuro was not limited to painting; it was also essential in printmaking and drawing, where artists like Albrecht Dürer and Rembrandt used it to powerful effect. By manipulating light and shadow, chiaroscuro allows artists to direct the viewer's gaze, enhance realism and imbue a scene with mood or tension.

In a nutshell
The use of strong contrasts between light and dark to model form.

Why it matters
It adds depth, drama and realism to artworks.

Key figures
Caravaggio, 1571–1610
Artemisia Gentileschi, 1593–1653
Rembrandt, 1606–69
Georges de La Tour, 1593–1652

Make the connection
Renaissance, p.16
Baroque, p.18
shadow/tone, pp.62–3
imagination, p.95
oil paint, p.125

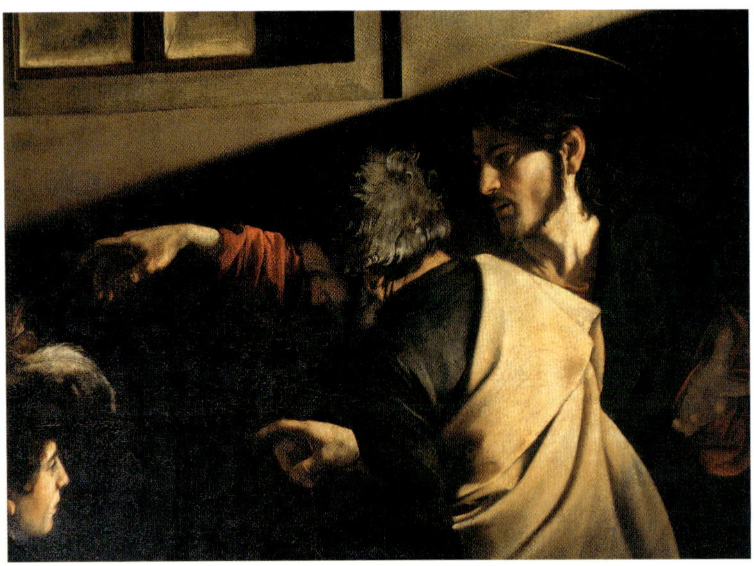

Caravaggio, *The Calling of Saint Matthew* (detail), 1599–1600
Contarelli Chapel, San Luigi dei Francesi, Rome

sfumato

A painting technique that creates soft, gradual transitions between tones and colours, sfumato creates a hazy, smoky or blurred effect. The term derives from the Italian word *sfumare*, meaning 'to evaporate' or 'to vanish like smoke', and the technique allows forms to merge subtly, creating a naturalistic, atmospheric appearance.

In oil painting, sfumato requires skilful layering of translucent glazes. The technique demands patience and precision. With other materials, such as pencil or pastel, a steady hand and careful layering are needed. The results mimic how the human eye perceives form, especially under diffused light.

Sfumato is particularly effective in rendering flesh and facial features. Leonardo da Vinci is the most celebrated practitioner. In the *Mona Lisa* (below), for example, the transitions between light and shadow lend the figure its famously enigmatic expression and ethereal presence. Leonardo's scientific studies of light and anatomy informed his application of the technique. Other Renaissance artists, such as Correggio and Raphael, also employed it to achieve softness and naturalism in their works.

While chiaroscuro creates volume, sfumato produces soft transitions, giving forms a more atmospheric and delicate appearance.

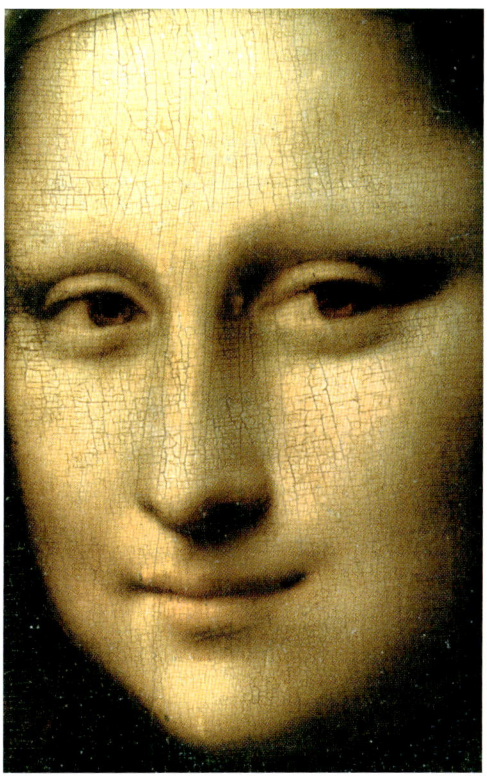

Leonardo da Vinci, *Portrait of Lisa Gherardini, Wife of Francesco del Giocondo*, known as the *Mona Lisa* (detail), *c.*1503–6
Musée du Louvre, Paris

In a nutshell
A painting technique that softly blends colours and tones, for hazy transitions without harsh lines.

Why it matters
It brings subtlety, depth and lifelike realism to portraits.

Key figures
Antonio Allegri da Correggio, 1489–1534
Jean-Auguste-Dominique Ingres, 1780–1867
Raphael, 1483–1520
Leonardo da Vinci, 1452–1519

Make the connection
High Renaissance, p.15
shadow/tone, pp.62–3
life drawing, p.139

woodcut

With origins in China dating back to the 8th century CE, and later flourishing in Europe from the 14th century onwards, woodcut is one of the earliest forms of printmaking. The qualities of woodcut prints are distinctive: bold contrasts, strong lines and a graphic immediacy that makes them visually striking.

The process begins with a block of wood. The design or image is usually drawn or transferred onto the surface in reverse. Because the image is printed from the surface, lines must be bold and simplified, and intricate shading is relatively difficult to achieve. The areas to remain unprinted are cut away with knives or gouges, while the raised surfaces are inked and pressed onto paper or fabric, transferring the image. Because blocks could be reused, woodcuts enabled the production of multiple impressions of the same design.

In Europe, woodcuts gained particular significance in the 15th and 16th centuries, used for religious images, playing cards and book illustrations. Artists such as Albrecht Dürer elevated the medium, demonstrating its capacity to convey detail and tonal variation.

Later, in Japan, woodblock printing reached extraordinary levels of sophistication, especially during the Edo period (17th – 19th centuries), when Ukiyo-e masters (see p.26) created dynamic, colourful scenes of landscapes, actors and everyday life.

In a nutshell
A relief printmaking method in which artists carve images into woodblocks, leaving raised areas to receive ink and be printed.

Why it matters
It democratized art and communication, especially in early book illustration and mass media.

Key figures
Albrecht Dürer, 1471–1528
Utagawa Hiroshige, 1797–1858
Katsushika Hokusai, 1760–1849
Hans Holbein the Younger, 1497/8–1543

Make the connection
Post-Impressionism, p.23
Japonisme, p.28
Art Nouveau, p.32
Pop art, p.46
contrast, p.92

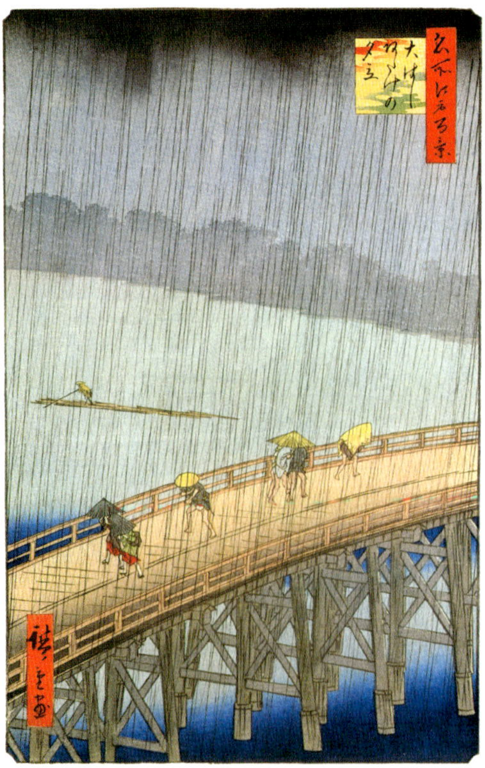

Utagawa Hiroshige, *Great Bridge, Sudden Shower at Atake*, c.1857

etching

A process that involves using acid to bite lines into a metal plate – usually made of copper, zinc or steel – etching dates back to the 3rd millennium BCE, when it was used to decorate carnelian, or quartz, beads by the Indus Valley civilization. By the 16th century, artists such as the Swiss Urs Graf and the Italian Parmigianino were exploring its expressive potential as an art form.

The process begins with the artist coating the metal plate with an acid-resistant ground made of wax or resin. With a pointed etching needle, the artist draws into the ground, or base layer, to expose the metal beneath. Once the design is complete, the artist submerges the plate in acid, which eats into the exposed lines, creating grooves that will hold ink. The ground is cleaned off, ink is worked into the etched lines (and wiped from the rest of the surface), and a sheet of damp paper is placed over the plate. Both are passed through a press, which pushes the paper into the recessed lines to pick up the ink.

Producing more than 300 etchings, Rembrandt revolutionized the medium in the 17th century, and – often combined with engraving and aquatint, a printmaking technique that creates the resemblance of watercolours – the technique flourished in Venice and France.

Etching enables artists to create fine, fluid lines and subtle tonal contrasts, and allows for corrections and reworking at various stages.

In a nutshell
Acid bites lines into a metal plate through a protective ground; when printed, these allow for fluid, expressive marks.

Why it matters
Revolutionized printmaking, allowing greater artistic freedom and reproducibility.

Key figures
Albrecht Dürer, 1471–1528
Francisco Goya, 1746–1828
Rembrandt, 1606–69
James McNeill Whistler, 1834–1903

Make the connection
Baroque, p.18
Romanticism, p.20
line, p.56
tone, p.63

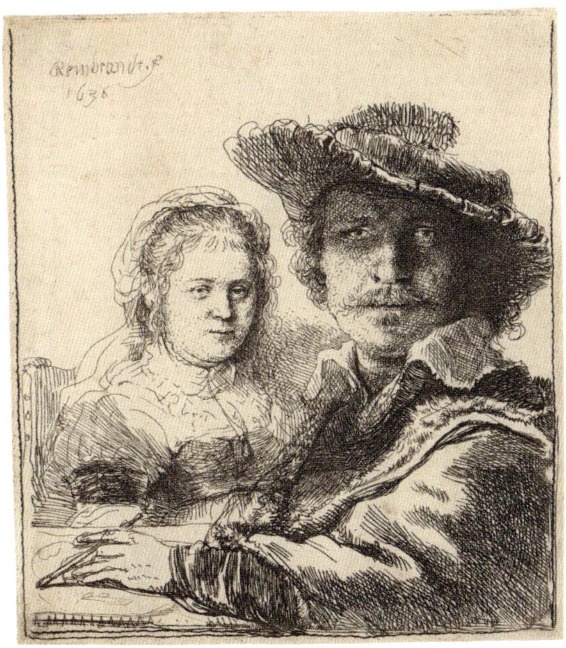

Rembrandt, *Self-Portrait with Saskia*, 1636
National Galleries of Scotland

bas-relief

Widely used across civilizations – from ancient Egypt and Mesopotamia to Renaissance Europe, and in Modern art – bas-relief, also known as low relief, is a sculptural technique in which some parts of an image or design project slightly from the background surface. The projection is often only a few centimetres, which gives the artwork a subtle, slightly textured appearance. Skilled artists use foreshortening (see p.85), overlapping and fine detail to suggest three-dimensionality within the constrained space.

Bas-relief is particularly well-suited to architectural decoration and large narrative panels, where visual clarity from a distance is crucial and precision and legibility take precedence over dramatic physical effects. The restrained projection allows it to integrate with walls or structures, emphasizing linear detail over dramatic shadow. High relief can create a sense of movement and intensity, whereas bas-relief relies on subtle variations in depth and texture.

Bas-relief has been used for temple carvings, architectural friezes, coins and commemorative plaques. In ancient Egyptian art, for example, it was used to depict gods, pharaohs and mythological scenes. These works were typically carved into stone, which allowed them to withstand the elements.

An art form that lies between two-dimensional imagery and three-dimensional form, bas-relief is 'low sculpture' that allows artists to create expressive, subtle designs, conveying texture and depth.

In a nutshell
A sculptural technique in which figures are slightly raised from a flat background.

Why it matters
Used for storytelling and decoration, in architecture, on coins and on monuments.

Key figures
Mino da Fiesole, 1429–84
Lorenzo Ghiberti, 1378–1455
Augustus Saint-Gaudens, 1848–1907

Make the connection
ancient Roman/Romanesque art, pp.8–9
Renaissance, p.16

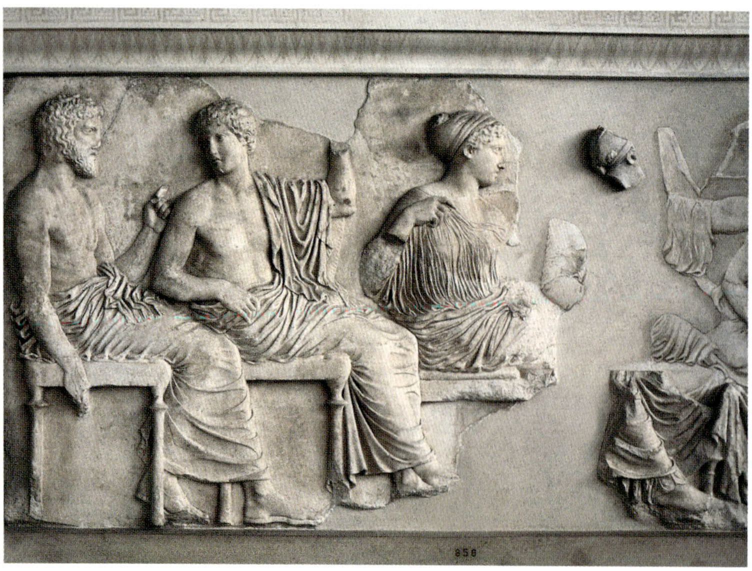

Alcamenes (attrib.), Poseidon, Apollo, Artemis and Aphrodite represented on the east frieze of the Parthenon, c.442–438 BCE
Acropolis Museum, Athens

high relief

High relief, or alto-relievo, is a sculptural technique in which some objects of the design – often figures – project prominently from the background. The sculpted elements that project significantly from the background in high relief often protrude by more than half their depth, which creates a noticeable three-dimensional effect. Offering greater depth and drama than bas-relief, high relief can convey a strong sense of realism, volume and physical presence, and the viewer can observe the artwork from different angles.

Artists creating high-relief artworks create a sculpture attached to a flat background. Because elements of a high-relief artwork protrude significantly from the picture plane, light and shadow are more intense than in bas-relief, giving the work immediacy, depth and dynamism. The work requires careful planning and often robust materials, such as stone or bronze, to support the intricate carving or casting.

Since antiquity, high relief has been a prominent feature in ancient Greek and Roman sculpture, Gothic cathedrals, Renaissance monuments and Baroque façades. It is often used in dynamic narrative scenes or for heroic figures, where movement, emotion and physical interaction between characters are important. While bas-relief is more about line and subtle depth, high relief prioritizes mass and space. Objects that are in high relief sometimes overlap or interact in complex ways, making them especially effective for narrative scenes.

In a nutshell
Comprises elements that project from the background or picture plane significantly, but are still attached.

Why it matters
With dramatic visual impact, high relief works well in stories or scenes that require expressive depth.

Key figures
Gian Lorenzo Bernini, 1598–1680
Antonio Canova, 1757–1822
Lorenzo Ghiberti, 1378–1455

Make the connection
Early Renaissance, p.14
Baroque, p.18
golden ratio, p.131

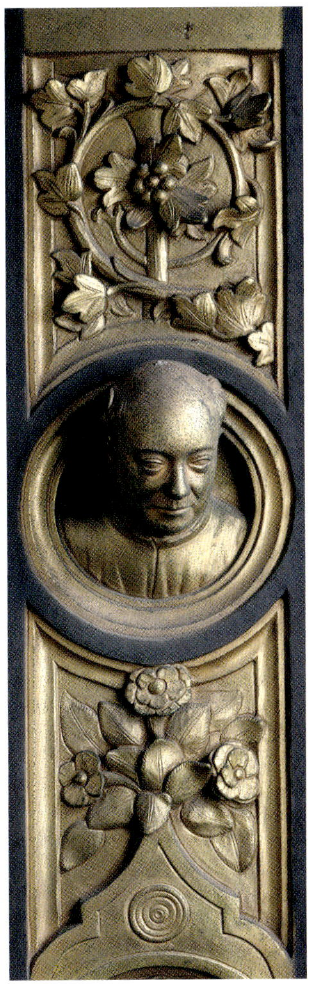

Lorenzo Ghiberti, Self-portrait on a roundel from the *Gates of Paradise* (East doors), 1425–52, in the Baptistery, Florence

drypoint

A type of intaglio printmaking technique in which an image is incised onto a plate, drypoint is traditionally made using copper, zinc or acrylic, and a sharp, pointed needle. The artist draws on the plate (rather than using acid, as in etching; see p.73) and the pressure of the tool creates a burr – or raised edge of metal – which holds ink and give drypoint its distinctive soft lines.

Inking a drypoint plate involves pushing ink into the incised lines and burrs, then carefully wiping the surface clean so only the recessed areas retain ink. The plate is then run through a high-pressure printing press with damp paper, transferring the image. Only a few strong, high-quality impressions can be made from a drypoint plate before the burr is flattened.

Each line reflects the pressure and speed of the artist's hand. There is no separation between the act of drawing and the creation of the printing surface. This closeness often gives drypoint prints a personal, spontaneous quality. Many artists, including Rembrandt, Käthe Kollwitz and Louise Bourgeois, effectively used drypoint.

While technically an intaglio technique, drypoint is uniquely immediate and tactile. Artists can embrace imperfections as part of their work.

In a nutshell
A printmaking technique, drypoint involves scratching images directly into a plate, creating rich, soft lines.

Why it matters
Offers expressive, intimate prints with a handmade quality, valued for their texture and mood.

Key figures
Francisco Goya, 1746–1828
Käthe Kollwitz, 1867–1945
Rembrandt, 1606–69
James McNeill Whistler, 1834–1903

Make the connection
Baroque, p.18
Romanticism, p.20
Impressionism, p.22,
line/mark, pp.56–7

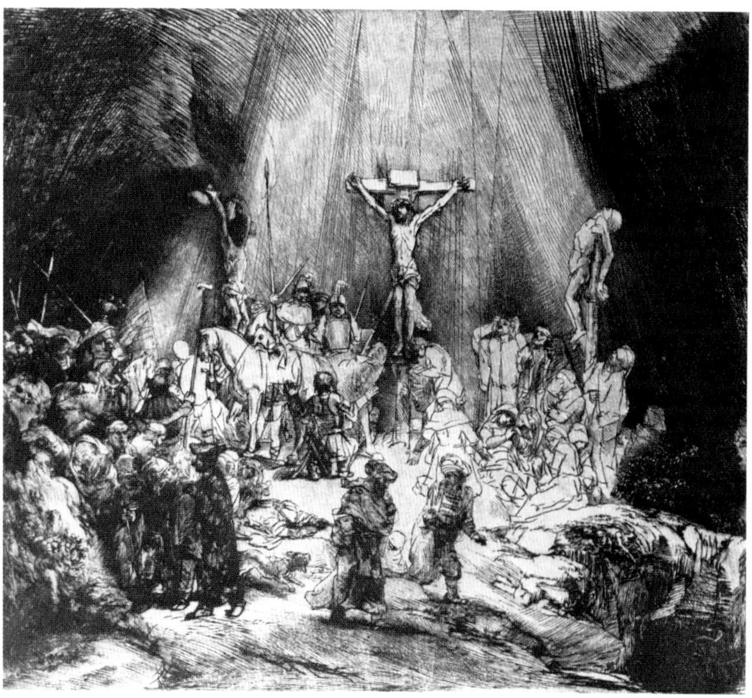

Rembrandt, *The Three Crosses*, 1653
Private collection

engraving

A traditional printmaking technique in which lines are cut directly into a metal plate – usually copper or steel – an engraving is made using a sharp, V-shaped tool called a burin. The artist pushes the burin into the surface to carve precise grooves by hand. These lines hold ink, which is transferred to paper when the plate is printed. Unlike drypoint, engraving produces no burrs or soft, fuzzy edges; the lines are clean and sharply defined.

In contrast to etching (see p.73), which uses acid to bite lines into the plate, engraving relies entirely on the artist's manual control. Every mark must be carefully planned, as errors are difficult to correct. By varying pressure and angle, the engraver can create lines of different depths and widths, producing crisp detail, strong contrast and, in skilled hands, a wide tonal range. Artists such as Albrecht Dürer and William Blake elevated engraving into a highly expressive and intricate art form.

Because engraved lines are deep and durable, plates produce many high-quality impressions, making engraving ideal for large editions. Before modern printing technologies, it was used for illustrations, maps and banknotes. Today, fewer artists practise the method, which is more technically demanding than etching or drypoint.

In a nutshell
A printmaking method in which lines are cut into metal plates to produce detailed images with ink and pressure.

Why it matters
Precise, durable images are created, which have been historically vital in art and reproduction.

Key figures
Gustave Doré, 1832–83
Albrecht Dürer, 1471–1528
Marcantonio Raimondi, 1480–1534
Martin Schongauer, 1448–91

Make the connection
Early/High Renaissance, pp.14–15
Romanticism, p.20
line/mark, pp.56–7
drawing, p.59

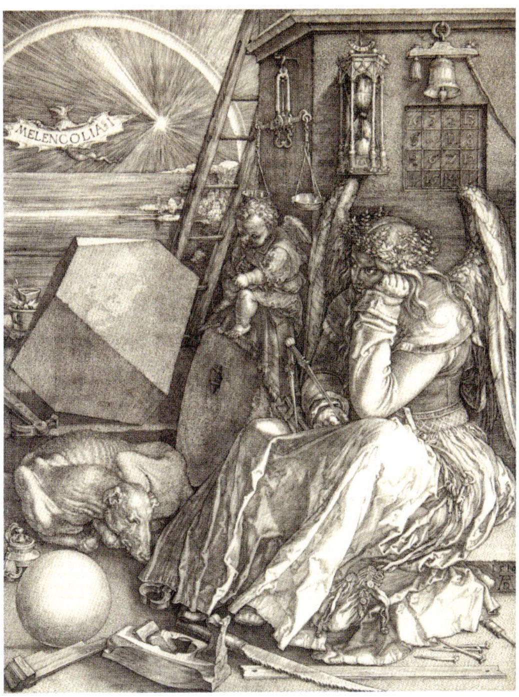

Albrecht Dürer, *Melencolia I*, completed in 1514
Private collection

atmospheric perspective

Alternatively known as aerial perspective, atmospheric perspective is often used in art to create the illusion of distance and depth by simulating how the atmosphere affects the appearance of objects. Unlike linear perspective, which relies on geometry and vanishing points, atmospheric perspective is created through colour and detail (or their absence).

This technique is based on a natural optical phenomenon: as objects recede into the distance, the air between the viewer and the object scatters light, making distant forms appear lighter in tone, less saturated and blurrier than those in the foreground. Details fade, edges soften, and colours appear cooler or bluer. Artists create the sense of atmospheric perspective by lightening and softening the colours and edges of distant elements, while keeping foreground objects brightly coloured, detailed and sharply defined. It is particularly effective for scenes that aim to convey a sense of space, depth and distance.

Artists have used atmospheric perspective for centuries. Chinese painters applied it in ink landscapes as early as the 8th century, using layers of mist and tonal variation to suggest great distances. In the West, the technique became more systematic during the Renaissance. Leonardo da Vinci famously wrote about it in his notebooks, noting how mountains in the distance appear pale and blue-ish compared to the warm, sharp details in the foreground.

In a nutshell
Distant objects appear lighter, bluer and less detailed due to the scattering of light by the atmosphere.

Why it matters
Adds the notion of depth, distance and realism to images.

Key figures
Leonardo da Vinci, 1452–1519
Claude Monet, 1840–1926
J. M. W. Turner, 1775–1851
Jacob van Ruisdael, 1628–82

Make the connection
ancient Roman art, p.8
High Renaissance, p.15
Romanticism, p.20
Impressionism, p.22

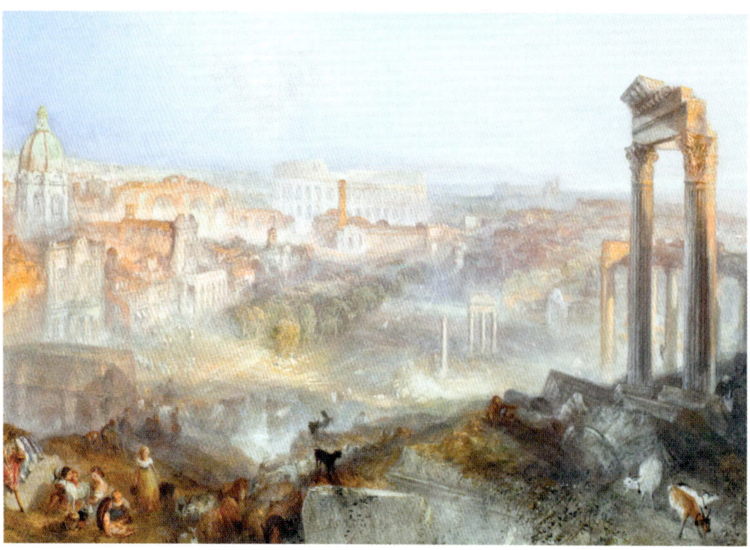

J. M. W. Turner, *Modern Rome – Campo Vaccino*, 1839
J. Paul Getty Museum, Los Angeles

linear perspective

Linear perspective is a system used in art to create the illusion of depth and space on flat surfaces. Although earlier artists used a form of linear perspective, the technique was first established in its mathematical form during the Italian Renaissance to help artists convey the notion of three-dimensional space. Filippo Brunelleschi is credited with developing the first formal rules of linear perspective in the early 15th century, and Leon Battista Alberti later documented them in his treatise *On Painting* (1435).

In linear perspective, the horizon line represents the viewer's eye level, and it is also where the vanishing points are located, where parallel or receding lines converge. In one-point perspective, when there is a direct, central viewpoint, lines converge at a single vanishing point. Two-point perspective has two vanishing points, and three-point perspective introduces a vertical vanishing point, often employed to convey dramatic height or depth.

Formal linear perspective allowed artists to bring realism to painting and to explore new scientific investigations into proportion and human vision; used skilfully, linear perspective allows the artist to guide the viewer's gaze and emphasize spatial relationships. While movements such as Cubism (p.36), Futurism (p.37) and Expressionism (p.30) moved away from the rules of linear perspective, the principles still reinforce much of how depth is represented in art today.

In a nutshell
Parallel lines meet at vanishing points to simulate depth and distance.

Why it matters
Linear perspective revolutionized spatial accuracy in art.

Key figures
Filippo Brunelleschi, 1377–1446
Raphael, 1483–1520
Jan van Eyck, 1390–1441
Johannes Vermeer, 1632–75

Make the connection
Renaissance/ Mannerism, pp.16–17
Art Nouveau, p.32
line, p.56

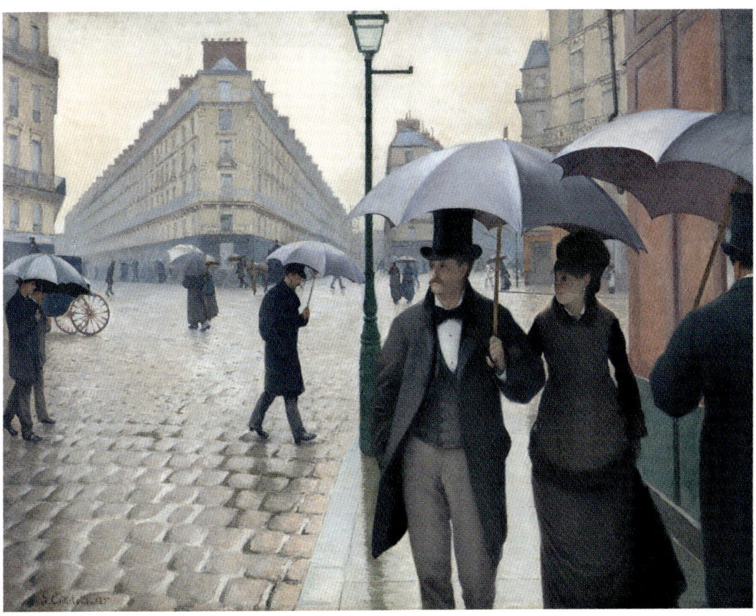

Gustave Caillebotte, *Paris Street, Rainy Day*, 1877
The Art Institute of Chicago

grisaille

A painting technique that is executed entirely in shades of grey, or in another neutral monochrome palette, grisaille is often used to imitate the appearance of sculpture or as a preparatory stage for a larger work. The term originates from the French word *gris*, meaning 'grey'. Although it became especially popular during the Renaissance, grisaille has roots in medieval manuscript illumination and stained glass, where it was used to create depth and volume within a limited colour palette.

In oil painting, grisaille allows artists to establish the tonal structure of a composition before adding colour. This emphasizes value over hue, helping the artist build form and spatial illusion through contrast and shading. Grisaille can also stand on its own as a finished technique. In decorative schemes – especially in fresco and architectural painting – grisaille is usually used to simulate sculptural relief. In altarpieces, it has sometimes served to differentiate sacred visions from the colourful 'real' world. In the 18th and 19th centuries, artists used grisaille for studies and maquettes, or even to achieve the effect of subdued realism.

Grisaille demands a strong understanding of light and form. Because there is no colour to rely on, the painter must carefully model volume and texture using only gradients of tone. This makes it a useful exercise in visual analysis and a valuable foundation for more complex techniques.

In a nutshell
A monochrome painting technique, typically in greys, used to simulate sculpture or build tonal structure.

Why it matters
Helps artists and viewers to focus on light, form and depth without the distraction of colour.

Key figures
Pieter Bruegel the Elder, d.1569
Robert Campin, 1378/9–1444
Hans Memling, d.1494
Peter Paul Rubens, 1577–1640

Make the connection
Renaissance, p.16
drawing, p.59
tone, p.63

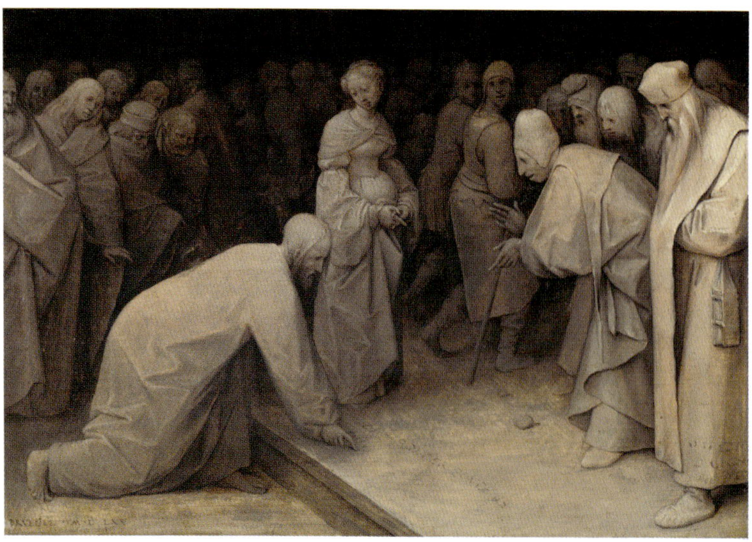

Pieter Bruegel the Elder, *Christ and the Woman taken in Adultery*, 1565
The Courtauld, London

underpainting

A first layer of paint laid down before the main painting is undertaken, underpainting provides structure to guide an artwork's values, depth and overall tone. Used with oils, acrylics, gouache and tempera, underpainting serves to create a tonal map, helping the artist judge tone and colour relationships. Several underpainting approaches are common: grisaille in greys, verdaccio in greenish hues and imprimatura (see p.101). Each method subtly shapes how subsequent layers of colour look and ultimately unifies the finished painting.

One of the most common reasons artists use underpainting is to block in darker values and establish the deepest tones of a painting – often with a single colour, such as burnt umber, raw sienna or a cool green (as in verdaccio). However, depending on the artist's process, underpainting can also take the form of a more complete rendering of the entire composition in limited tones. In traditional art schools, some painters produced quite detailed monochrome versions of their final image before adding any colour. This is often referred to as a 'dead layer'.

Underpainting speeds the painting process, as the artist establishes where highlights and shadows should fall. In more experimental or expressive approaches, parts of the underpainting may even be deliberately allowed to show through for aesthetic effect.

In a nutshell
A foundational layer of paint, often in a single tone, which helps the artist establish tonal values in the final painting.

Why it matters
Ensures strong structure, tonal balance and adds a sense of dimension.

Key figures
Leonardo da Vinci, 1452–1519
Rembrandt, 1606–69
Peter Paul Rubens, 1577–1640
Titian, d.1576

Make the connection
Renaissance, p.16
Baroque, p.18
Romanticism, p.21
scumbling/glazing, pp.86–7

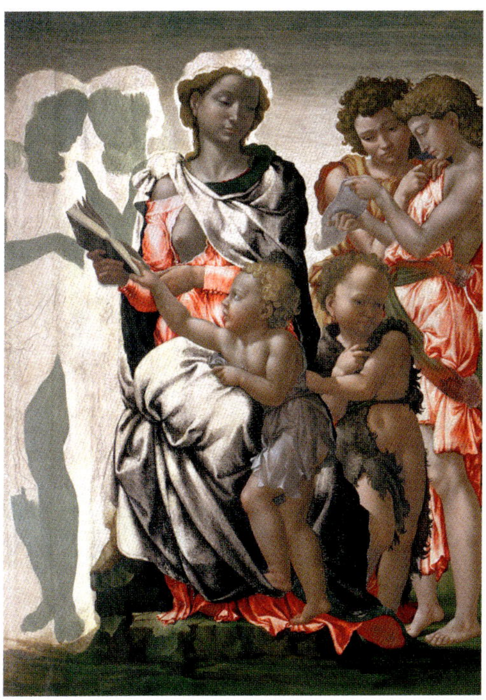

Michelangelo, *The Manchester Madonna*, *c.*1494 National Gallery, London

sculpture

Unlike painting, sculpture is a three-dimensional art that occupies real space. Traditional materials used by sculptors include stone, wood, metal and clay. Contemporary sculptors also utilize materials such as plastic, found objects, polyester resin, fibreglass and silicone. Traditional sculpture methods include carving, modelling, casting (in bronze, via the lost-wax process) and assembling.

Historically, sculpture has served both aesthetic and functional roles. In ancient civilizations, such as Egypt, Greece and Rome, sculpture was used to honour deities, commemorate leaders and decorate architecture. In addition to conveying a sense of balance and proportion, ancient Greek marble figures often emphasized idealized human forms. Gothic cathedral carvings and Renaissance and Baroque statues often blended realism and naturalism with spiritual symbolism. By the 19th century, sculptors such as Auguste Rodin (see *The Thinker*, below) and Camille Claudel introduced expressive surfaces and emotional depth to their work, while others, including Constantin Brâncuși, Henri Matisse, Barbara Hepworth and Henry Moore, explored abstraction and organic forms. Other artists began using unconventional materials to create sculpture. Some artists, such as Alexander Calder and Jean Tinguely, have produced kinetic (moving) sculpture.

Sculptors explore volume, balance and surface, while the viewer experiences a direct relationship with the artwork in the area and location it inhabits.

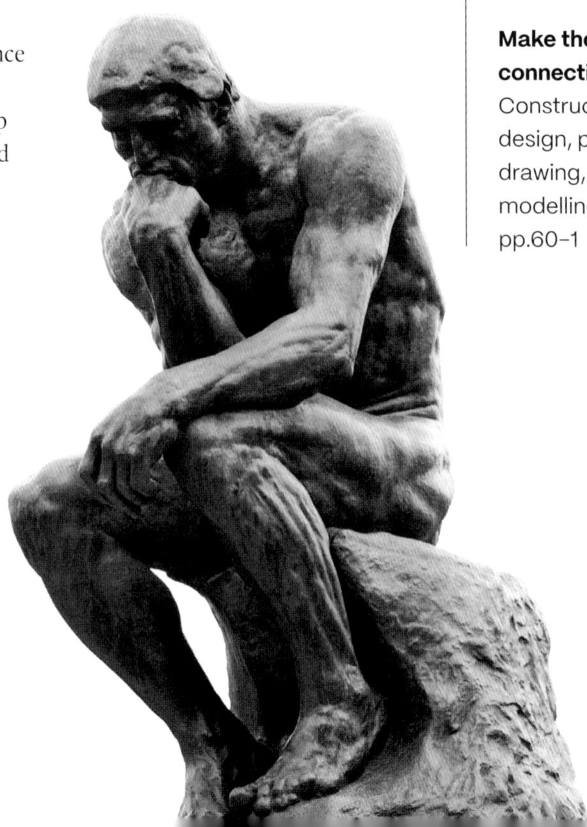

Auguste Rodin,
The Thinker, 1903
Rodin Museum, Paris

In a nutshell
Through carving, modelling, casting or assembling, sculptors create forms in three dimensions.

Why it matters
Captures physical presence, emotion and cultural identity across time.

Key figures
Constantin Brâncuși, 1876–1957
Camille Claudel, 1864–1943
Michelangelo, 1475–1564
Auguste Rodin, 1840–1917

Make the connection
Constructivism, p.39
design, p.55
drawing, p.59
modelling/carving, pp.60–1

installation

Like freestanding sculpture, an installation can often be experienced from multiple angles. Typically large-scale, immersive, and site-specific, installations are often made in and responding to a particular environment.

Installations can be created from conventional or unexpected materials. They may be situated in art galleries, museums, outdoor spaces or unusual locations. The space surrounding these artworks is often important, and in installations, artists often aim to blur the distinction between fine art and the broader environment. While conventional artworks are usually permanent, installations are generally temporary, and frequently arresting, theatrical and time-based. Some encourage viewer interaction.

In 1991, Cornelia Parker created *Cold Dark Matter: An Exploded View* (below). She suspended fragments of a garden shed that had been blown apart from a gallery ceiling. Lit by a single bulb, the floating debris cast dramatic shadows, transforming destruction into a contemplative experience concerned with fragility and memory.

Installation art shifts the emphasis from the object to the experience. It is always about the present, the space and the viewer.

In a nutshell
Using mixed media, installations are usually grand in scale, immersive, and site-specific.

Why it matters
Challenges perception, invites interaction and redefines the viewer's role.

Key figures
Agnes Denes, b.1931
Olafur Eliasson, b.1967
Yayoi Kusama, b.1929
Cornelia Parker, b.1956

Make the connection
imagination, p.95
assemblage, p.102
innovation, p.133

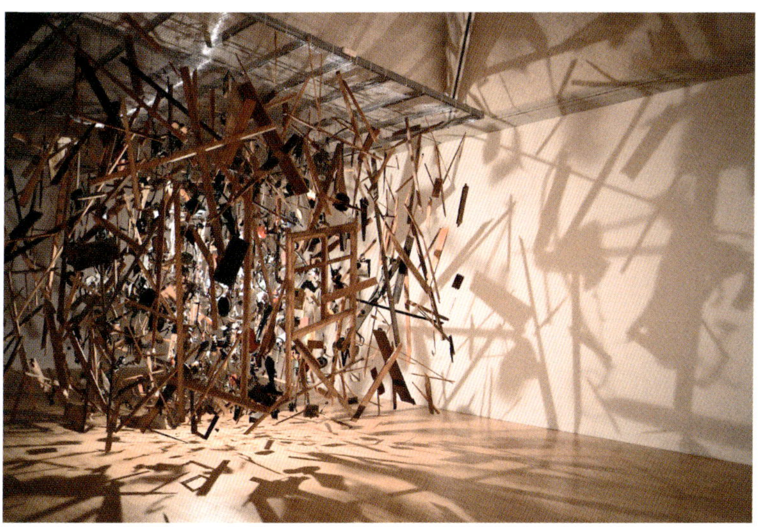

Cornelia Parker, *Cold Dark Matter: An Exploded View*, 1991, installed at Tate Britain, London, 2022

distortion

Exaggeration, stretching, expanding, changing shape or proportions – all are forms of distortion, which in art can be subtle or extreme. Distortion is usually a deliberate tool, and it can encourage viewers to see beyond the literal and engage with deeper, often subjective interpretations of a subject or theme. Distortion is one way artists break away from naturalistic representation, often to express inner feelings, create stylistic effects or critique social norms.

Distortion has been an essential part of art in movements such as Expressionism, Cubism and Surrealism (see p.43). Artists such as Egon Schiele, Giorgio de Chirico and Edvard Munch elongated limbs and torsos, twisted facial features and tilted buildings to convey psychological intensity and inner turmoil. In Cubism, objects appear to be fragmented, redefining spatial logic, while Surrealists warped reality to explore the subconscious and dream states.

Distortion can also result from cultural or political influences. During the Renaissance, anamorphism became a visual art technique in which images appear distorted when viewed from a specific angle. See, for example, the skull in *The Ambassadors* (below) by Hans Holbein the Younger, which comes into focus only when viewed from an angle. Anamorphism allows artists to explore perception and illusion and display their technical skills.

Distortion enables artists to move beyond the constraints of realism, challenging conventional artistic norms and societal expectations.

In a nutshell
Alters form, proportion and, often, perspectives.

Why it matters
Challenges realism, deepens expression and reshapes our perception of truth.

Key figures
Francis Bacon, 1909–92
Edvard Munch, 1863–1944
Jenny Saville, b.1970
Egon Schiele, 1890–1918

Make the connection
Renaissance, p.16
Expressionism, p.30
Cubism, p.36
linear perspective, p.79

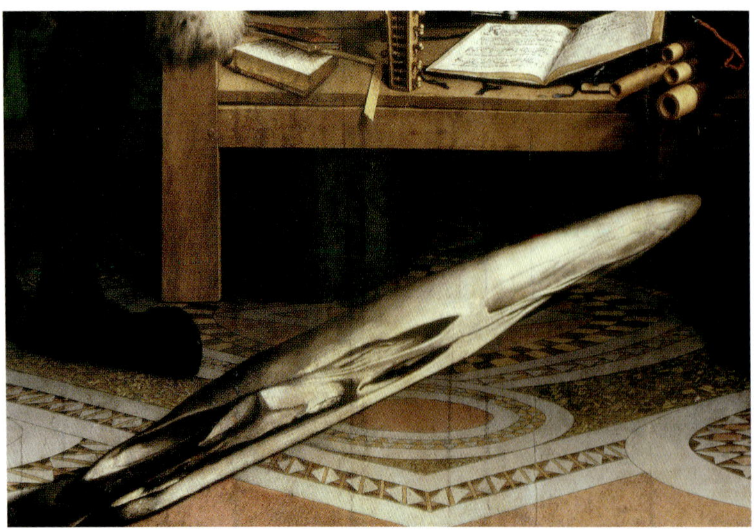

Hans Holbein the Younger, *The Ambassadors* (detail), 1533
National Gallery, London

foreshortening

Part of the broader technique of perspective, foreshortening creates the illusion of depth by altering an object's proportions. Parts that are closer to the viewer are drawn larger, while those further away are reduced in size, allowing the artist to mimic, on a two-dimensional surface, how the human eye perceives three-dimensional space.

While technically the artist is altering the proportions of objects or figures, often to quite intense or dramatic effect, foreshortening differs from distortion in that these alterations are used to capture objects as the eye perceives them (typically in close-up or from an unusual angle). The object or figure is distorted to make it look realistic. For example, if we are looking at a hand or foot coming towards us, it will appear far larger than the rest of the body. When viewing an object from above, the part that is meant to be closest to us will appear larger in proportion to the rest of the object. Think of comic book illustrations and animations, which often employ foreshortening for dramatic purposes, showing, for example, a superhero's fist seeming to project towards the viewer.

The technique of foreshortening became prominent in Western art from the Renaissance and Baroque periods.

In a nutshell
The distortion of objects or figures to make them appear to realistically recede or advance

Why it matters
Creates a dramatic sense of space and perspective.

Key figures
Caravaggio, 1571–1610
Andrea Mantegna, *c.*1431–1506
Michelangelo, 1475–1564
Jacopo Tintoretto, *c.*1518–94

Make the connection
sketching/drawing, pp.58–9
linear perspective, p.79
observation, p.94
figurative, p.129

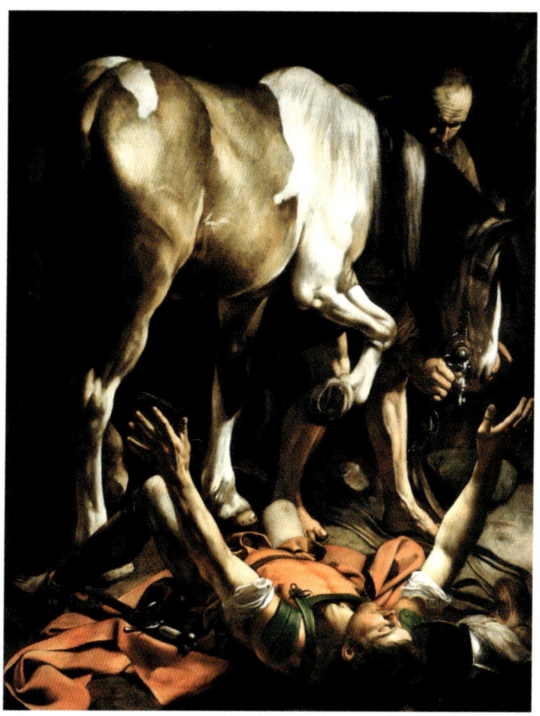

Caravaggio, *The Conversion of St Paul on the Way to Damascus*, *c.*1600–01
Santa Maria del Popolo, Rome

scumbling

A dry-brush painting technique in which a thin, opaque or semi-opaque layer of a lighter colour is brushed over (usually) a darker, dry underlayer, allowing parts of the base to show through. Scumbling is achieved by dragging a brush with minimal paint across a surface of dried paint, catching the raised textures of the earlier layer.

Scumbling is especially effective for depicting mist, clouds, aged surfaces or subtle transitions in skin tones. Additionally, the hazy or textured effects of scumbling can suggest atmosphere, light diffusion or interesting textures. Scumbling can add highlights to dark backgrounds, soften transitions between colours, or create broken-colour effects. Although it is mainly used in oil painting, scumbling can also be worked with other materials, including pastels, acrylics and coloured pencils.

A Western technique, scumbling was first seen in the Renaissance and later used by Rembrandt, J. M. W. Turner and the Impressionists. Turner's *Snow Storm: Steam-Boat off a Harbour's Mouth* (below) exemplifies the technique in the hazy effects that veil the stormy sea, creating muted radiance and atmospheric depth.

Unlike glazing, which is transparent, scumbling tends to mute and soften underlying tones rather than intensifying them. Scumbling and glazing can complement each other, however: one shrouds, the other unveils. Both techniques enhance the resonance and richness of paintings.

In a nutshell
The application of a thin, opaque layer of colour over a dry base.

Why it matters
Creates atmosphere, depth, textures, shadows and highlights.

Key figures
John Constable, 1776–1837
Rembrandt, 1606–69
Jacopo Tintoretto, *c.*1518–94
J. M. W. Turner, 1775–1851

Make the connection
Romanticism/Realism, pp.20–1
Impressionism, p.22
chalk/oil pastel, pp.114–15
oil paint, p.125

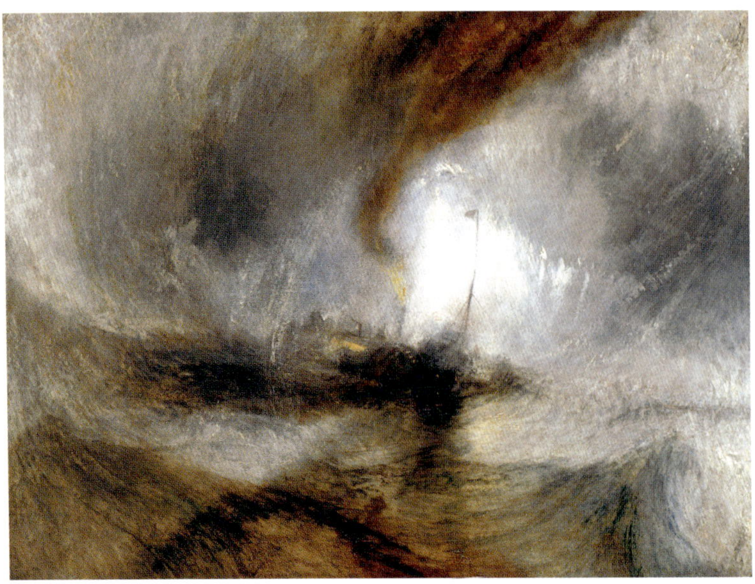

J. M. W. Turner, *Snow Storm: Steam-Boat off a Harbour's Mouth*, 1842
Tate

glazing

Glazing is the application of sheer, translucent layers of paint over a dry, opaque base, enhancing the colour and luminosity of the underlying layer. It is particularly used in oil painting, where slow drying times allow for effective layering.

During the Renaissance and Baroque periods, artists such as Jan van Eyck and Titian refined the glazing technique. The application of multiple glazes can create the effects of complex skin tones, luminous fabrics and atmospheric backgrounds. Each layer modifies the one beneath it, creating nuanced transitions.

Glazing requires a medium, such as linseed oil or alkyd, to thin the paint and maintain transparency. Each layer must dry before the next is applied, making the process time-consuming. The result is a glowing effect with subtly shifting colours.

In modern practice, glazing is used to evoke mood and realism. It can unify disparate elements, tone down overly bright areas or add warmth and complexity to shadows. Acrylic painters also use the technique, often with special glazing mediums that slow down drying times.

In a nutshell
Transparent paint is layered over dry colour to enrich luminosity and hue.

Why it matters
Adds depth, clarity and a glowing surface to paintings.

Key figures
Jan van Eyck, d.1441
Rembrandt, 1606–69
Titian, d.1576
Johannes Vermeer, 1632–75

Make the connection
High Renaissance, p.15
Baroque, p.18
acrylic/oil paint, pp.124–5

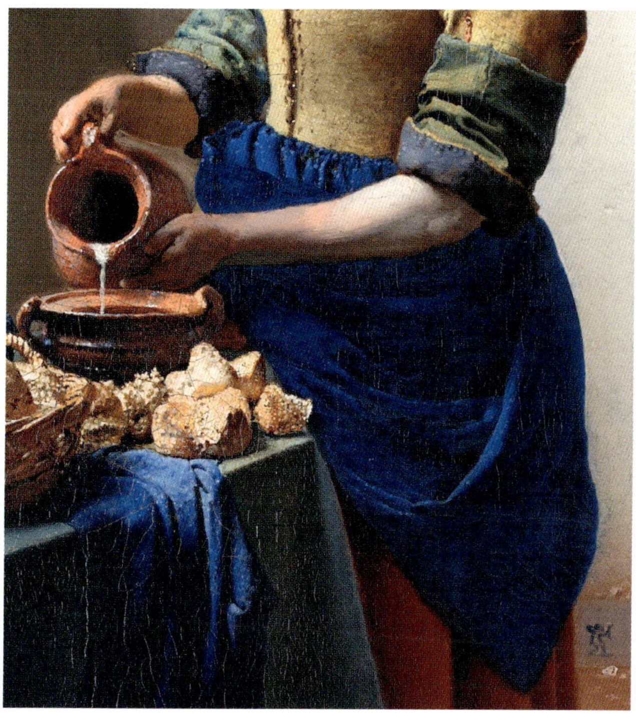

Johannes Vermeer, *The Milkmaid* (detail), *c.*1658–60 Rijksmuseum, Amsterdam

screenprinting

Also known as silkscreen printing or serigraphy, screenprinting is an ancient but enduringly popular printing technique used in both fine and commercial art, in which ink is pushed through a mesh screen onto a variety of materials, including posters, textiles and signage.

The basic process of screenprinting involves stretching a fine mesh (traditionally silk, now often polyester) over a frame to create a screen. A stencil is applied to this screen, obscuring the areas to be ink-free. The screen is then placed over the surface to be printed, and thick ink is spread across the screen using a squeegee (a tool with a rubber 'blade' that presses the ink through the screen). The ink passes through the mesh, around the stencil, transferring the image or design onto the surface beneath. Each colour in a screenprint is applied separately, so a new screen and stencil are required for every colour layer.

The bold, vivid effect of screenprinting – often with strong contrast and flat areas of colour – has made it popular in commercial contexts and among artists such as Andy Warhol and Eduardo Paolozzi. The technique, however, requires planning and precision. Registration (aligning different colour layers) can be challenging, especially for detailed designs. Despite this, the adaptability and visual impact of screenprinting have made it a lasting and influential technique.

In a nutshell
A printing technique where thick, often brightly coloured ink is pushed over stencils through a mesh screen.

Why it matters
Versatile, ideal for vibrant imagery and widely used in both art and industry.

Key figures
Sister Corita Kent, 1918–86
Roy Lichtenstein, 1923–97
Eduardo Paolozzi, 1924–2005
Andy Warhol, 1928–87

Make the connection
Pop art, p.46
line, p.56
woodcut, p.72
contrast, p.92

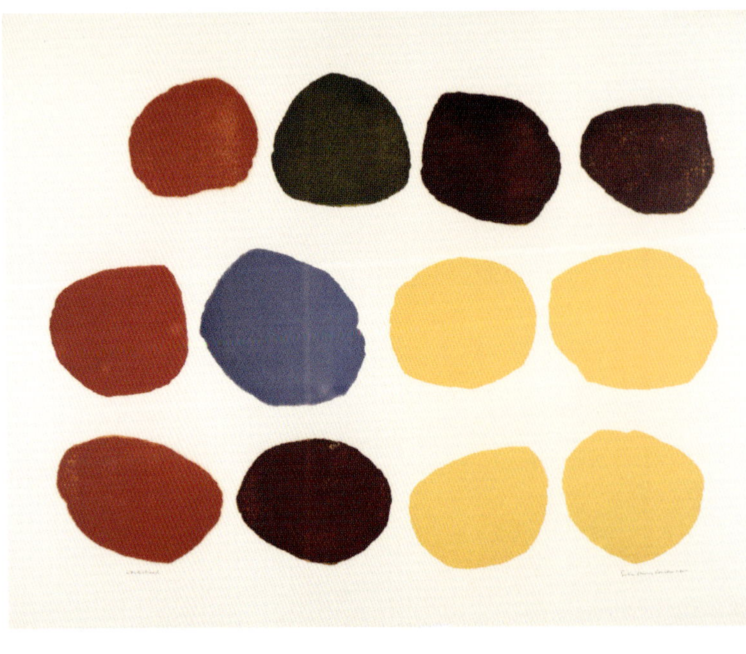

Corita Kent, *Wonderbread*, 1962
Corita Art Center

lithography

Based on the mutual repulsion of oil and water, lithography was invented in the late 18th century by the German inventor and playwright Alois Senefelder and quickly became popular for both artistic and commercial purposes. Unlike relief or intaglio methods (see pp.74–5, 76), lithography is a 'planographic' technique, meaning that the image is printed from an entirely flat surface.

In traditional lithography, the artist draws directly onto a smooth limestone block using a greasy substance, such as a special lithographic crayon or ink. This stone is then treated with a solution of gum arabic and nitric acid, which makes the greasy areas attract an (oil-based) ink while the untreated (and water-coated) areas repel it. When the stone is moistened and inked, the ink sticks only to the drawing, and this image is then transferred onto paper using a press. Modern lithography often uses metal plates, usually aluminium. Colour lithographs require separate stones or plates for each colour, which, as in screenprinting, requires precise registration.

Lithography allows artists to capture delicate textures, soft shading and precise lines, qualities often lost in screenprinting. The resulting prints can appear as immediate as pencil, crayon or ink: for example, in the evocative lithographs by Käthe Kollwitz (below). Because of the method, lithography preserves the nuance and spontaneity of the original drawing in multiple impressions.

In a nutshell
A printmaking method that transfers drawn images from a flat surface onto paper, based on the repulsion of oil and water.

Why it matters
Allows for detailed, expressive prints; revolutionized both art and commercial printing.

Key figures
Käthe Kollwitz, 1867–1945
Alphonse Mucha, 1860–1939
Pablo Picasso, 1881–1973
Henri de Toulouse-Lautrec, 1864–1901

Make the connection
Post-Impressionism, p.23
Expressionism, p.30
line/mark, pp.56–7
drawing, pp.59

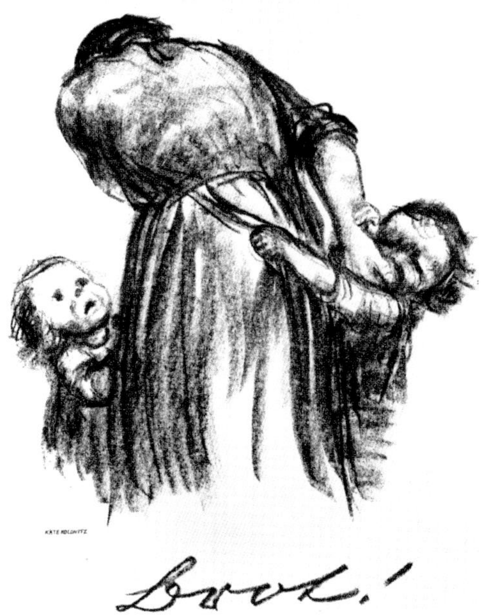

Käthe Kollwitz, *Bread!*, 1924
British Museum, London

photography

Formally invented in the early 19th century by Nicéphore Niépce, who produced the first permanent photograph around 1826–7, photography is the practice of creating images by capturing light, initially through chemical processes (now primarily through digital sensors). Louis Daguerre improved the process with the daguerreotype (1839), making photography more accessible.

Photography revolutionized the visual arts. Because it could record reality with unprecedented accuracy, it challenged painters to rethink their role, contributing to new artistic movements such as Impressionism and Cubism. Artists also quickly embraced it as an expressive medium, using light and composition to convey emotion, and to document the visible world.

Today's photographers use tools such as long exposures, high-speed capture, studio lighting, post-processing software and mobile devices to shape their images. Photography informs journalism, shapes social media, drives advertising and continues to thrive in fine art contexts. It remains a powerful art form because it blends technical skill with personal vision, enduring as a creative and cultural force.

In a nutshell
The creative capture of light and time, by chemical or digital means.

Why it matters
Enabled the immediate capture of fleeting moments, preserving visual experiences with clarity and permanence.

Key figures
Ansel Adams, 1902–84
Julia Margaret Cameron, 1815–79
Dorothea Lange, 1895–1965
Edward Weston, 1886–1958

Make the connection
Impressionism, p.22
Cubism, p.36
Surrealism, p.43
Photorealism, p.50

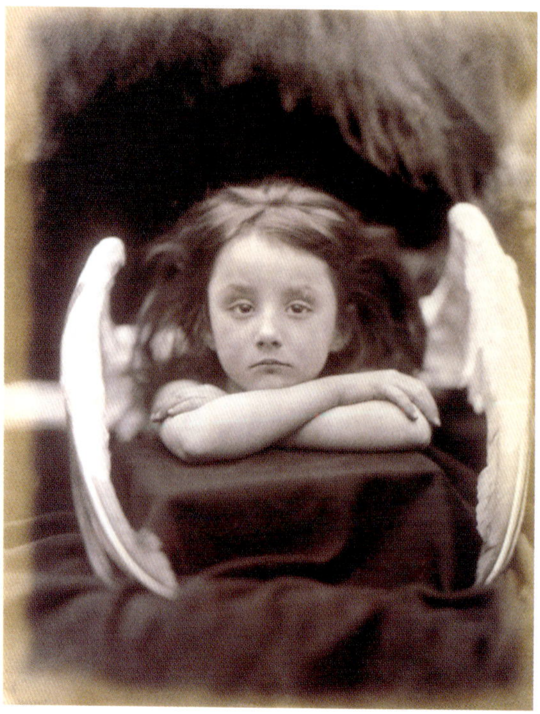

Julia Margaret Cameron, *I Wait (Rachel Gurney as an Angel)*, 1872
Private collection

photomontage

Photomontage is the art of assembling disparate photographic elements into a single, unified composition. It is usually created by cutting, arranging and sticking down parts of several photographs to form a new image. By juxtaposing unrelated elements, artists create visual metaphors, construct imagined realities and generate commentaries on reality and its representation in the media.

Emerging in the early 20th century, photomontage was embraced by Dadaists and later by the Surrealists, who used it to challenge traditional aesthetics and critique political and social values. One of the earliest practitioners was Hannah Höch, whose satirical collages explored gender roles and the values of Weimar society.

Although traditionally created manually, photomontages can also be made digitally, using photo-editing software. Cut-outs, overlays and digital manipulation allow for playful or radical reimaginings of space, identity and meaning in contemporary photomontage.

The technique is especially potent in exploring themes of media saturation, fragmentation and cultural hybridity. It extends photography's legacy by challenging the 'truths' the medium seems to present.

In a nutshell
The collage of multiple photographic elements into a single composition.

Why it matters
Disrupts realism, amplifies symbolism and enables bold commentary on identity, politics and media.

Key figures
John Heartfield, 1891–1968
Hannah Höch, 1889–1978
David Hockney, b.1937
Martha Rosler, b.1943

Make the connection
Cubism, p.36
Dada/Surrealism, pp.42–3
contrast, p.92
collage, p.103

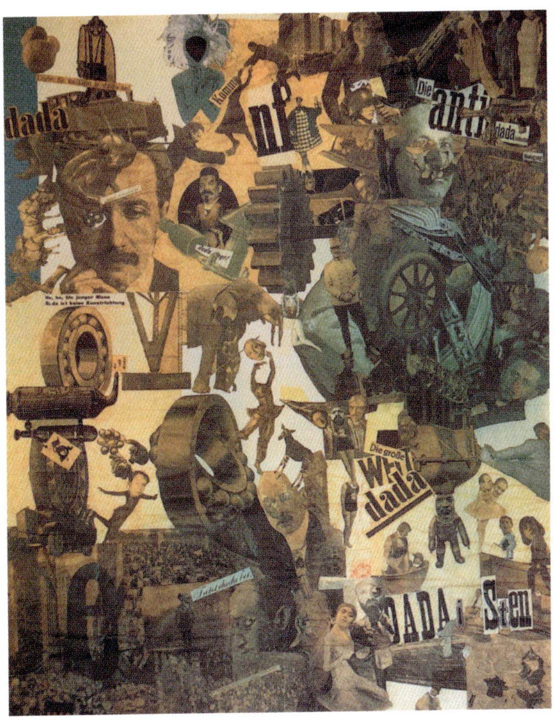

Hannah Höch, *Cut with the Kitchen Knife through the Last Epoch of Weimar Beer-Belly Culture in Germany*, 1919 Staatliche Museen, Berlin

contrast

By placing elements that differ, oppose or clash near each other in a work of art, artists can create visual interest or tension. Contrast is a fundamental principle that artists use to guide the viewer's eye and evoke emotional responses.

Contrast in art can manifest in many forms: light and dark, rough and smooth, warm and cool, complementary colours (opposite colours on the colour wheel), and even realism and abstraction. Textural contrasts, such as combining smooth surfaces with rough or shiny with matte, add tactile richness. Stark contrasts can create tension or drama, while softer contrasts may evoke a sense of calmness or harmony. Caravaggio's chiaroscuro technique – his use of strongly contrasting light and dark – is a powerful form of contrast. Equally powerful is the placement of opposing colours close together, which can make the two appear either calmer or more vibrant. Picasso contrasted black, white and shades of grey to dramatic effect in his vast painting *Guernica* (1937), which portrays the atrocities of the Spanish Civil War.

Contrast can also be conceptual, and relates to the presentation of art as well as its content. A serene landscape might be disrupted by a vibrant sun or a dark cloud, for example, creating narrative tension. Or a sculpture might be placed in a contrasting environment to amplify its presence.

In a nutshell
The use of opposing elements, such as light and dark, or rough and smooth, to create visual interest.

Why it matters
Guides the viewer's eye, adds depth and enhances mood or drama.

Key figures
Caravaggio, 1571–1610
Artemisia Gentileschi, 1593–1654
Henri Matisse, 1869–1854
Rembrandt, 1606–69

Make the connection
Renaissance, p.16
Baroque, p.18
shadow/tone, pp.62–3
chiaroscuro, p.70

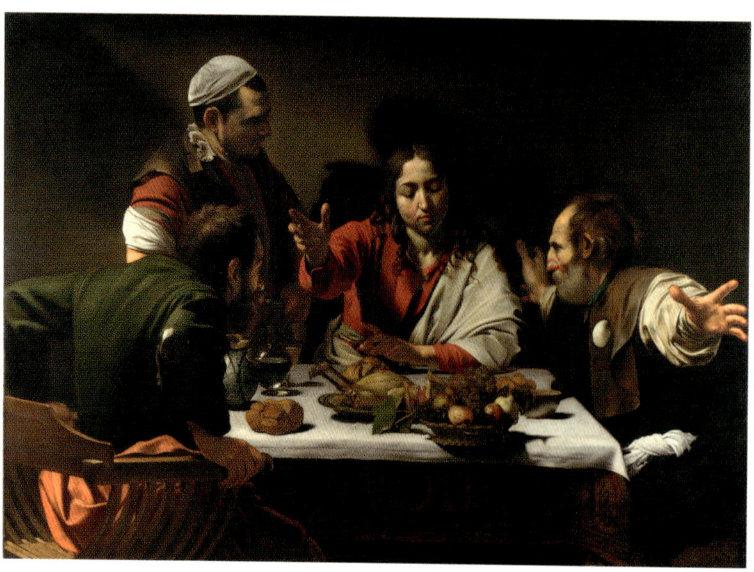

Michelangelo, *The Supper at Emmaus*, 1601
National Gallery, London

unity

Unity is when all aspects of a work of art seem to belong together. Even if contrast is involved, unity refers to the overall sense of harmony that makes an artwork feel cohesive.

Artists employ various techniques to achieve unity. Repeating shapes or lines throughout a composition can help create a sense of rhythm and consistency. Elements placed close together often feel connected, helping to organize space and meaning. One of the most familiar ways to create unity is through colour. A limited or carefully chosen palette can give an artwork consistency. Similarly, using comparable textures or brushstrokes helps surfaces appear unified. Using continuous, flowing brushstrokes and harmonious colour palettes, Monet's *Water Lilies* series (below) conveys a sense of unity by merging water, light and reflection.

Importantly, unity is about balancing different elements. A work can include contrast, variety and even surprise, but when unified, these elements work together rather than competing for attention. For instance, a landscape might use repeating tree shapes, a consistent colour scheme and similar painting techniques throughout. Even if the scene includes a lot of detail or movement, the viewer still experiences it as one connected image. Good artists often strive for a particular balance, including enough variety to keep the artwork interesting while maintaining enough unity to make the work feel cohesive and consistent.

In a nutshell
When all elements in a work of art seem connected and harmonious.

Why it matters
A clear, cohesive visual experience that helps an artwork to feel complete and balanced.

Key figures
Katsushika Hokusai, 1760–1849
Claude Monet, 1840–1926
Georges Seurat, 1859–91
James McNeill Whistler, 1834–1903

Make the connection
Ukiyo-e, p.26
Suprematism, p.38
Bauhaus, p.41
sublime, p.152

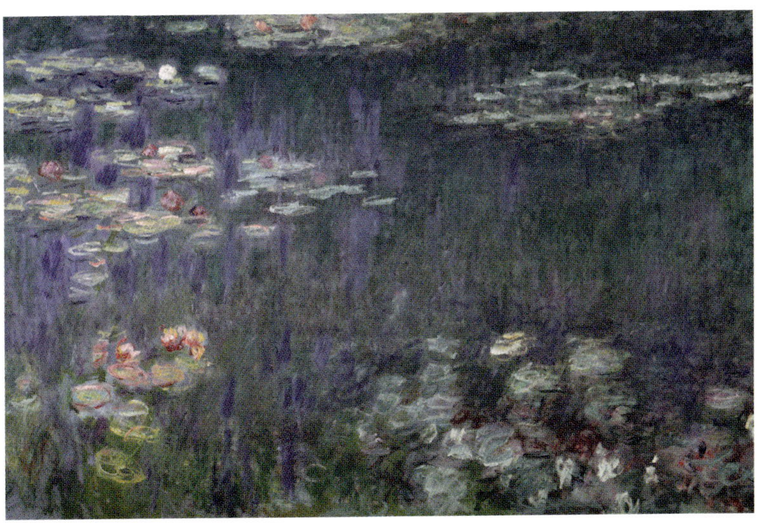

Claude Monet, *Waterlilies: Green Reflections*, 1914–18
Musée de l'Orangerie, Paris

observation

The careful, deliberate act of studying the visual world to capture its details accurately and sensitively in a work of art: observation is how artists perceive and interpret the world. As the foundation of creation, observation involves engaging deeply with visual stimuli, noticing subtleties in light, form, texture, proportion, spatial relationships and movement, and translating those impressions into visual art.

Technically, observation allows artists to replicate proportions, perspectives and anatomical accuracy. Intuitively, it helps them capture mood, emotion and atmosphere. Even abstract artists, who may not depict recognizable subjects from the world around us, use observation to assess balance, contrast and rhythm within their work. By training the eye to see, observation also cultivates awareness, helping artists to make connections and consciously recognize patterns. While observational art is based on what is seen, it also invites interpretation and expression through each artist's unique perspective and handling of materials. Artists filter what they see through their own experiences, emotions and cultures, then they interpret and shape how they represent reality.

Developing observational skills is a lifelong process. To improve their technical ability, artists often sketch, take notes, or revisit subjects repeatedly to deepen their understanding. Observation is the foundation of nearly all art, enabling artists to transform fleeting moments into enduring expressions.

In a nutshell
Artists study real subjects – primary sources – to capture accurate details.

Why it matters
Develops technical skill and enables artists to create lifelike, believable images.

Key figures
John Constable, 1776–1837
Leonardo da Vinci, 1452–1519
Clara Peeters, c.1588/90–d. after 1621
Grant Wood, 1891–1942

Make the connection
sketching/drawing, pp.58–9
figurative, p.129
still life/life drawing, pp.138–9
negative space, p.140

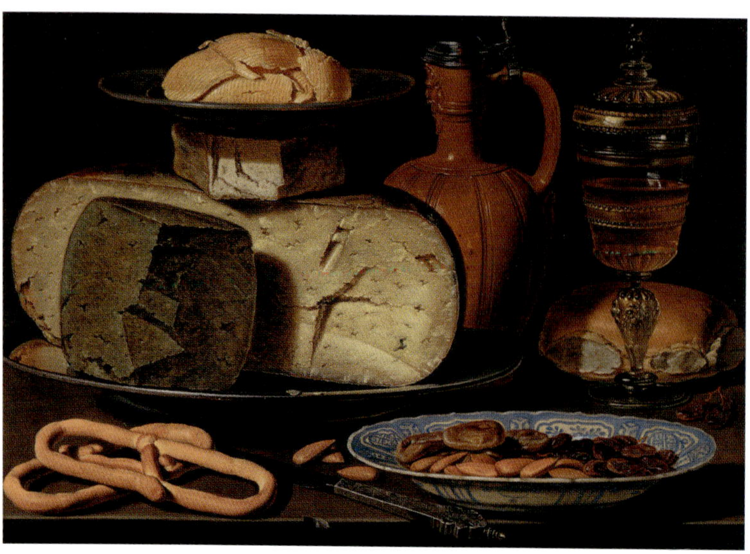

Clara Peeters, *Still Life with Cheeses, Almonds and Pretzels*, c.1615
Mauritshuis, The Hague

imagination

By inventing images or concepts, artists transcend physical reality and express their own inner visions, emotions or abstract ideas. Many artists begin with observation – studying and drawing what they see – then use their imagination to create final artworks.

Imaginative art gives form to the intangible and invites the viewer to enter worlds shaped by the artist's mind; it offers artists the freedom to distort realities. Edvard Munch's *The Scream* (below) exemplifies this freedom, transforming an ordinary moment into a distorted landscape that visualizes inner anxiety rather than literal reality. Through imagination, artists can construct mythical creatures, symbolic compositions, fictional characters and more.

While inspiration comes from external stimuli, the imagination evolves through an artist's personal experiences, memories or dreams. Where observational art stays close to what's real, imaginative art breaks free from those boundaries.

Imaginative art invites wide interpretation, and it is also typically innovative and experimental. Imaginative art serves as a conduit between the internal and external worlds, the real and the fictional, allowing creativity and transformation to flourish.

In a nutshell
Imagination in art involves creating images, ideas or scenes that transcend visible reality.

Why it matters
Enables artists to express abstract thoughts, emotions and fantasies.

Key figures
William Blake, 1757–1827
Judy Chicago, b.1939
Wassily Kandinsky, 1866–1944
Henri Matisse, 1869–1854

Make the connection
Expressionism, p.30
Surrealism, p.43
line/mark, pp.56–7
innovation, p.133

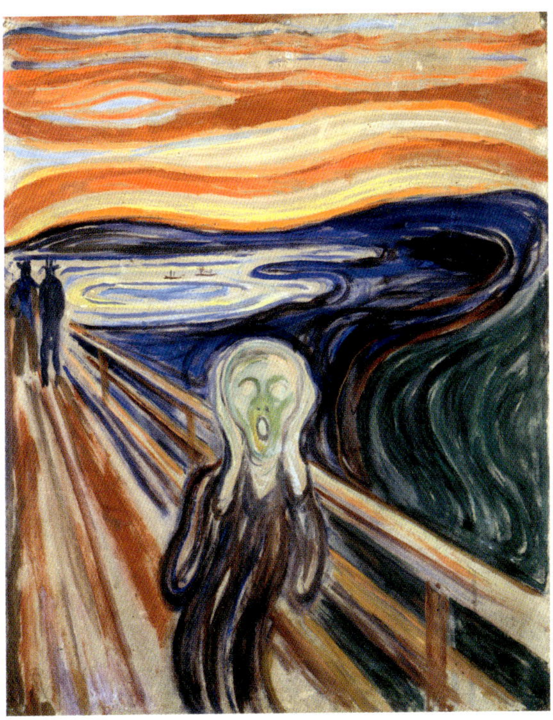

Edvard Munch,
The Scream, 1893
National Museum, Oslo

pointillism

A painting technique developed by Georges Seurat in 1886, pointillism evolved from Impressionism. Building on the Impressionists' preoccupation with colour and light, Seurat developed a scientifically ordered, analytical system of painting, in which dots of pure colour are placed side by side so that, when viewed from a distance, they blend into tones and forms.

Rather than the traditional mixing of pigments on a palette, pointillism relies on optical colour mixing; the viewer's eye fuses the dots into a cohesive image, an effect the artists believed would make colours appear brighter. Pointillists often used complementary colours (see p.151), placed side by side to enhance their vibrancy. This gave paintings a shimmering, almost vibrating quality.

As each dot contributes to the overall composition and colour balance, pointillism demands careful planning and patience. Unlike stippling, which is mostly monochromatic and concerned with tone and texture, pointillism is primarily used in painting rather than drawing, aiming to create depth and atmosphere through colour.

The term 'pointillism' was initially coined by critics who sought to deride the method, but it later became an accepted label. The broader movement came to be known as Neo-Impressionism, which encompassed pointillism and divisionism – the theory of separating colours into individual, pure components that are placed side by side.

In a nutshell
Tiny dots of pure colour, placed adjacent to each other, blend visually at a distance.

Why it matters
Pointillism was built on colour theory and optical mixing, influencing modern painting techniques.

Key figures
Henri-Edmond Cross, 1856–1910
Camille Pissarro, 1830–1903
Georges Seurat, 1859–91
Paul Signac, 1863–1935

Make the connection
Post-Impressionism, p.23
shadow, p.62
contrast, p.92
warm/cool colours, pp.148–9

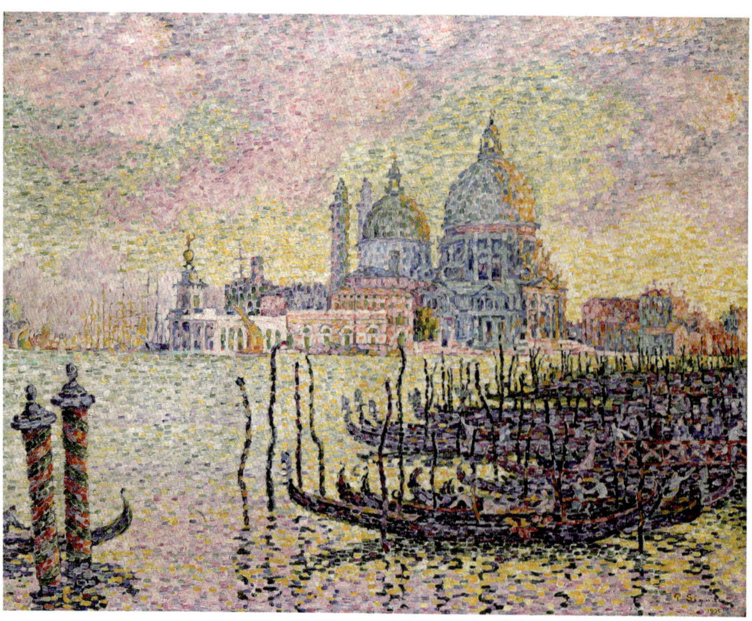

Paul Signac, *Entrance to the Grand Canal, Venice*, 1905
Toledo Museum of Art

stippling

The technique of using small dots to create the impressions of shading, texture and form, stippling is usually undertaken in monochrome and often created with pen and ink, but can also be achieved using other media. Dots placed closer together create darker areas, and dots spaced farther apart create lighter areas. Unlike pointillism, which uses coloured dots to blend hues optically, stippling relies on variations in density to build value and form.

Because stippling entails the application of many small dots to build up tone, texture and form, stippling is usually painstaking and time-consuming, requiring patience and control. Due to its clarity and the level of control and detail possible, this method is commonly used in illustrations – especially in scientific drawings.

A wide range of artistic expression is possible, however. The placement of individual dots across an image or design relies on the viewer's eye to blend them visually, as in pointillism. Subtle transitions between light and dark are possible; historically, stippling was used in engraving and etching (see pp.73, 77), where it evoked soft tonal contrasts. A stippled drawing or design generally appears softer than a traditional drawing, as outlines and conventional shading are not typically used. Artists often use the technique to convey different textures, such as rough stone, long hair or soft fur.

In a nutshell
Artists apply many tiny dots to create the illusion of texture, depth and shading.

Why it matters
It can create the appearance of precision, softness, detail and other striking visual effects.

Key figures
Giulio Campagnola, c.1482–1516
Xavier Casalta, b.1992
Albrecht Dürer, 1471–1528
Georges Seurat, 1859–91

Make the connection
Renaissance, p.16
mark, p.57
drawing, p.59
tone, p.63

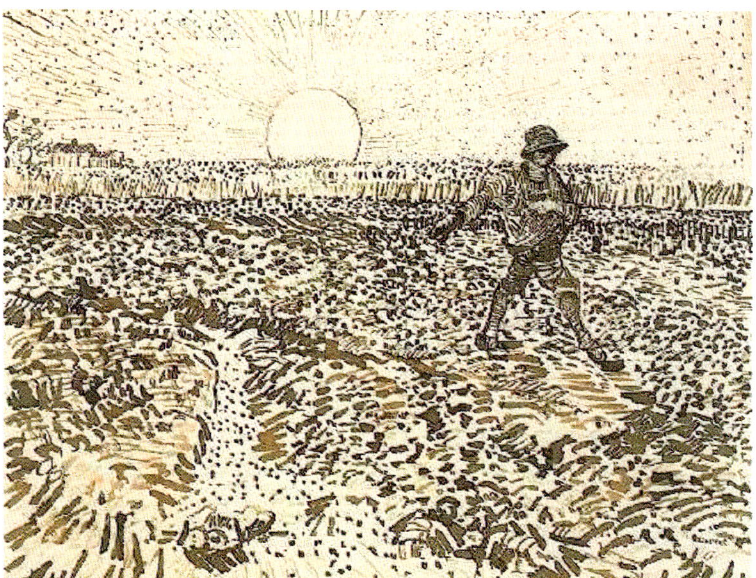

Vincent Van Gogh, *Sower in a Wheatfield with Setting Sun*, 1888
Private collection

dry brushing

Widely used in both fine art and, especially, miniature painting – including model making or decorative furniture painting – dry brushing is a technique in which a small amount of dry paint is taken on a brush and applied by lightly dragging it across a surface. The 11th-century painting *Travellers Among Mountains and Streams* by Fan Kuan (below) used a dry brush, with lightly dragged ink strokes that evoke rock faces and atmospheric depth.

Dry brushing imparts a textured effect, with the underlying surface still partially visible. Controlled handling is required: successful dry brushing is achieved when hardly any paint is on the brush. The brush, now nearly dry, is then skimmed over the surface, catching only raised areas. Soft highlights are created, or rough, grainy textures that mimic natural surfaces such as weathered wood, stone, skin or fabric.

In fine art, dry brushing is usually used in oil and acrylic painting, often to create a sense of atmosphere or texture. It is particularly effective for highlighting details in miniature painting. It can add richness and interest to a painting without the need for heavier methods like impasto or thick layers. Well-known examples of dry brushing are seen in Turner's watercolours, particularly in *The Blue Rigi, Sunrise* (1842), which creates delicate textures on the mountains and reflections, allowing the paper's texture to show through.

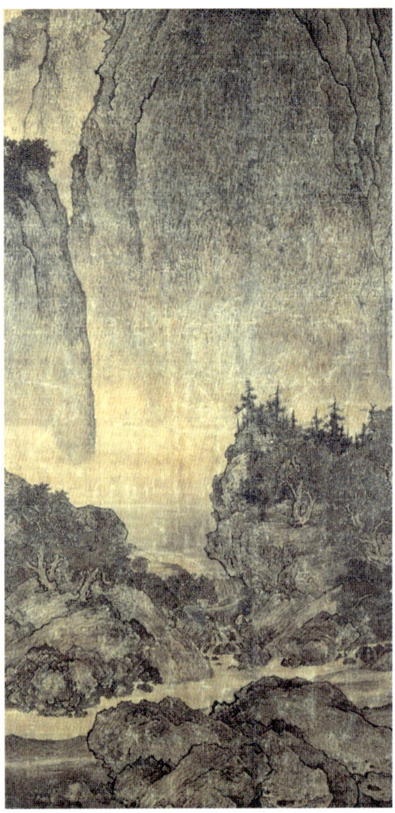

In a nutshell
Using a brush loaded with a small amount of (fairly dry) paint, artists create textured, scratchy effects.

Why it matters
Adds depth, highlights and texture efficiently, enhancing realism and expression.

Key figures
William-Adolphe Bouguereau, 1825–1905
John Constable, 1776–1837
John Singer Sargent, 1856–1925
J. M. W. Turner, 1775–1851

Make the connection
Tang/Song Dynasty art, pp.12–13
Romanticism, p.20
impasto, p.100
acrylic/oil paint, pp.124–5

Fan Kuan, *Travellers among Mountains and Streams*, 960–1279
National Palace Museum, Taipei

sgraffito

A technique that involves scraping through a surface layer to reveal a contrasting colour beneath, sgraffito is used in painting and drawing, as well as wall decoration and ceramics. The word comes from the Italian *sgraffiare*, meaning 'to scratch'. As with dry brushing, the result is a broken or disrupted surface that can convey motion or express detail, although the techniques are quite different. Paul Klee incised sgraffito lines through layers of paint to reveal luminous forms, animating *Fish Magic* (below) with symbolic textures.

Artists working with sgraffito apply multiple layers of colour, usually contrasting, onto a surface such as plaster, clay, wood or canvas. Once the top layer is partially dry, particular areas are scratched away to create designs, textures or images. The technique has been used since antiquity: architectural façades of the Italian Renaissance were decorated with it, with dark-coloured plaster revealed beneath a lighter surface layer; in Islamic, Italian and Eastern European ceramic traditions, sgraffito has been used to create bold patterns in coloured slip (a liquid clay mixture) before glazing.

In painting, sgraffito is especially suited to the thick consistency of oil or acrylic paint. Painters use palette knives, brush handles or other tools to scratch into wet or tacky layers of impasto paint, resulting in energetic lines, rough textures or unexpected visual contrasts.

In a nutshell
Layers of contrasting materials are scraped or scratched, revealing colours and designs beneath the top layer.

Why it matters
Across cultures, sgraffito enriches painting, architecture and ceramics.

Key figures
Jean Dubuffet, 1901–85
Shōji Hamada, 1894–1978
Paul Klee, 1879–1940
Bernard Leach, 1887–1979

Make the connection
Early/High Renaissance, pp.14–15
Expressionism, p.30
impasto, p.100
acrylic/oil paint, pp.124–5

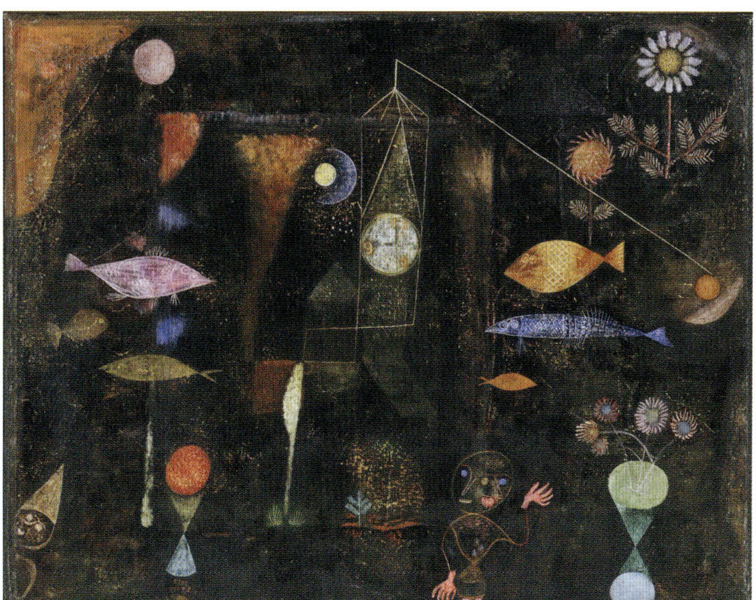

Paul Klee, *Fish Magic*, 1925
Philadelphia Museum of Art

impasto

Rather than smoothly blended paint, impasto paint is thickly applied, with artists sometimes squeezing it straight from the tube or mixing it with other materials to create texture, as seen in *Self-Portrait* by Rembrandt (below). Created with thick, textured paint, typically oil or acrylic, impasto stands out from a painting's surface, and often retains the marks of the brush or palette knife.

The tactile surface of impasto allows light to interact with the crests and dips of pigment, adding depth and dynamism to the composition. Contrasting with the imperceptible brush marks that have generally been preferred by official art academies, impasto allows artists to convey textures, emotions and movement. The term comes from the Italian *impastare*, meaning 'to paste' or 'to knead', which aptly describes the sculptural quality of the method.

Historically, impasto gained prominence during the Baroque period, allowing painters to create the dramatic effects they sought. Impressionist artists such as Claude Monet embraced impasto to capture fleeting light and atmosphere in plein-air scenes. Van Gogh, perhaps the most iconic impasto artist, used thick swirls and swathes of impasto paint to convey expressive intensity. Abstract Expressionists such as Hans Hofmann, Jackson Pollock and Willem de Kooning also used impasto extensively. More recently, Frank Auerbach and Anselm Kiefer often used extremely heavy impasto.

In a nutshell
Paint is laid thickly to create texture and depth.

Why it matters
Adds expression, dimension, emotion and movement to paintings, enhancing the tactile experience.

Key figures
Willem de Kooning, 1904–97
Vincent van Gogh, 1853–90
Jackson Pollock, 1912–56
Rembrandt, 1606–69

Make the connection
Post-Impressionism, p.23
Abstract Expressionism, p.31
plein-air painting, p.104
oil paint, p.125

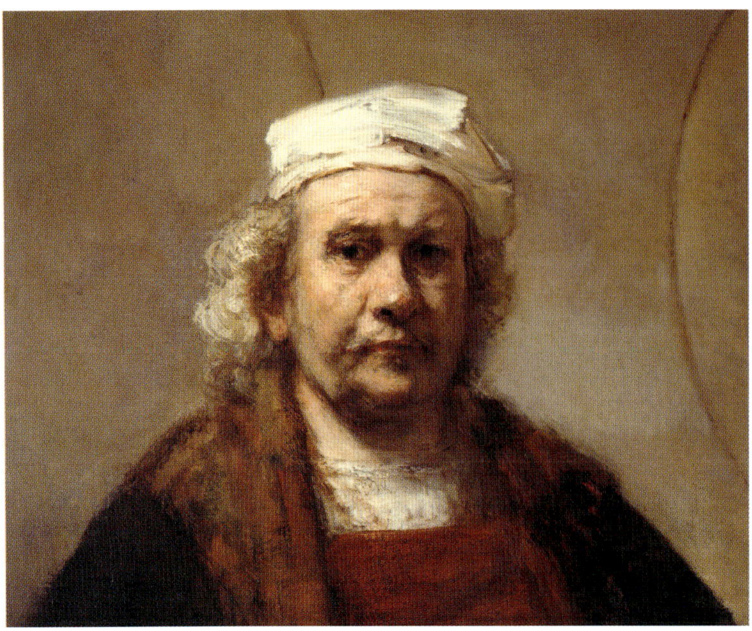

Rembrandt, *Self-Portrait with Two Circles*, c.1665
The Iveagh Bequest, Kenwood House, London

imprimatura

An Italian term meaning 'first paint layer', imprimatura refers to the thin, transparent wash of colour applied to a primed canvas or panel before a painting begins. This tonal base reduces glare from the white ground, sets the overall mood and helps unify the composition.

Typically applied in oil or diluted pigment and allowed to dry before further work, imprimatura is often made with warm earth tones such as burnt or raw umber. Establishing a mid-tone from the outset allows the artist to model form more effectively, working both towards lighter areas through highlights and towards darker areas by deepening shadows. This practice was widely used during the Renaissance and Baroque periods, particularly in paintings that rely on chiaroscuro or dramatic lighting.

Imprimatura differs from underpainting (see p.81), which is a more developed preliminary layer that establishes composition and values. Imprimatura also contrasts with impasto; where impasto emphasizes materiality and expression, imprimatura remains subtle and unobtrusive.

Often visible through later, more transparent layers of paint, imprimatura can lend a soft, glowing undertone to the finished work. As a foundational oil-painting technique taught for centuries, it enables artists to build depth, cohesion and luminosity in layered compositions.

In a nutshell
A translucent, toned base layer that is applied to a primed canvas before painting begins.

Why it matters
Unifies the composition, reduces glare from the white ground and helps to establish tonal values.

Key figures
Leonardo da Vinci, 1452–1519
Caravaggio, 1571–1610
Artemisia Gentileschi, 1593–1654
Rembrandt, 1606–69

Make the connection
mark, p.57
shadow/tone, pp.62–3
contrast, p.92
oil paints, p.125

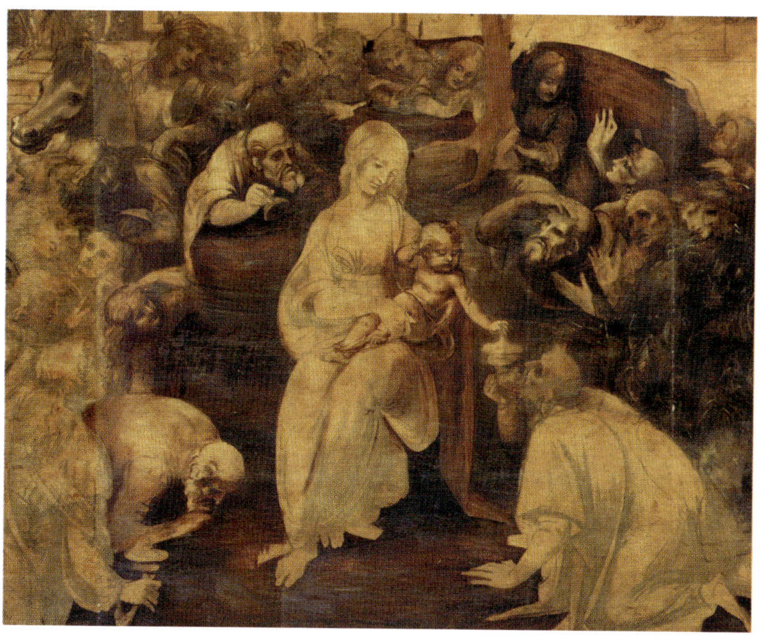

Leonardo da Vinci, *Adoration of the Magi* (unfinished, detail), *c.*1482
Gallerie degli Uffizi, Florence

assemblage

The combination of found objects, everyday materials and non-traditional art components distinguishes assemblage from collage, which is typically a two-dimensional medium. Similarly, an assemblage differs from a readymade – a found object designated as art – as it combines found objects to create a new, larger artwork.

The origins of assemblage can be traced back to the early 20th century, with Pablo Picasso often credited as one of its pioneers. In 1912, Picasso created an artwork titled *Guitar* from cardboard, and later remade it in sheet metal. Visitors to his studio were confused; Picasso had invented something new. Soon after, artists associated with Dada, such as Kurt Schwitters, further developed the assemblage technique. Schwitters used scavenged scrap materials to create collages and assemblages that he called 'Merz' (see below).

The term 'assemblage' was popularized in the 1950s by American artist Jean Dubuffet, who used it to describe his own use of unusual materials, and the concept gained prominence in the later 20th century, with artists like Robert Rauschenberg and Louise Nevelson, who used discarded materials to reflect aspects of contemporary life.

Assemblage art is ultimately about transformation, turning the ordinary or the discarded into something meaningful or provocative, inviting the viewer to see everyday objects in entirely new ways.

In a nutshell
An art form that combines found or everyday objects into three-dimensional compositions.

Why it matters
Gives discarded materials new meaning, challenging traditional artistic hierarchies.

Key figures
Marcel Duchamp, 1887–1968
Louise Nevelson, 1899–1988
Pablo Picasso, 1881–1973
Robert Rauschenberg, 1925–2008

Make the connection
Expressionism, p.30
Dada, p.42
installation, p.83
imagination, p.95

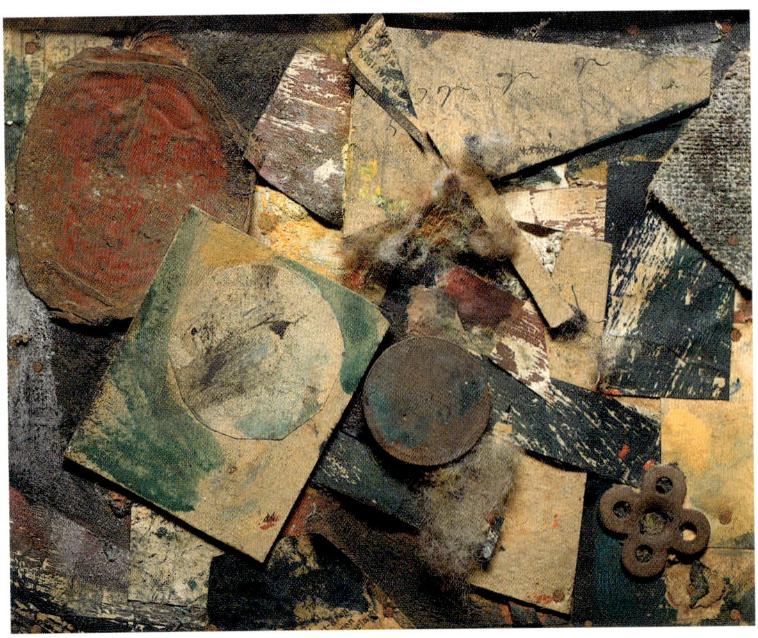

Kurt Schwitters, *Merz Picture 9A, Picture with Checker*, 1919
Private collection

collage

Collage has been used by artists since ancient times, but it gained significant popularity in the 20th century, when Pablo Picasso and Georges Braque began incorporating collage into their Cubist works, adding newspaper clippings, wallpaper and other materials to their paintings. Deriving from the French *coller*, meaning 'to glue', the word 'collage' describes the technique of assembling materials such as pieces of paper, photographs or fabric, then sticking them down onto a supporting surface; it also refers to the resulting work of art.

Collage can be playful, political, poetic or personal. It allows artists to mix textures, colours and meanings in unexpected ways. Some collages are flat and made from paper; others are layered with paint, fabric and other materials, though they stop short of the full three-dimensionality of assemblage. In his late cut-out *The Sorrows of the King* (below), Matisse assembled boldly coloured paper shapes into a rhythmic, jazz-like composition, creating a poignant meditation on creativity, memory and mortality. Later, Pop artists such as Richard Hamilton created collages incorporating mass media imagery.

Both assemblage and collage remain powerful tools for artists. Whether used to make political statements, dreamlike landscapes or experiments, they invite the viewer to see the world differently.

In a nutshell
Art form created by combining different materials, such as paper, photos or fabric, to produce something new.

Why it matters
It breaks rules, mixes ideas and lets artists tell layered, personal stories.

Key figures
Georges Braque, 1882–1963
Richard Hamilton, 1922–2011
Hannah Höch, 1889–1978
Pablo Picasso, 1881–1973

Make the connection
Cubism, p.36
Dada/Surrealism, pp.42–3
Pop art, p.46
photomontage, p.91

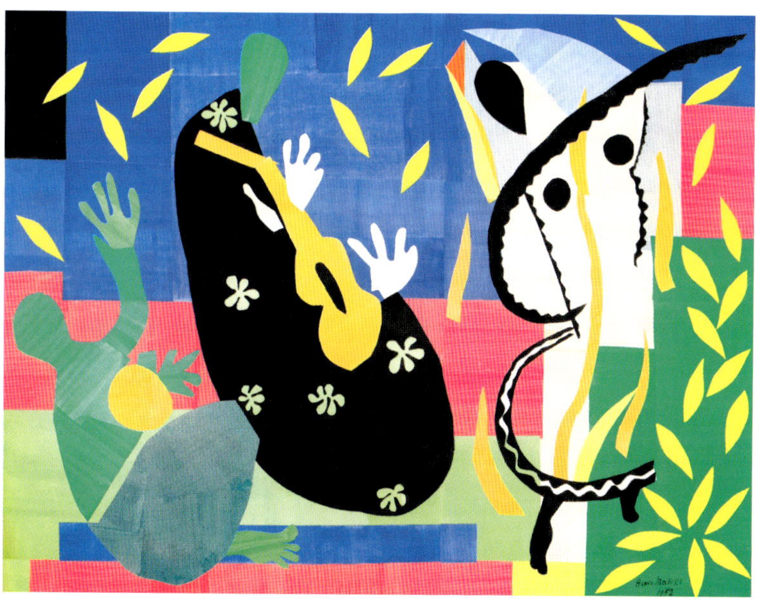

Henri Matisse, *La Tristesse du roi* (The Sorrows of the King), 1952
Musée National d'Art Moderne, Paris

plein–air painting

Describing the practice of painting finished pictures outdoors, the French term *en plein air* means 'in the open air'. Artists who paint *en plein air* work directly in the landscape rather than in a studio, aiming to capture the natural light, colours, atmosphere and changing conditions of a scene as they experience it.

Although artists have sketched outdoors for centuries, painting *en plein air* became particularly popular in the 19th century. Painters such as Camille Corot, Claude Monet, Pierre-Auguste Renoir and Camille Pissarro took their canvases into the countryside to observe how light and colour changed throughout the day. Inventions such as portable easels and paint in metal tubes made this work easier. Artists in Britain, particularly watercolourists, had been painting from nature outdoors long before this period, though the term was not used at the time. Today, 'plein air' can be used to refer to any medium used outdoors, not just oil.

Plein-air painting encourages spontaneity and direct observation. Instead of carefully planning every detail, plein air artists often work quickly to capture fleeting effects. These artworks often appear fresh, lively, and connected to nature, though plein-air painting is not limited to landscapes and can include city scenes, seascapes, gardens and even figures in outdoor settings.

In a nutshell
Refers to creating art outdoors, directly capturing natural light, colour and atmosphere as they are seen.

Why it matters
Brings immediacy, freshness and a deep connection to nature.

Key figures
Mary Cassatt, 1844–1926
Claude Monet, 1840–1926
Camille Pissarro, 1830–1903
Pierre-Auguste Renoir, 1841–1919

Make the connection
Romanticism, p.20
Impressionism, p.22
sketching, p.58
watercolour, p.122

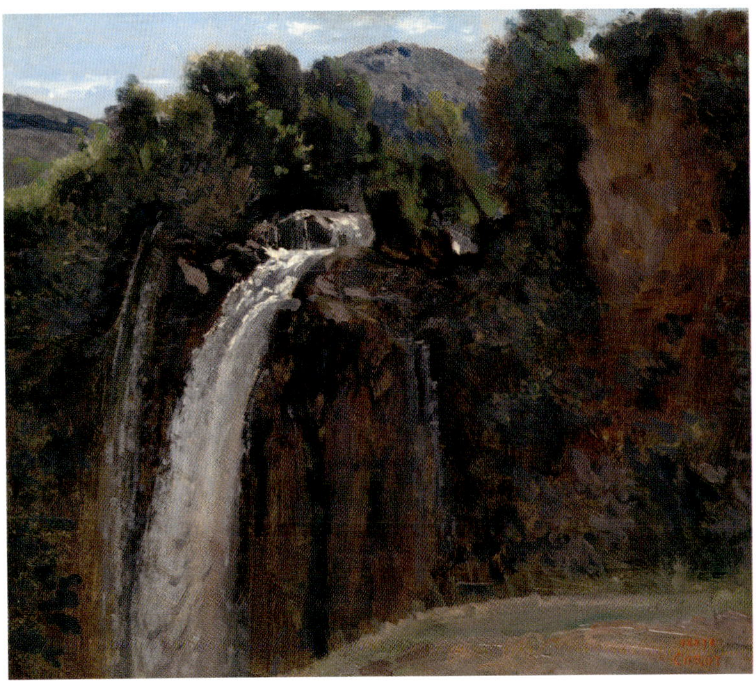

Camille Corot, *Waterfall at Terni*, 1826
Metropolitan Museum of Art, New York

studio painting

Studio paintings are created indoors, rather than on location. In the studio, an artist can usually plan and compose work at his or her own pace, often using sketches, photographs or studies made elsewhere (perhaps *en plein air*) as references.

Historically, studio painting was especially important in academic art traditions, where artists often worked on large, grand history paintings, portraits or religious scenes that required precise methods. In this context, models can be posed for hours under ideal lighting, and landscapes or backgrounds can be constructed from a range of sources. Famous studio painters include Diego Velázquez, Rembrandt and Johannes Vermeer, all of whom used their studios to develop detailed, layered works over weeks or months. Even artists associated with plein-air techniques, such as Claude Monet, often returned to the studio to refine or reinterpret their outdoor sketches.

In their studios, artists can control temperature and lighting and use a wide range of materials. They can refine details and experiment with ideas and techniques at their leisure, which is why studio painting remains the preferred medium for many artists, from traditional oil portraits to conceptual works. While plein-air painting is valued for its spontaneity and direct observation, studio painting offers a more reflective, deliberate process.

In a nutshell
Artworks are created in a controlled indoor setting; technique, composition and academic styles are emphasized.

Why it matters
Shaped Western art traditions, influenced artistic training and enabled refinement of detail and narrative.

Key figures
Caravaggio, 1571–1610
Jacques-Louis David, 1748–1825
Jean-Auguste-Dominique Ingres, 1780–1867
Raphael, 1483–1520

Make the connection
drawing, p.59
history/genre painting, pp.136–7
still life/life drawing, pp.138–9

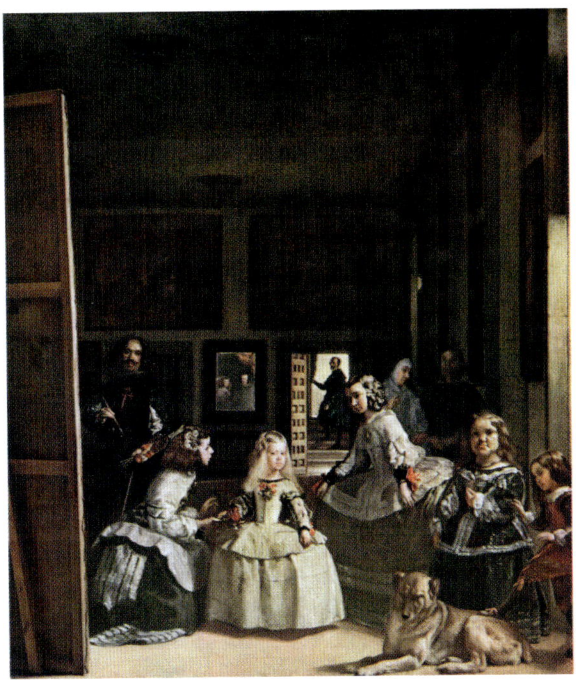

Diego Velázquez, *Las Meninas*, 1656
Museo Nacional del Prado, Madrid

trompe l'oeil

While many artists focus on illusion, trompe l'oeil – a French term meaning 'to deceive the eye' – is the ultimate example of artistic trickery. Artists employing trompe l'oeil use painstaking detail, accurate linear and atmospheric perspective, and tonal contrasts to convince viewers that painted objects or scenes are real.

Although the term 'trompe l'oeil' was not widely used until the early 19th century, the illusionistic technique was employed in ancient Greece and Rome. Although none of his artworks survive, Zeuxis, an ancient Greek artist, is famed for his realistic paintings; one of his grape paintings was reportedly so lifelike that birds attempted to peck at it. Some ancient Greek and Roman domestic murals depicted architectural features such as windows, doors or openings into other rooms, creating the illusion of larger or more appealing homes. During the Renaissance, artists such as Melozzo da Forlì and Andrea Mantegna painted trompe-l'oeil ceiling frescoes, meticulously rendering perspective to convey a sense of architectural depth.

Now, trompe l'oeil appears in street art, graffiti and digital media, as artists continue to create lifelike illusions that confuse viewers about the boundaries between painting, perception and reality.

In a nutshell
Creates lifelike illusions that make flat surfaces appear three-dimensional.

Why it matters
Challenges perception and celebrates artistic skill.

Key figures
Pere Borrell del Caso, 1835–1910
Pietro da Cortona, 1596–1669
Samuel van Hoogstraten, 1627–78
Juan Sánchez Cotán, 1560–1627

Make the connection
Renaissance, p.16
Baroque/Rococo, pp.18–19
atmospheric/linear perspective, pp.78–9
observation, p.94

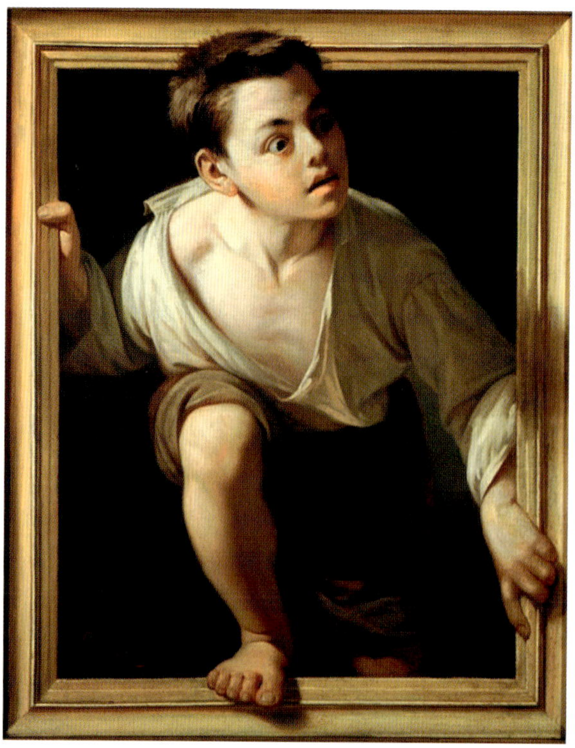

Pere Borrell del Caso, *Escaping Criticism*, 1874
Collection of the Banco de España, Madrid

verisimilitude

Deriving from the Latin *veri similis*, which means 'like the truth', the word 'verisimilitude' describes the appearance of reality; it suggests the convincing illusion of reality. This concept is central to many artistic traditions, particularly those aiming for realism, or at least naturalism, and including trompe l'oeil.

Artists achieve verisimilitude through accurate proportions, perspective, lighting and texture. For example, some High Renaissance artists began studying anatomy, light and shadow to make their paintings and drawings of human figures appear lifelike. During the Baroque period, artists further pushed the boundaries of realism, employing dramatic contrasts and illusionistic techniques to create immersive, believable scenes. Verisimilitude is not limited to visual accuracy. It also encompasses emotional or psychological realism. A painting or sculpture may not depict a real person but can still feel 'true' if it conveys authentic emotion or behaviour.

Ultimately, verisimilitude is about creating a bridge between the viewer's and the artwork's worlds (even if that is through trickery, as in trompe l'oeil). It invites the viewer to suspend disbelief and engage with the art on a deeper level.

In a nutshell
The artistic pursuit of realism, verisimilitude involves creating depictions that appear true to life.

Why it matters
Deepens viewer engagement by fostering emotional resonance and believability in visual storytelling.

Key figures
Gustave Courbet, 1819–77
William Holman Hunt, 1827–1910
Ilya Repin, 1844–1930
Andrew Wyeth, 1917–2009

Make the connection
Baroque, p.18
Realism, p.21
observation, p.94
studio painting, p.105

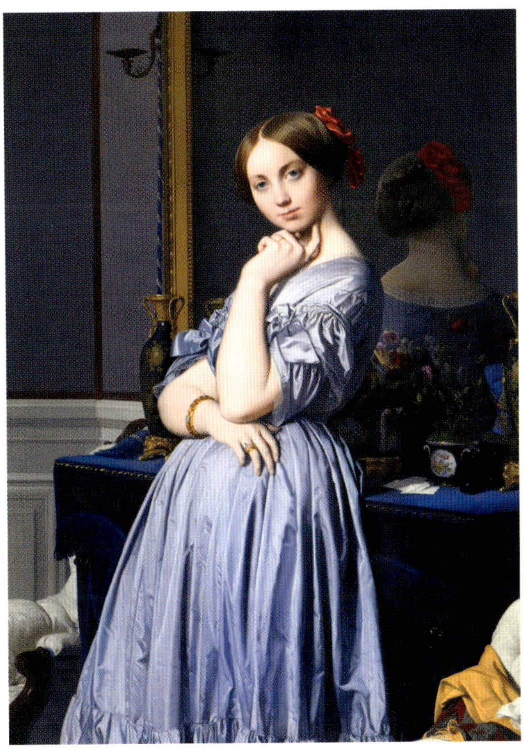

Jean-Auguste-Dominique Ingres, *Portrait of Comtesse d'Haussonville*, 1845
The Frick Collection, New York

symmetry

A balanced and proportional arrangement of visual elements can generate a sense of stability and regularity, giving the impression of logic, balance and calm. Artists use symmetry to guide the viewer's eye, emphasize focal points and establish visual coherence.

Technically, there are several types of symmetry, including bilateral (mirror-like reflection across a vertical axis), radial (elements radiating from a central point), and approximate (when equilibrium is achieved without perfect reflection), as in *The Two Fridas* by Frida Kahlo (below). Many artists who incorporate symmetry into their artworks also use techniques such as the golden ratio (see p.131) or the rule of thirds, which can help in achieving effective symmetry.

For thousands of years, symmetry has been associated with ideal proportions and divine order. Ancient Egyptian, Greek and Roman art often employed symmetrical compositions in architecture, sculpture and frescoes to convey power and perfection. Symmetry was also a key feature in much Renaissance art, reflecting the period's interest in order, harmony, proportion, the revival of Classical ideals and the development of linear perspective. Many Renaissance artists used mathematical symmetry and geometric balance to create intellectually grounded compositions.

In a nutshell
The balanced arrangement of visual elements creates harmony and order.

Why it matters
Symmetry in art reflects ideals of beauty, stability and perfection.

Key figures
Piero della Francesca, *c.*1415/20–92
Georgia O'Keeffe, 1887–1986
Pietro Perugino, d.1523
Frank Stella, 1936–2004

Make the connection
Renaissance, p.16
linear perspective, p.79
unity, p.93

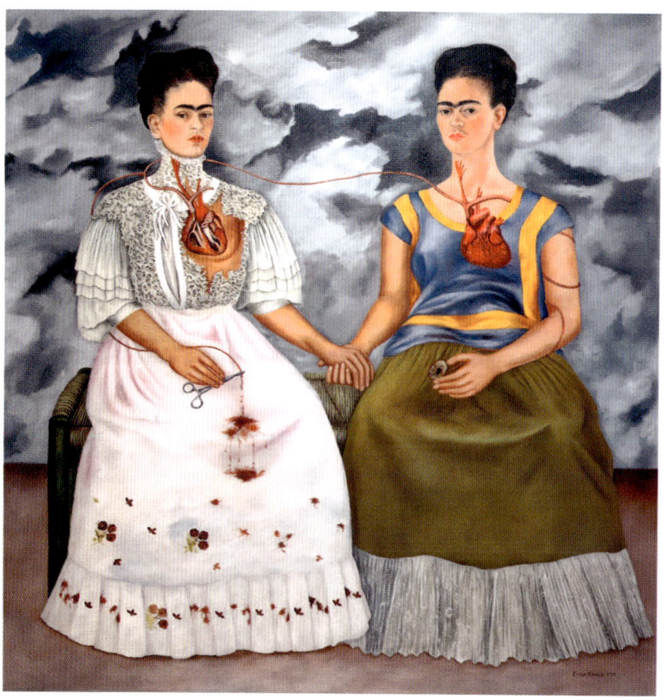

Frida Kahlo, *The Two Fridas*, 1939
Museo de Arte Moderno, Mexico City

asymmetry

The natural counterpoint to symmetry, asymmetry creates contrast, variation and a sense of dynamic interplay. When artists use it intentionally, differing elements on each side of a composition can generate tension, evoke emotion and introduce movement and rhythm, drawing the eye across an artwork.

In Japanese art, asymmetry has always played a significant role; the principle of *wabi-sabi* embraces imperfection and asymmetry as expressions of natural beauty. Ukiyo-e compositions were frequently asymmetrical. A Western example is *Arrangement in Grey and Black No.1* by James McNeill Whistler (below). The figure is slightly off-centre, balanced by the careful orchestration of tonal areas; the dark dress contrasts with the pale wall, and the vertical curtain stabilizes the composition.

Asymmetry is not necessarily about imbalance, therefore. It suggests an intuitive equilibrium. This is often referred to as 'informal balance', where disparate elements are arranged and empty spaces utilized to achieve a sense of stability without direct mirroring. The eye is guided across the work in a more exploratory manner, leading to a deeper interaction between viewer and artwork. Ultimately, both symmetry and asymmetry in art aim to achieve balance.

In a nutshell
Uneven, unbalanced compositions that create visual interest and dynamic movement.

Why it matters
Challenges traditional balance and evokes emotion through contrast and tension.

Key figures
Edward Hopper, 1882–1967
Utagawa Hiroshige, 1797–1858
Sesshū Tōyō, 1420–1506
Kitagawa Utamaro, 1753–1806

Make the connection
Ukiyo-e, p.26
Japonisme, p.28
Art Nouveau, p.32
contrast, p.92

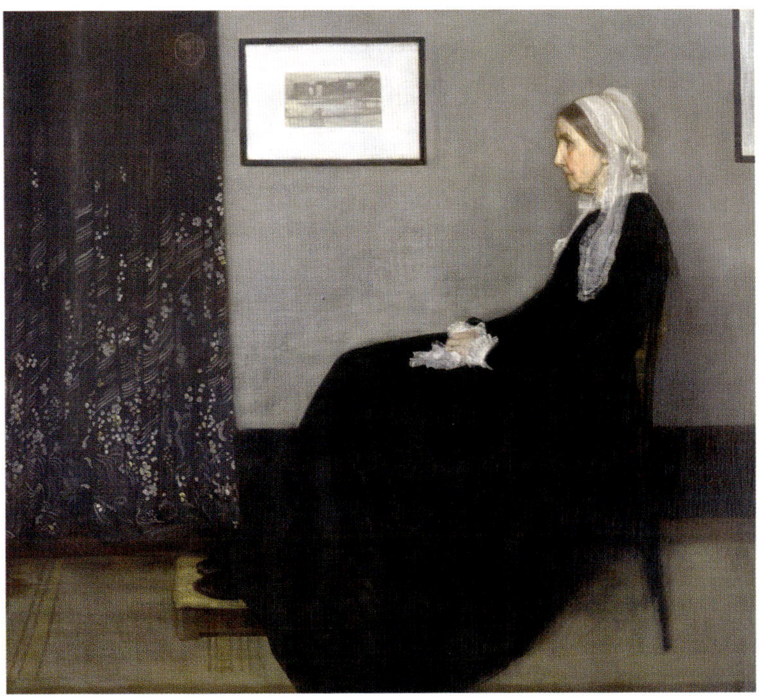

James McNeill Whistler, *Arrangement in Grey and Black No.1*, 1871
Musée d'Orsay, Paris

paint

Paint is a substance composed of pigment (colour) suspended in a binder, such as oil, water or acrylic polymer, which allows it to adhere to surfaces. In fine art, paint is both a medium of expression and a material with rich historical and cultural significance. Its evolution reflects humanity's changing relationship with creativity.

The earliest known use of paint dates back over 40,000 years, to prehistoric cave paintings, where artists used natural pigments such as ochre, charcoal and hematite, mixed with animal fat or water, to depict animals and hunting scenes. The ancient Egyptians refined the art of paint-making by using minerals such as malachite and azurite, often combining them with egg whites or tree resins to decorate tombs and temples. The Greeks and Romans expanded this palette, introducing fresco techniques and more vivid, mineral-based colours.

During the Middle Ages, artists used egg tempera (see p.120) – a mixture of pigment and egg yolk – for religious iconography. The Renaissance saw the rise of oil paint, which offered richer colour and slower drying times, allowing for more detailed and layered compositions. In the 20th century, synthetic paints such as acrylics emerged, offering brilliant colours; these modern materials empowered movements like Abstract Expressionism (p.31) and Pop art (p.46).

Paint continues to evolve, with innovations like digital colour matching and sustainable, non-toxic formulas.

In a nutshell
One of humanity's oldest artistic tools, paint is pigment mixed with a binder.

Why it matters
Paint gives form to emotion, ideas and culture, turning imagination and observation into vibrant, enduring expression.

Key figures
Helen Frankenthaler, 1928–2011
Giotto, c.1267/76–1337
Vincent van Gogh, 1853–90
Frida Kahlo, 1907–54

Make the connection
Renaissance, p.16
Impressionism, p.22
plein-air painting, p.104
acrylic/oil paint, pp.124–5

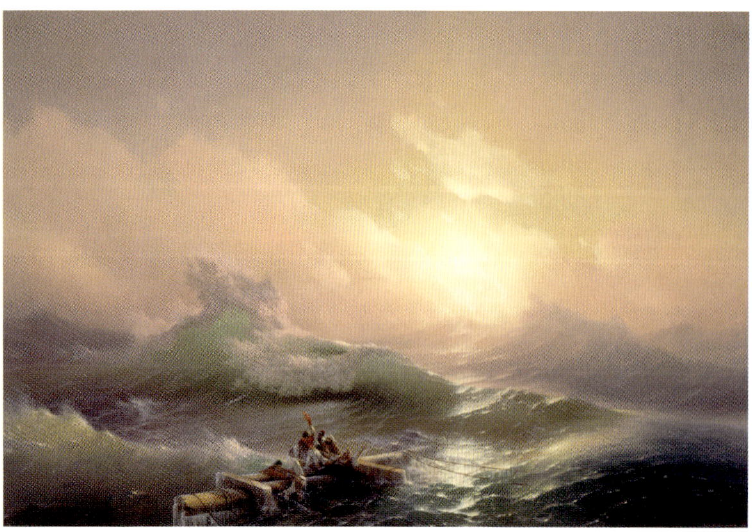

Ivan Konstantinovich Aivazovsky, *The Ninth Wave*, 1850
State Russian Museum, St Petersburg

pigment

Pigment gives paint its colour. Derived from natural sources, including minerals, plants and even insects, pigments have shaped artistic expression for tens of thousands of years.

Early humans used earth pigments such as ochre, charcoal and chalk to create cave and rock paintings, grinding these into powder and mixing them with water or animal fat. Ancient Egyptians expanded the palette with malachite green and Egyptian blue, the first known synthetic pigment. The Renaissance saw the rise of oil painting and a demand for richer, more stable colours. Lapis lazuli, imported from Afghanistan, was ground into ultramarine, the most expensive pigment of its time, often reserved for the robes of the Virgin Mary.

The Industrial Revolution transformed pigment production as chemists developed affordable, consistent synthetic alternatives, such as chrome yellow and Prussian blue. In the 20th century, acrylic paints introduced new synthetic colours and durable pigments that dried quickly and resisted fading. Today, artists often use non-toxic, lightfast pigments, and some experiment with unconventional sources, such as bacteria or recycled materials.

In a nutshell
Derived from minerals, plants or synthetics, pigments are colour-giving substances used in paint.

Why it matters
Pigments shape visual language, evoke emotion and reflect cultural, scientific and historical shifts.

Key figures
Yves Klein, 1928–62
Georgia O'Keeffe, 1887–1986
Mark Rothko, 1903–70
Johannes Vermeer, 1632–75

Make the connection
Minoan art, p.6
Renaissance, p.16
Baroque, p.18
Impressionism, p.22

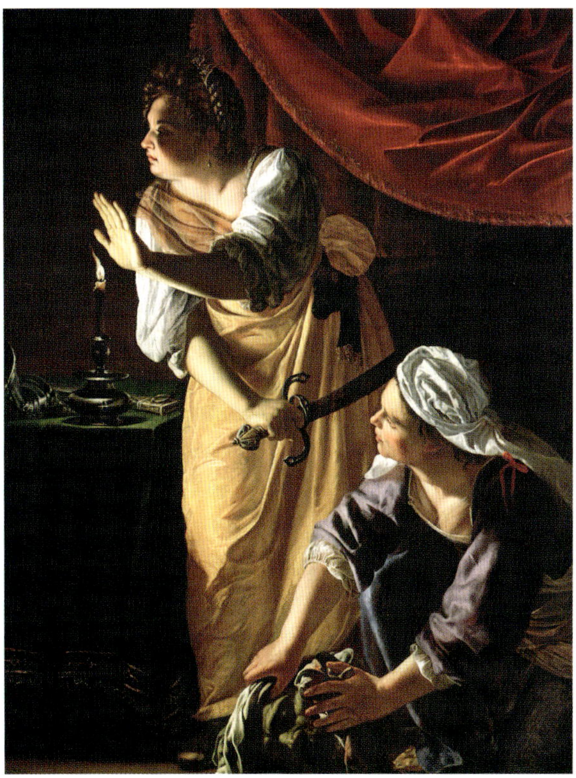

Artemisia Gentileschi, *Judith and Maidservant with the Head of Holofernes*, *c.*1625
Detroit Institute of Arts

charcoal

One of the oldest, most elemental materials in art history, charcoal is prized for its expressive range, immediacy and tactile richness. Made from burnt organic materials – typically willow, vine or compressed wood – charcoal has been used by artists for millennia.

The earliest use of charcoal dates back over 30,000 years, when early humans sketched animals and symbols on cave walls using charred sticks. During the Renaissance, charcoal became a vital tool for preparatory sketches and compositional studies. Artists utilized it to explore form, anatomy and light, often combining it with chalk. For many years, powdered charcoal was used for 'pouncing', a method for transferring designs from one surface to another; this was useful for scaling up designs for frescoes, tapestries and altarpieces.

During the late 19th and early 20th centuries, artists such as Edgar Degas and Käthe Kollwitz used charcoal to capture the essence of gesture, emotion and atmosphere. Contemporary artists like Robert Longo have pushed the boundaries of charcoal, creating hyperrealistic drawings that rival photography in detail and drama.

Charcoal allows artists to make marks freely and expressively.

In a nutshell
A dry, easily smudged drawing medium made from burnt wood.

Why it matters
Allows artists to explore tone, texture and gesture with immediacy, creating expressive, dynamic marks.

Key figures
Théodore Géricault, 1791–1824
Käthe Kollwitz, 1867–1945
Édouard Manet, 1832–83
Odilon Redon, 1840–1916

Make the connection
mark, p.57
shadow/tone, pp.62–3
observation, p.94

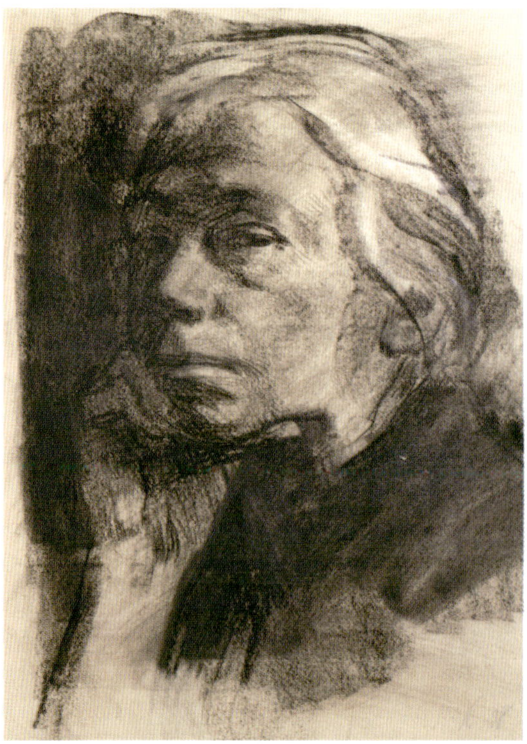

Käthe Kollwitz, *Self-portrait*, 1908
Albertina, Vienna

pencil

Pencils were perfected in 1795 by Nicolas-Jacques Conté, who mixed graphite with clay to produce varying degrees of hardness or softness, and encased this mixture in wood. This innovation allowed artists to control tone and texture with assurance. While pencils were initially used primarily for preliminary sketches, they soon gained popularity for creating finished artworks.

In the 19th century, artists such as Jean-Auguste-Dominique Ingres and Edgar Degas created refined graphite portraits characterized by elegant line work and tonal sensitivity. Pierre-Auguste Renoir frequently began his paintings with pencil sketches. In the 20th century, Andrew Wyeth brought pencil drawing into the spotlight, producing highly detailed, atmospheric compositions using graphite.

Modern graphite pencils are graded from soft (in the B range) to hard (in the H range). HB is in the middle. Coloured pencils use a mixture of pigments with wax or oil, and are usually used for artistic colour work. In general, pencil offers more precise, controlled lines and fine detail than charcoal, which provides rich, velvety tones and expressive, gestural marks. They are complementary in artistic practice – many artists use both in their sketches and drawings.

In a nutshell
A graphite-based writing and drawing implement sheathed in wood or plastic.

Why it matters
Prized for its precision and ability to make a range of marks.

Key figures
Jean-Auguste-Dominique Ingres, 1780–1867
Adonna Khare, b.1980
Alphonse Mucha, 1860–1939
J. M. W. Turner, 1775–1851

Make the connection
Rococo, p.19
Romanticism, p.20
line/mark, pp.56–7
shadow/tone, pp.62–3

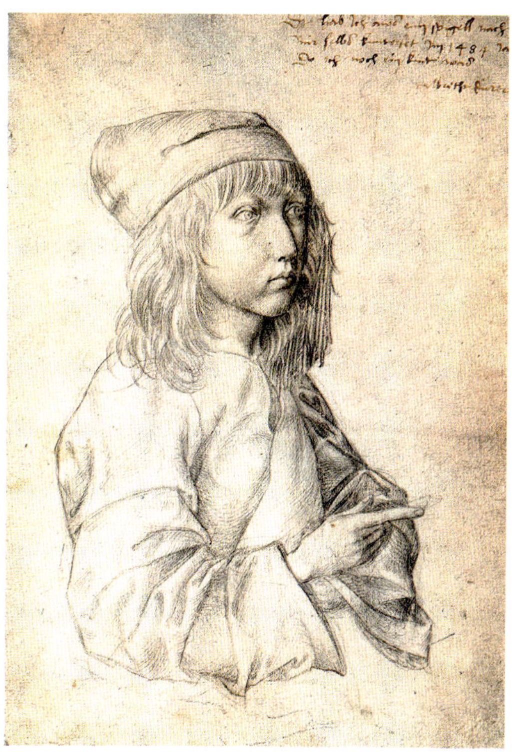

Albrecht Dürer, Self-*Portrait at 13*, 1484
Albertina, Vienna

chalk pastel

Despite the name, chalk pastels do not actually contain chalk (calcium carbonate). The term likely stems from their soft, dry consistency and their appearance, which resembles traditional chalk. They are often called soft pastels. Typically made from pure powdered pigment, a small amount of natural binder (such as gum arabic), and sometimes a filler (such as kaolin or gypsum), they are soft, smooth and prized for their vibrant colours and their ability to blend easily on paper.

These pastels allow artists to work quickly, applying colour directly to a surface without brushes or drying time. The colours can be layered, smudged or blended with tools to create a wide range of effects, from bold lines to hatched or stippled marks to subtle shading. Chalk pastel is, however, also delicate. Because the pigment sits loosely on the surface, pastel drawings are fragile and prone to smudging. Pastel artworks are best when created on textured or specially prepared paper – with a 'tooth' – which helps the pigment adhere to the surface. To protect the finished work, artists often use fixative spray.

In *The Ballet* (below), Edgar Degas used chalk pastel to capture the fluidity and grace of dancers with soft, layered strokes that blend colour and line. The medium enabled him to convey movement, light and the rehearsal space's ephemeral atmosphere with immediacy.

In a nutshell
Soft, pigment-rich sticks used for drawing, known for their vibrant, blendable colours.

Why it matters
Pastels offer expressive, painterly effects and are widely used in fine art and illustration.

Key figures
Mary Cassatt, 1844–1926
Edgar Degas, 1834–1917
Maurice Quentin de La Tour, 1704–88
Jean-François Millet, 1814–75

Make the connection
Romanticism/Realism, pp.20–1
Impressionism, p.22
mark, p.57
pigment, p.111

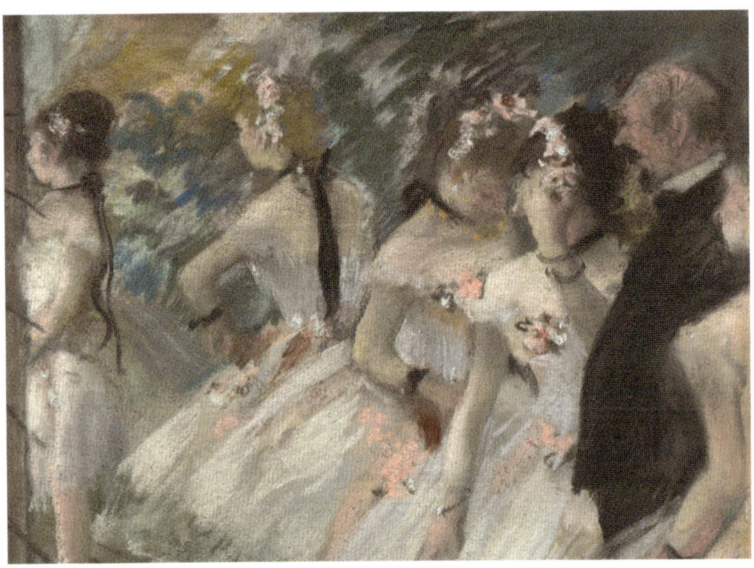

Edgar Degas, *The Ballet* (detail), *c.*1880
Corcoran Collection, National Gallery of Art, Washington D.C.

oil pastel

Offering a bridge between drawing and painting, oil pastels are made by mixing pigment with a wax binder and a non-drying oil, then forming the mixture into sticks. Unlike the dry, powdery consistency of chalk pastel, oil pastel has a creamy and slightly greasy texture, which creates rich, bright colours and a smooth, waxy finish.

Introduced in the 20th century, oil pastels were developed as a more durable and versatile alternative to chalk pastels. One of the main advantages of the medium is its permanence: the pigment adheres firmly to the surface. It does not require a fixative (though the effect is still strongest on a sturdy, textured surface, with a 'tooth' to catch and hold the pigment effectively). The colours remain intense over time and are resistant to smudging once set. The sticks themselves do not crumble or produce dust.

Oil pastels can be used in numerous ways: applied thickly for bold, impasto-style effects (see p.100), layered for depth, or thinned with solvents like turpentine to emulate the appearance of oil paint (p.125). They can be blended with tools or even a brush when dissolved, offering a wide range of expressive possibilities.

Colours often need to be softened or lightened with layers of white or lighter-coloured oil pastel, in a process similar to glazing with paint.

In a nutshell
Creamy sticks of pigment mixed with wax and oil.

Why it matters
Ideal for bold, vibrant artwork, they allow blending and layering without drying out or smudging.

Key figures
Henri Goetz, 1909–89
Shikō Munakata, 1903–75
Pablo Picasso, 1881–1973

Make the connection
tone, p.63
glazing, p.87
pigment, p.111
creativity, p.132

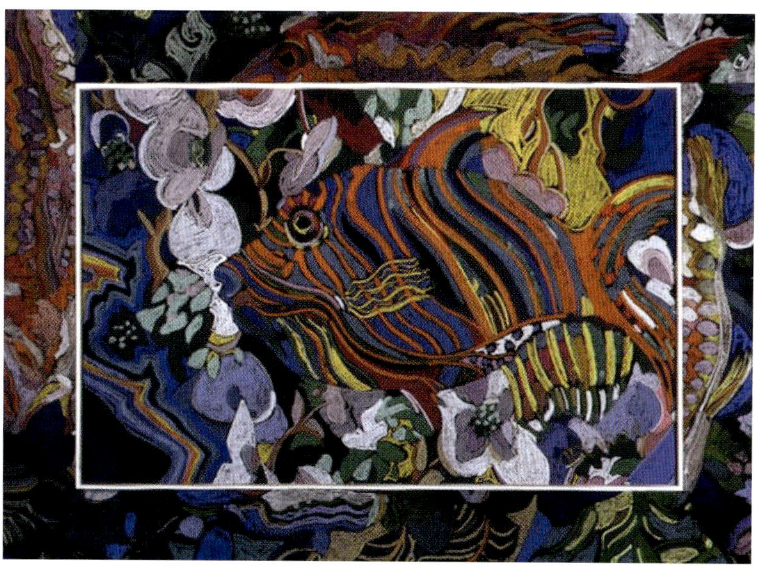

Frances Treanor, *Golden Fish*, c.1993
Private collection

tapestry

The world's most famous tapestry is not a tapestry at all – the 'tapestry' at Bayeux is actually an embroidery made with wool yarn stitched onto linen. An authentic tapestry is made by weaving threads on a loom, unlike embroidery, where the design is applied to the surface of a finished fabric. Tapestry involves creating an image or design by interweaving coloured weft threads through fixed warp threads.

From the medieval to the Renaissance periods, tapestry was a prestigious art form, typically commissioned by royalty and the nobility for use in castles, cathedrals and grand manors. Tapestries served as both adornment and insulation, usually depicting biblical, mythological or historical scenes. One of the most iconic examples is the series *The Lady and the Unicorn* (see below), probably designed in Paris and woven in Brussels.

The creative process for a tapestry began with a full-scale, coloured drawing, known as a cartoon, produced by an artist. This cartoon would be placed behind a high-warp (vertical) or beneath a low-warp (horizontal) loom, and the design transferred to the warp threads by pouncing. The tapestry was woven by hand using shuttles, following the design. Weavers worked in reverse, as the back of the tapestry faced them. Once complete, the tapestry was cut from the loom, edges were hemmed, and sometimes a lining added.

In a nutshell
A woven textile art form: images or patterns are created by interlacing coloured threads on a loom.

Why it matters
Combines craftsmanship, storytelling and interior design.

Key figures
Francisco de Goya, 1746–1828
William Morris, 1834–96
Raphael, 1483–1520
Peter Paul Rubens, 1577–1640

Make the connection
design, p.55
line, p.56
drawing, p.59
warm/cool colours, p.148–9

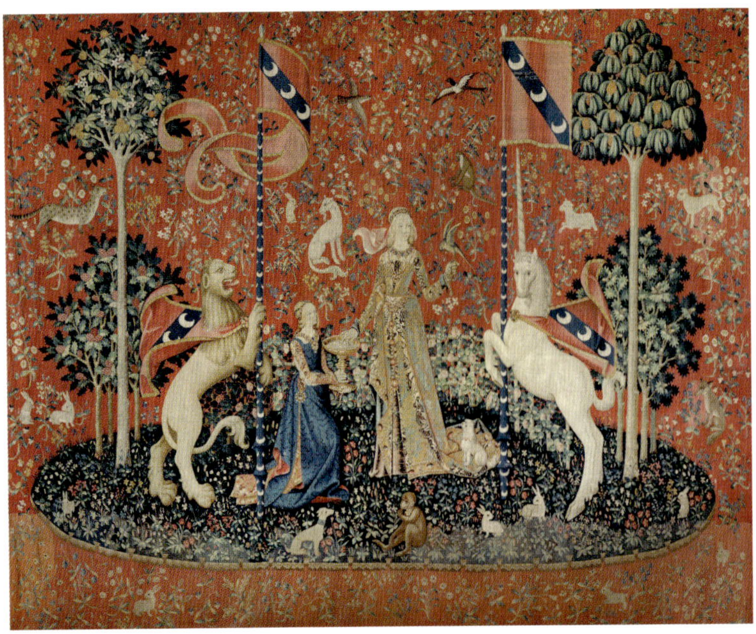

'Taste' (tapestry), from *The Lady and the Unicorn*, c.1500
Musée de Cluny, Paris

embroidery

Using a needle with (usually coloured) thread or yarn, embroidery is a technique for embellishing fabrics. While tapestry is woven, embroidery is stitched onto an existing fabric, sometimes incorporating other trimmings. Appliqué is a related technique in which additional fabric is sewn or embroidered onto a base.

Embroidery originated in ancient Egypt, China and the Near East, and was traditionally used to decorate various textiles. Historically, it was often seen as a domestic, 'feminine' craft and dismissed in the male-dominated art world. Since the Feminist art movement began in the 1960s, many women artists have embraced embroidery to challenge gender norms and explore identity, history and feminism.

The perception of embroidery as craft rather than fine art has shifted significantly; now several artists use it as a means to explore memory, cultural heritage and personal narrative. May Morris (below) was an early advocate for treating embroidery as a serious art form, emphasizing creative design and expressive stitchwork rather than purely decorative use. Judith Scott expanded the medium in the second part of the 20th century by integrating embroidery with fibre sculpture to explore memory, identity and materiality. In *Everyone I Have Ever Slept With 1963–1995* (1995) by Tracey Emin, hand-stitched text conveys personal stories. Embroidery is increasingly recognized as fine art for its tactile intimacy and enduring expressive power.

In a nutshell
The art of decorating fabric with stitched designs using a needle and thread.

Why it matters
Historically undervalued, embroidery is now often employed in fine art as a means of exploring identity, memory and gender.

Key figures
Louise Bourgeois, 1911–2010
Tracey Emin, b.1963
Sheila Hicks, b.1934
May Morris, 1862–1938

Make the connection
Art Nouveau, p.32
line/mark, pp.56–7
contrast/unity, pp.92–3

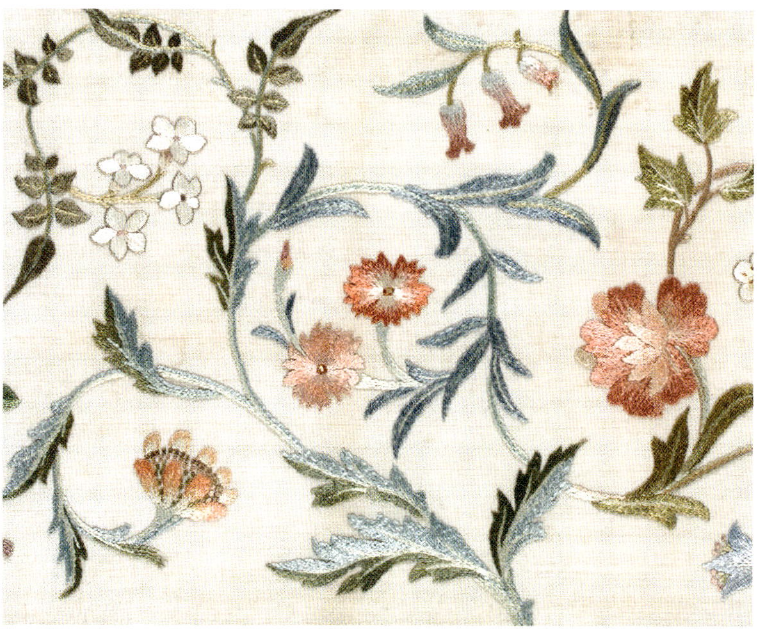

May Morris, *A Garden Piece* (detail), 1938
Private collection

mosaic

Mosaic art originated around the 3rd millennium BCE in Mesopotamia, where small pieces of coloured stones, shells and ivory were used to decorate floors and walls. The technique spread to ancient Greece, where pebble mosaics were popular. In ancient Rome, mosaics were crafted from small pieces of stone, glass or ceramic – called tesserae – and arranged to form intricate images and patterns in villas and palaces.

During the Byzantine era, artists created mosaics on the walls and ceilings of churches and cathedrals. Made *c.*526 and 547, the mosaics of San Vitale Basilica in Ravenna (see below) are shimmering images that blend imperial grandeur and spiritual symbolism, most famously depicting Emperor Justinian and Empress Theodora in richly adorned processions. Gold tesserae were made using glass backed with gold leaf, to convey divine presence and heavenly light. Islamic cultures also embraced mosaics, utilizing complex geometric and floral patterns to adorn mosques and palaces.

Artists and designers in the Arts and Crafts movement, Art Nouveau and Modernism also utilized mosaics. The Spanish architect Antoni Gaudí is renowned for his use of *trencadís*, a mosaic technique that utilizes broken ceramic tiles, as seen in Park Güell in Barcelona.

In a nutshell
Artworks made by assembling small pieces of stone, glass or tile into decorative images or patterns.

Why it matters
Durable and expressive storytelling becomes possible, particularly in architecture and religious spaces.

Key figures
Dioskourides of Samos, late 2nd–early 1st century BCE
Antoni Gaudí, 1852–1926
Laurel True, b.1968
Gaius Julius Volusenus, *fl.*mid-1st century BCE

Make the connection
ancient Roman art, p.8
Byzantine, p.10
design, p.55
contrast, p.92

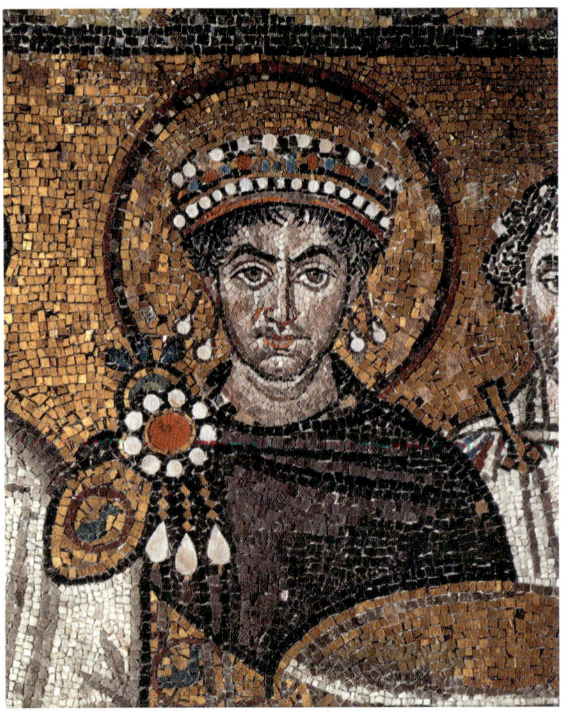

Mosaic (detail), Basilica of San Vitale, 545–547 BCE

tilework

While mosaics are created by assembling small tesserae to form patterns or images, tilework involves decorating surfaces with thin, hard slabs, usually square or rectangular – combining functionality with adornment. The tiles might be decorated or plain, and arranged in set patterns.

In Islamic art, tiles express geometric, floral and calligraphic patterns, especially in mosques and palaces across the Middle East, North Africa and Spain, where the repetition of patterns evokes ideas of the infinite or the underlying harmony of creation. The 19th-century Kasbah of Thami El Glaoui in Morocco features glazed *zellij* (also spelt *zellige*) tiles, traditional Moroccan ceramic pieces, cut into geometric shapes and assembled into elaborate patterns.

Many tile traditions exist across cultures. Often painted in blue and white, *azulejo* tiles have been a feature of Portuguese architecture since the 16th century. In the Netherlands, blue-and-white Delft tiles feature painted scenes on white backgrounds. Italian *majolica* tiles are known for their painted scenes and glossy finishes. In China, during the Tang and Ming dynasties, glazed roof tiles were used in imperial buildings, providing both symbolic and protective benefits.

Both mosaics and tilework create vibrant, patterned surfaces, but tilework emphasizes surface decoration and pattern repetition. Both focus on colour, geometry and rhythm.

In a nutshell
Tiles are small, often ceramic, shapes used to embellish walls, floors and architecture.

Why it matters
Blends function with beauty, preserving cultural, religious and artistic traditions across centuries.

Key figures
Art Nouveau and Art Deco designers
Chinese potters
Islamic artisans
Portuguese *azulejo* makers

Make the connection
Art Nouveau, p.32
design, p.55
line, p.56
warm/cool colours, pp.148–9

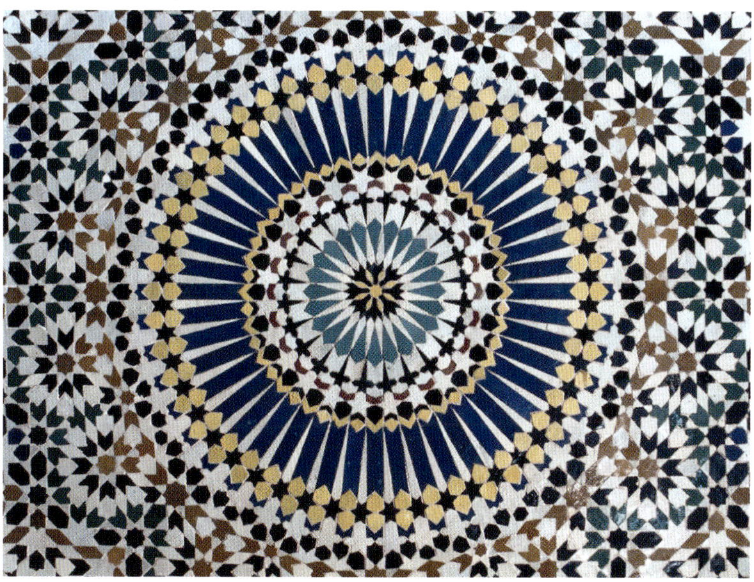

Zellige tilework (detail)
Kasbah of Thami El Glaoui, Télouet

tempera

Used extensively from antiquity to the Renaissance, tempera (from the Latin *temper*, meaning 'to adjust something to the right consistency') is a paint medium traditionally applied in thin, semi-opaque layers on rigid surfaces such as wood panels, often prepared with gesso – a smooth chalk-and-glue ground. Tempera consists of dry pigments mixed with a binding agent, usually egg yolk, which dries rapidly to form a durable surface.

For centuries, tempera dominated Western painting, before oil paint gained favour in the late 15th century. Many ancient artists, in Egypt, Greece and Rome, used tempera, and it remained central in early Christian, medieval and Early Renaissance art. Its quick-drying nature required careful planning, fine brushwork and a highly disciplined technique.

Tempera produces a luminous yet matte finish and is stable: it can survive for hundreds of years with minimal cracking, fading or yellowing. Its precision and clarity made it well-suited to artists who prized crisp contours and intricate detail. *The Battle of San Romano* (detail below) by Paolo Uccello is made with egg tempera, which heightens the sharp outlines, jewel-like colours and meticulous surface effects that give the scene its almost enamelled brilliance.

Tempera has enjoyed periodic revivals, particularly among icon painters and artists drawn to its clarity, discipline and radiant colour.

In a nutshell
A fast-drying painting medium made by mixing pigment with egg yolk.

Why it matters
Its fine detail and luminosity dominated European painting for centuries.

Key figures
Sandro Botticelli, *c.*1445–1510
Duccio, d.1319
Fra Angelico, d.1455
Giotto, *c.*1267/76–1337

Make the connection
Early Renaissance, p.14
shadow/tone, pp.62–3
pigment, p.111

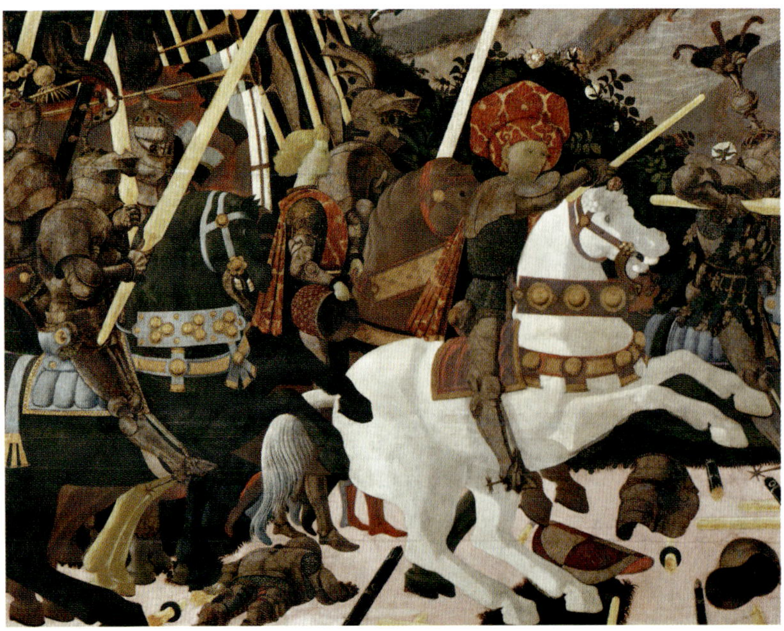

Paolo Uccello, *The Battle of San Romano* (detail), 1432
National Gallery, London

encaustic

From the Greek *enkaustikos* ('to burn in'), the term encaustic refers to a technique in which heated wax is mixed with pigment and applied in molten form to a surface such as wood, canvas or marble. Once the wax is laid down, the artist reheats it to fuse the layers, creating a surface that can be built up, scraped back or reworked.

Encaustic is typically made from beeswax and damar resin combined with powdered pigments, although some artists also incorporate inks or oil paints. Metal tools and special brushes are used to shape the wax, while heated instruments help manipulate and bind the surface as it cools. The earliest surviving examples of encaustic are the Fayum mummy portraits from the 1st to 3rd centuries CE.

In the 20th century, encaustic experienced a revival, most notably through Jasper Johns. In *Three Flags* (1958), Johns used encaustic to build up layered, textured surfaces, embedding newsprint and brushstrokes beneath translucent wax. This gave the work its dense physical presence and emphasized the tension between an everyday symbol – the American flag – and its material, handcrafted construction.

Unlike tempera, its equally ancient counterpart, encaustic allows for rich blending, texture and an almost sculptural quality. Although encaustic is unsuited to fine linear detail, it remains stable, with its colours retaining brilliance for decades and even centuries.

In a nutshell
A painting method using pigment mixed with hot beeswax.

Why it matters
Yields vibrant, textured, long-lasting works and enables sculptural effects.

Key figures
Lynda Benglis, b.1941
Jasper Johns, b.1930
Martin Kline, b.1964

Make the connection
Byzantine, p.10
sgraffito, p.99
pigment, p.111
oil pastel, p.115

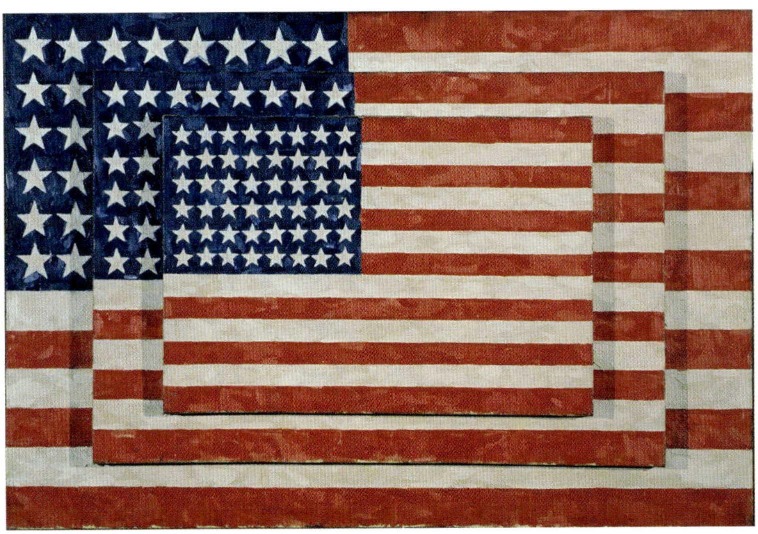

Jasper Johns, *Three Flags*, 1958
Whitney Museum of American Art, New York

watercolour

Watercolour is a transparent medium made by suspending ground pigments in a water-soluble binder, usually gum arabic. It is activated when mixed with water and applied to paper. When light passes through its translucent layers, it reflects off the paper beneath, resulting in a luminous, often delicate effect. While other paints, such as gouache, are also water-soluble, watercolour is uniquely characterized by this transparency; it relies on the whiteness of the paper, sometimes left bare, to provide highlights and luminosity.

Although it was used in ancient Egypt and China, watercolour flourished especially in Europe during the Renaissance – it was often used for botanical illustration, map-making and preparatory sketches. By the 18th and 19th centuries, artists including J. M. W. Turner, Paul Sandby and John Singer Sargent were carrying their portable watercolours outdoors to capture landscapes directly from nature, recording changing light, atmosphere and colour on site.

The medium is favoured for its quick drying time and minimal set-up. It cannot be easily corrected once applied, however, and its fluidity and unpredictability make it challenging. Artists often build their watercolour images through glazing or wet-on-wet techniques to create soft transitions.

Despite its reputation for being unforgiving, watercolour offers a unique expressive range, from light washes to rich, controlled details.

In a nutshell
A transparent, water-based medium, usually applied to paper, known for its luminous washes.

Why it matters
Allows for expressive, spontaneous work; long-prized for its transparency and subtlety.

Key figures
Winslow Homer, 1836–1910
John Singer Sargent, 1856–1925
J. M. W. Turner, 1775–1851

Make the connection
glazing, p.87
unity, p.93
dry brushing, p.98
plein-air painting, p.104

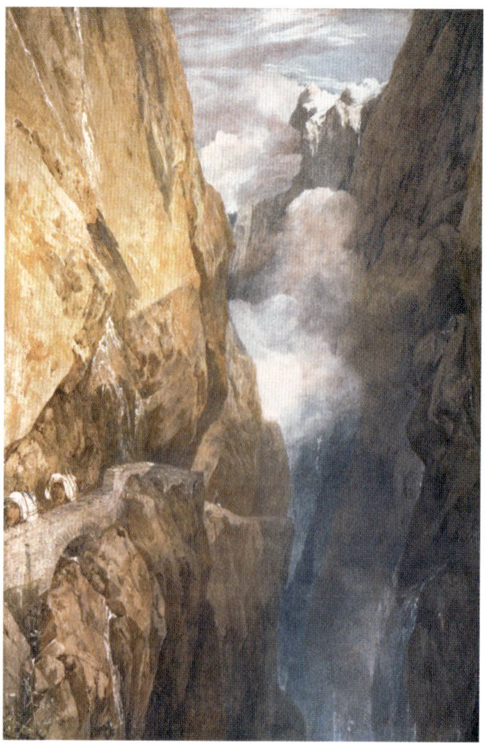

J. M. W. Turner, *Passage of Mount St Gothard from the Centre of Devil's Bridge*, 1804
Abbot Hall Art Gallery, Kendal

gouache

An opaque, water-based painting medium made of pigment, water, gum arabic and (sometimes) additional fillers like chalk to increase its density, gouache produces solid, flat, matte areas of colour. It combines the spontaneity and ease of watercolour with the possibility of bolder, more graphic effects (and the capacity for reworking and correction).

The term 'gouache' was first used to describe opaque watercolour enhanced with white pigment in 18th-century France, and by the 20th century, this term had become standard, superseding the alternative 'bodycolour', which had been common from the 17th to late 19th centuries in English-speaking regions. The medium is much older, however: it was used in ancient Egyptian art and Persian miniatures. Its opacity was suited to detailed, vibrant illustrations.

In the 20th century, gouache was popular among artists, illustrators and designers for its bold, flat colours and quick-drying properties. Henri Matisse famously used it for his vividly coloured paper cut-outs and it is a preferred medium for graphic work, illustration and poster art. Like watercolour, gouache is activated with water and usually used on paper, but it is heavier and more controllable. Its opacity means it can be applied in layers, allowing mistakes to be corrected and light colours to be applied over dark.

In a nutshell
An opaque, matte, water-based paint that offers solid, vibrant colours.

Why it matters
Favoured by illustrators and designers, it combines the ease of watercolour with the boldness of acrylic or oil.

Key figures
Paul Klee, 1879–1940
Camille Pissarro, 1830–1903
Henri de Toulouse-Lautrec, 1864–1901
J. M. W. Turner, 1775–1851

Make the connection
paint/pigment, pp.110–11
tempera, p.120

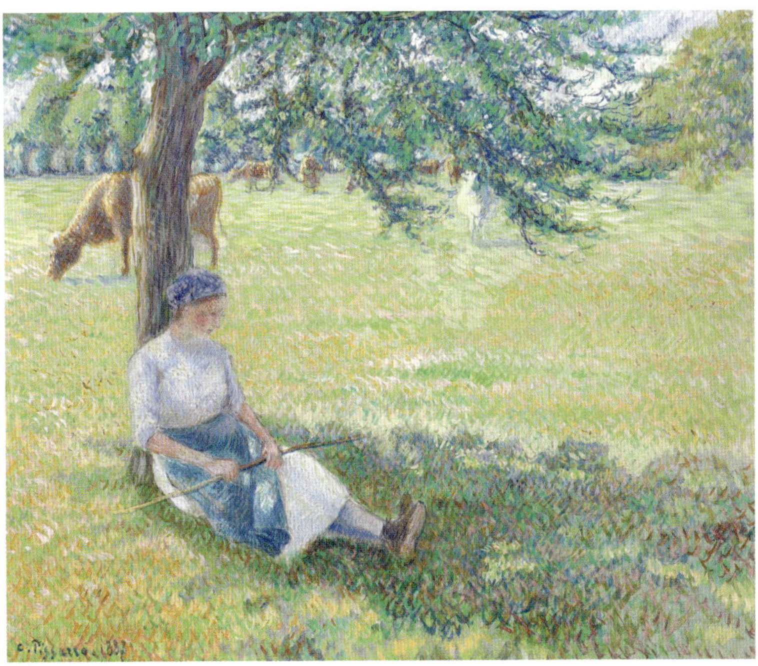

Camille Pissarro, *Gardeuse de vaches, Eragny*, 1887
Private collection

acrylic paint

Developed in Germany in 1934, initially as a house paint, acrylic paint gained popularity among artists from the mid-1950s. In many ways, it was seen as an alternative to oil paint, becoming known for its versatility and ability to emulate the appearance of oils, gouache or watercolours, depending on how it is diluted and applied.

Acrylic paint, consisting of three main components – pigment, binder and vehicle – is easy to clean up, has little odour and, once dry, becomes water-resistant and flexible. The binder is an acrylic polymer emulsion, and the paint can be used to create detailed work with textured impasto effects (see p.100). It is available in a wide range of colours and adheres to many surfaces – even fabric.

Because acrylics are synthetic, manufacturers have developed a wide range of mediums and additives. These can alter the paint's texture, sheen, drying time and transparency, giving artists great control over the outcome. However, the fast drying time can be frustrating for those accustomed to working more slowly with oil paint.

Historically, acrylics were popular among abstract and Pop artists, drawn to their bright, synthetic colours and adaptability. These same qualities suit bold, graphic styles, such as that of Malcolm Jagamarra Maloney (see below), who works in the tradition of Aboriginal art.

In a nutshell
A synthetic painting medium, known for its boldness, versatility and wide range of colours.

Why it matters
Ideal for quick work, layering and modern techniques, it is widely used in contemporary and educational settings.

Key figures
Helen Frankenthaler, 1928–2011
David Hockney, b.1937
Malcolm Jagamarra Maloney, b.1955
Andy Warhol, 1928–87

Make the connection
Abstract Expressionism, p.31
Pop art, p.46
underpainting, p.81
impasto/imprimatura, pp.100–1

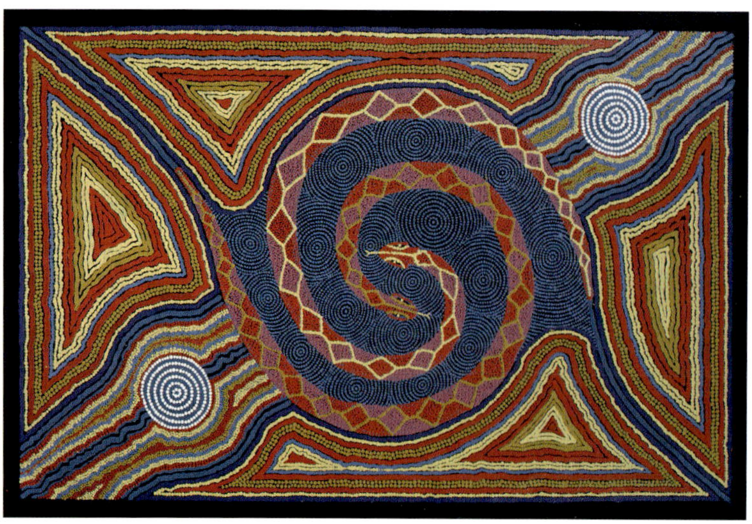

Malcolm Jagamarra Maloney, *Wantapari*, 1992
Horniman Museum, London

oil paint

The richness of oil paint stems from its binder. Oil suspends pigment particles more densely than water-based mediums, resulting in saturated colours and a natural gloss.

It is likely that Buddhist artists in 7th-century Afghanistan used a form of oil paint, although it was not used in Europe until about the 11th century, primarily for painting wooden statues. Oil paint came into widespread use in Europe during the 15th century, as an alternative to tempera (see page p.120). Its slow drying time and versatility – for layering, blending, glazing and scumbling – made it popular, and it has remained the dominant medium in Western art.

Unlike acrylics, oil paints dry through oxidation, a chemical process, rather than evaporation, allowing artists to manipulate paint for hours or even days. This enables subtle transitions in tone and colour, as well as corrections. However, oil paints require solvents for thinning and cleaning, many of which are toxic. Finished works can take months to dry completely and may yellow or crack over time, although many have survived centuries with minimal degradation.

In *The Wedding at Cana* (detail below), Paolo Veronese uses oil paint to achieve jewel-like colours, intricate detailing and rich, layered depth.

In a nutshell
Pigment mixed with natural oils, offering slow drying and rich blending.

Why it matters
Central to classical Western art, oil paint creates detailed, atmospheric, long-lasting work with unmatched depth of colour.

Key figures
Vincent van Gogh, 1853–90
Georgia O'Keeffe, 1887–1986
Peter Paul Rubens, 1577–1640
Paolo Veronese, 1528–88

Make the connection
underpainting, p.81
foreshortening, p.85
scumbling/glazing, pp.86–7
pigment, p.111

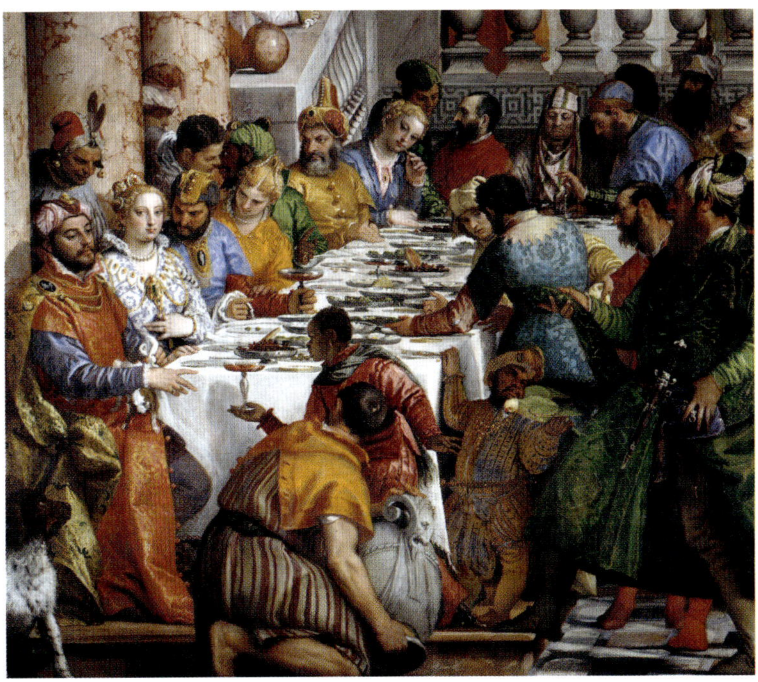

Paolo Veronese, *The Wedding at Cana* (detail: The Meal of the Princes), 1562–3
Musée du Louvre, Paris

subject

The primary focus or identifiable content of a work of art is its subject. If the question is, 'what is this artwork about at first glance?' the answer is 'the subject'.

Subjects in art can be grouped into general categories, such as portraiture (people), landscape (nature or settings), still life (inanimate objects), genre scenes (everyday life), history painting (significant events) or abstract forms (where representation is minimal or non-existent). For example, the subject of *American Gothic* by Grant Wood (below), is a woman, a man and their house. (The theme, however, is rural American identity of the period.) In the many paintings of waterlilies by Claude Monet, the subject is a pond with lilies and reflections.

The subject is not necessarily the same as the meaning, message or theme of the artwork. A painting of a woman may be a portrait, but it may carry symbolic or emotional significance, depending on the context. The subject is what is seen, not necessarily what is implied. In abstract and conceptual art, identifying the subject can be more difficult; it may be the form, colour or material itself.

A clear, definite subject in a work of art helps the viewer understand it more effectively.

In a nutshell
Usually, the artwork's visible focus is a person, object or scene – this is its subject.

Why it matters
Anchors the viewer's attention and provides a starting point for interpretation.

Key figures
Frida Kahlo, 1907–54
Grant Wood, 1891–1942
Diego Velázquez, 1599–1660
Kara Walker, b.1969

Make the connection
tone, p.63
sfumato, p.71
atmospheric/linear perspective, pp.78–9
distortion, p.84

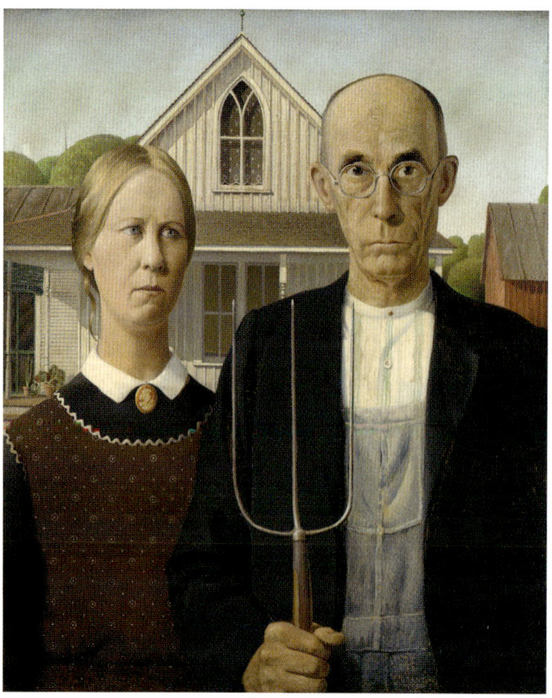

Grant Wood, *American Gothic*, 1930
The Art Institute of Chicago

theme

An artwork's underlying idea, message, or emotional core is its theme: what the work is ultimately about, beyond its visible subject matter. While the subject is what is shown, the theme is why it matters. Themes are often abstract and universal, encompassing ideas such as love, identity, power, nature, mortality or the human condition. These concepts may not be explicitly stated but are conveyed through composition, symbolism and context. For example, although the subject of *Self-Portrait with Thorn Necklace and Hummingbird* (below) is a self-portrait, its deeper themes include fractured identity, emotional resilience, loss and personal trauma.

A single subject can sustain multiple themes: a painting of a woman might explore femininity, strength or maternal love, for example, depending on how she is represented. Conversely, one theme may appear across varied subjects; the theme of death, for instance, might be expressed in vanitas still lifes – a genre that emphasizes the futility of life and the inevitability of death through symbolic representations – in scenes of conflict, or in portraits reflecting ageing.

Themes give artworks depth and emotional resonance, shaped by the artist's viewpoint and experiences and the historical moment. They encourage the viewer to interpret not only what is depicted but also what is implied, through colour, form, setting and symbolism. Themes may also articulate broader social, political or philosophical ideas, as seen in Kahlo's explorations of identity and suffering, or in Barbara Kruger's interrogation of power and gender.

In a nutshell
The underlying idea or message an artwork conveys, such as love, identity, maternity or mortality.

Why it matters
Gives emotional or intellectual depth, connecting the viewer to broader meanings.

Key figures
Jean-Michel Basquiat, 1960–88
Frida Kahlo, 1907–54
Barbara Kruger, b.1945
Wassily Kandinsky, 1866–1944

Make the connection
Baroque, p.18
shadow, p.62
imagination, p.95
creativity, p.132

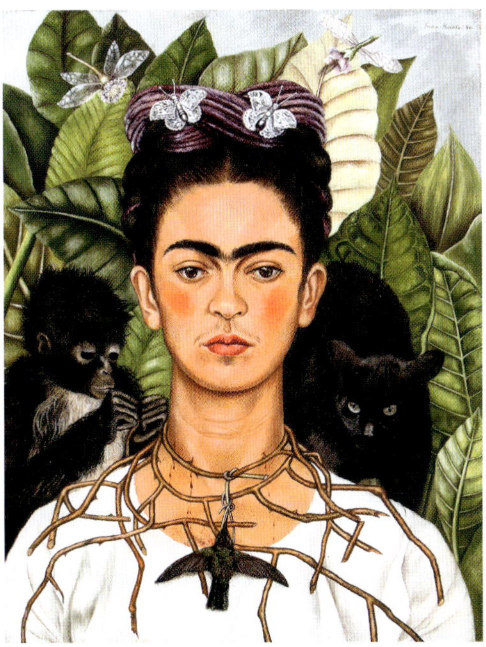

Frida Kahlo, *Self-Portrait with Thorn Necklace and Hummingbird*, 1940
Harry Ransom Center, Austin

abstract

Although much art around the world – for example, Islamic art – has been abstract, it was not until the early 20th century that abstraction appeared in Western art. Without representing the physical world, abstract art comprises shapes, colours, lines and forms. It does not aim to depict reality, but explores visual language, independent of recognizable subjects.

One of the first abstract Western artists, working in the late 19th and early 20th century, was Swedish painter Hilma af Klint. She said her work was guided by spirits she encountered during seances. Other artists who questioned traditional representation in this period included Wassily Kandinsky, Kazimir Malevich and Piet Mondrian, who each experimented with non-objective forms to explore spirituality, emotion and universal order through art.

There are various types of abstract art: geometric abstraction, for example, as in Mondrian's paintings (see p.40), or lyrical abstraction, which is more spontaneous and emotional. Abstract art enables artists to explore new dimensions of creativity and expression, free from the constraints of realistic representation. It challenges both the artist and the viewer to think beyond what is seen.

In a nutshell
Abstract art uses shape, colour and form to express ideas without representing real-world objects.

Why it matters
It encourages emotional and intellectual interpretation beyond literal meaning.

Key figures
Hilma af Klint, 1862–1944
Wassily Kandinsky, 1866–1944
Piet Mondrian, 1872–1944
Alma Thomas, 1891–1978

Make the connection
Expressionism/Abstract Expressionism, pp.30–1
Op art, p.47
installation, p.83
symmetry/asymmetry, pp.108–9
Land art, p.142

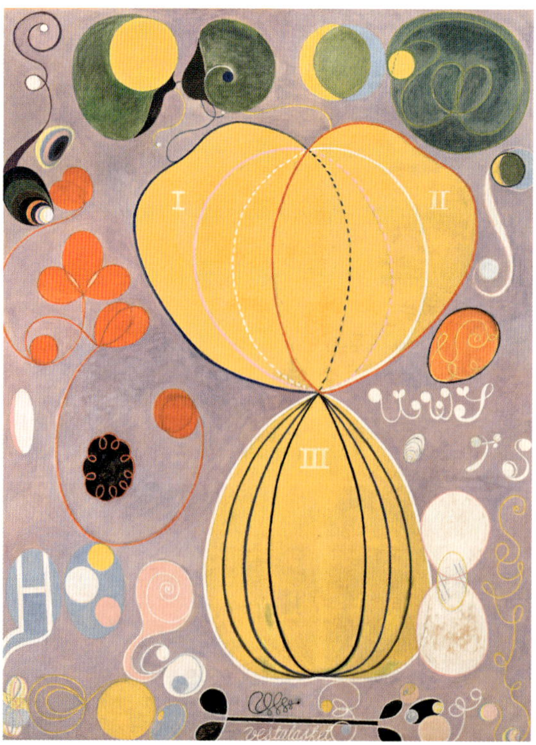

Hilma af Klint, *The Ten Largest, No. 7., Adulthood, Group IV*, 1907
Hilma af Klint Foundation

figurative

Art that is derived from the physical world around us is called figurative or representational. It depicts recognizable subjects, even if they are not necessarily portrayed in a realistic style. Unlike abstract art, figurative art maintains strong connections to reality.

Some of the earliest cave paintings and rock sculptures we know of are figurative, representing a world we recognize, and this tradition has continued throughout history. Representational art has evolved, reflecting changes in culture and society, but, for much of history, it has been the dominant form. During specific eras, such as the ancient Egyptian and Byzantine (see p.10) periods, art often appeared relatively static and diagrammatic, to convey messages as clearly as possible. Later, from the Renaissance onwards, artists were more inclined to depict the world with exacting, lifelike detail.

In the early 20th century, however, a significant shift towards abstraction occurred. By the late 19th and early 20th centuries, figurative art had come to be influenced by movements such as Cubism (p.36) and Expressionism (p.30). Yet it was never eliminated, and artists continue to include recognizable subjects in their work, sometimes blending them with abstract techniques.

In a nutshell
Depicts recognizable subjects from the physical world.

Why it matters
Has a profound connection to human experience, storytelling and cultural identity throughout history.

Key figures
Rosa Bonheur, 1822–99
Mary Cassatt, 1844–1926
Leonardo da Vinci, 1452–1519
Lucian Freud, 1922–2011

Make the connection
Tang Dynasty art, p.12
Baroque, p.18
foreshortening, p.85
observation, p.94

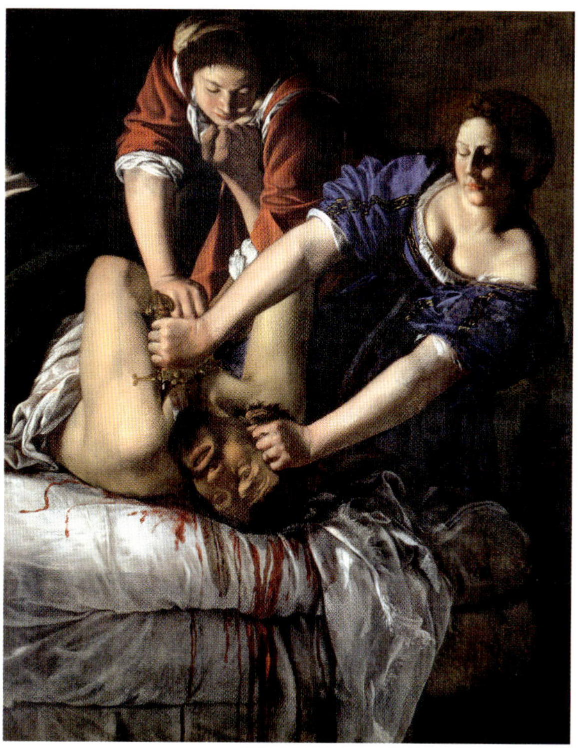

Artemisia Gentileschi, *Judith Beheading Holofernes*, *c.*1612–13
Museo di Capodimonte, Naples

Fibonacci sequence

Named after the Italian mathematician Leonardo Bonacci of Pisa, also known as Fibonacci (*c.*1170–*c.*1240–50), the Fibonacci sequence is a series of numbers that occurs in nature: for example, in the arrangement of leaves around a stem, or the number of spirals on a pinecone. Each number in the sequence is the sum of the two preceding numbers, with the ratio between successive numbers approaching the golden ratio (≈1.618) as the sequence progresses; for example, 4,181 (the 19th number in the sequence) divided by 2,584 (the 18th number) is 1.618 to three decimal places.

In nature, this sequence has been observed in growth patterns and reflects optimal packing and growth efficiency; for example, pinecone 'bracts' are arranged in two spirals, and the numbers of spirals in each direction are always two consecutive Fibonacci numbers, that is, 5 and 8. Although some mathematicians were, therefore, already aware of the sequence, Fibonacci's 1202 book *Liber Abaci* (Book of Calculation) introduced it more widely to Western Europe. But what is its relevance to art and design?

Less directly applied in art than the golden ratio, the Fibonacci sequence is nonetheless used by some artists and designers to determine dimensions, spacing or scaling, creating a sense of balance and harmony in compositions. See, for example, Raphael's *Madonna of the Goldfinch* (right), whose proportions can be mapped by a Fibonacci spiral.

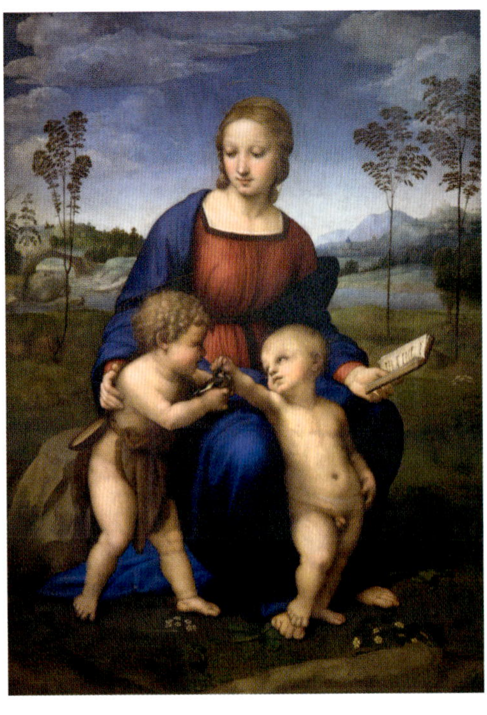

Raphael, *Madonna of the Goldfinch*, *c.*1505–6 Gallerie degli Uffizi, Florence

In a nutshell
A series in which each number is the sum of the two previous numbers: 0, 1, 1, 2, 3, 5, 8, and so on.

Why it matters
It models natural growth patterns and creates aesthetically pleasing proportions; therefore, it appears in nature, art and architecture.

Key figures
Sandro Botticelli, *c.*1445–1510
Leonardo da Vinci, 1452–1519
Piet Mondrian, 1872–1944
Raphael, 1483–1520

Make the connection
art, p.54
contrast/unity, pp.92–3
asymmetry, p.109

golden ratio

Often represented by the Greek letter Φ (phi), the golden ratio is a mathematical constant: a number (≈1.618) that connects two quantities or numbers in a specific way. Where a line is divided into two unequal parts such that the ratio of the whole segment to the longer part is equal to the ratio of the longer part to the shorter, this ratio is ... golden. The effect is generally considered aesthetically pleasing.

Also referred to as the golden section, the golden mean, the golden number, the divine proportion or the golden proportion, this vital ratio has been used as a structural device by artists, designers and architects for centuries, allowing them to create compositions that feel intuitively pleasing to the human eye. This is because – as with the Fibonacci sequence, with which it shares a connection – this ratio is found in nature: governing the branching patterns of trees and the spirals of seashells.

The horizon lines in Georges Seurat's paintings are often placed in relation to the canvas height according to the golden ratio, and the same relationship appears in *The Golden Stairs* (1880) by Edward Burne-Jones. These are just two examples of how artists have used the ratio to create balance, order and symmetry in their works.

In a nutshell
A mathematical proportion often found in nature and used in art, design and architecture.

Why it matters
Creates visual balance and harmony.

Key figures
Edward Burne-Jones, 1833–98
Leonardo da Vinci, 1452–1519
Michelangelo, 1475–1564
Georges Seurat, 1859–91

Make the connection
ancient Roman/Romanesque art, pp.8–9
Early/High Renaissance, pp.14–15
unity, p.93

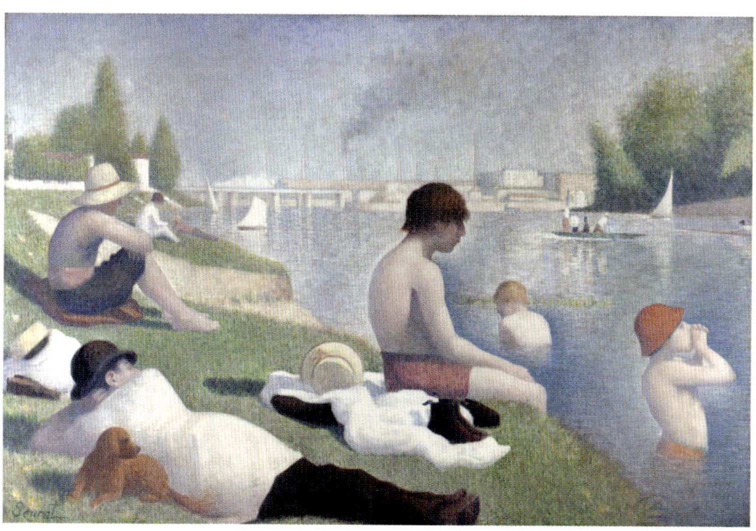

Georges Seurat, *Bathers at Asnières*, 1884
National Gallery, London

creativity

The power to imagine, express and represent the world in original ways, creativity involves thinking freely, experimenting and creating something unique, be it a new style, concept or emotional expression. Pablo Picasso, for example, demonstrated exceptional creativity, using a wide range of materials and contributing to the development of multiple art movements.

The most successful creativity includes purpose, cultural or historical context, and a willingness to challenge accepted conventions. Whether artists are reacting to tradition or completely redefining what art can be, creativity often reflects a spirit of intellectual freedom – thinking of new ideas, making connections where others might not and reimagining the familiar.

Psychologists often distinguish between divergent and convergent thinking in creative processes. Divergent thinking involves the generation of numerous ideas – exploring multiple paths. Convergent thinking, on the other hand, involves refining ideas and selecting the most effective solutions. Both are essential to creativity. Openness to experience, a willingness to take risks and courage are also essential.

In a nutshell
The ability to imagine and express ideas in original and meaningful ways.

Why it matters
Creativity challenges the expected. It can inspire emotion and drive artistic and cultural progress.

Key figures
Paul Cézanne, 1839–1906
Wassily Kandinsky, 1866–1944
Michelangelo, 1475–1564
Pablo Picasso, 1881–1973

Make the connection
Romanticism, p.20
Expressionism, p.30
installation, p.83
imagination, p.95

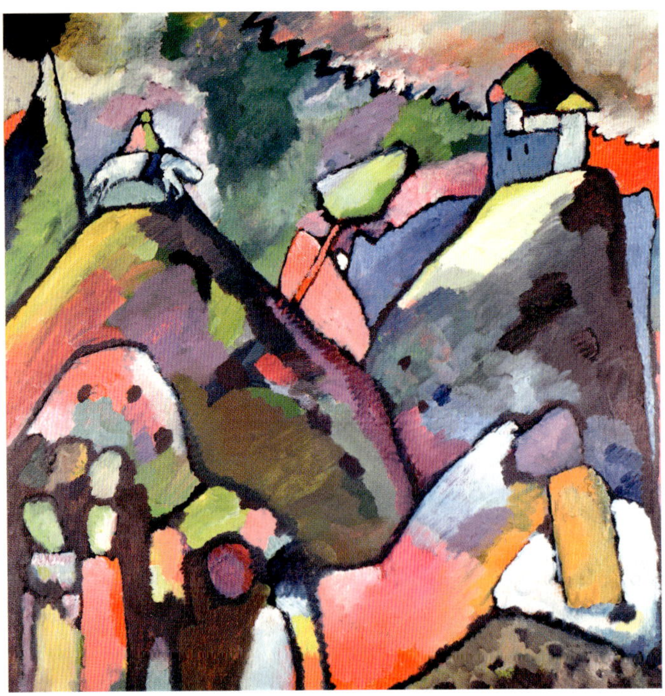

Wassily Kandinsky, *Improvisation 9*, 1910
Private collection

innovation

In 2003, Olafur Eliasson created *The weather project* (see p.53). This vast installation filled Tate Modern's Turbine Hall with a glowing artificial sun and fine mist. The work explored perception, environment and collective experience, merging technology, space and sensory engagement in ways that had not been considered before. Innovation is about applying creativity in pioneering ways, whether in technique, medium or message. While creativity in art is the ability to generate original ideass or forms, innovation is the act of transforming those ideas into new methods, approaches or practices that change how art is made or understood.

Some influential artistic innovations of the twentieth century include the painting *Nude Descending a Staircase, No.2* (below) and the readymade *Fountain* (1917), both by Marcel Duchamp. Blending elements of Cubism and Futurism (pp.36–7), *Nude Descending a Staircase* offered radically new ways of representing movement and the human body. *Fountain* proposed an entirely new definition of art, shifting attention from craftsmanship to concept. Although Duchamp's work provoked outrage – *Nude Descending a Staircase* was even denounced as immoral – it challenged convention and inspired others to move in new artistic directions.

In a nutshell
Development of new techniques, materials or concepts, which change artistic practice.

Why it matters
Shapes new movements and approaches.

Key figures
Christo, 1935–2020, and Jeanne-Claude, 1935–2009
Judy Chicago, b.1939
Marcel Duchamp, 1887–1968
Piet Mondrian, 1872–1944

Make the connection
Suprematism, p.38
De Stijl, p.40
Dada, p.42
abstract, p.128

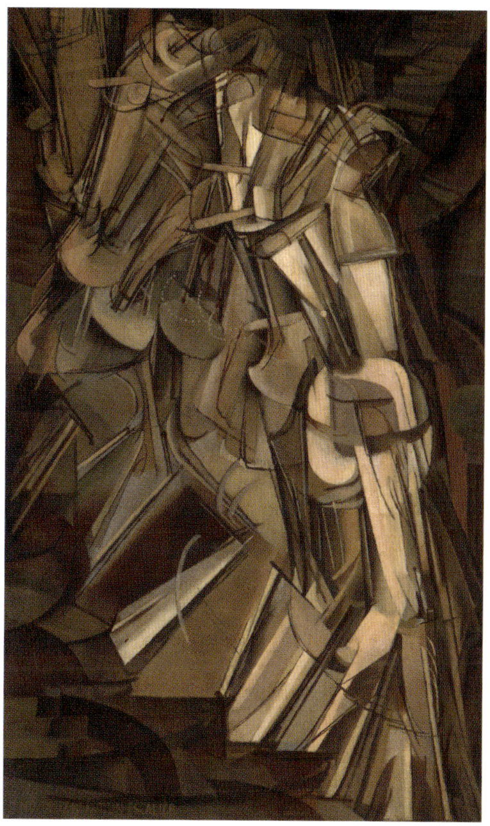

Marcel Duchamp, *Nude Descending a Staircase (No.2)*, 1912 Philadelphia Museum of Art

symbolism

Artists across all cultures and time periods have used symbolism, employing objects, colours or figures to represent ideas or emotions, suggesting meanings beyond their surface appearances.

Ancient Egyptian wall paintings used scale and colour to signal the status and divinity of individuals; Buddhist mandalas symbolize the universe and spiritual enlightenment; and Indigenous Australian art often encodes Dreamtime stories through symbolic shapes and patterns. Symbolic details were prevalent in medieval and Renaissance art: for example, lilies represented purity and apples stood for temptation or original sin. Artists such as Jan van Eyck and Piero della Francesca frequently incorporated ordinary-looking objects into their paintings to convey spiritual or moral messages.

Symbolism continued to be a key component of art throughout the 20th century and into the 21st, with artists such as Frida Kahlo, Jean-Michel Basquiat and Yayoi Kusama creating personal symbols to convey their perspectives on identity, memory and perception. Even in abstract or conceptual work, symbolism can suggest more than meets the eye. In *The Kiss* (below), Gustav Klimt employed symbolism in the figures' patterned gold robes, evoking ideas of unity, spirituality, transcendence and complementary energies.

In a nutshell
Visual elements – objects, colours and figures – are used to convey deeper meanings, emotions or ideas.

Why it matters
Enables artists to convey complex concepts – spiritual, emotional and political – often transcending language or time.

Key figures
Jan van Eyck, d.1441
Hans Holbein the Younger, 1497/8–1543
Frida Kahlo, 1907–54
Kerry James Marshall, b.1955

Make the connection
Renaissance, p.16
imagination, p.95
innovation, p.133
history painting, p.136

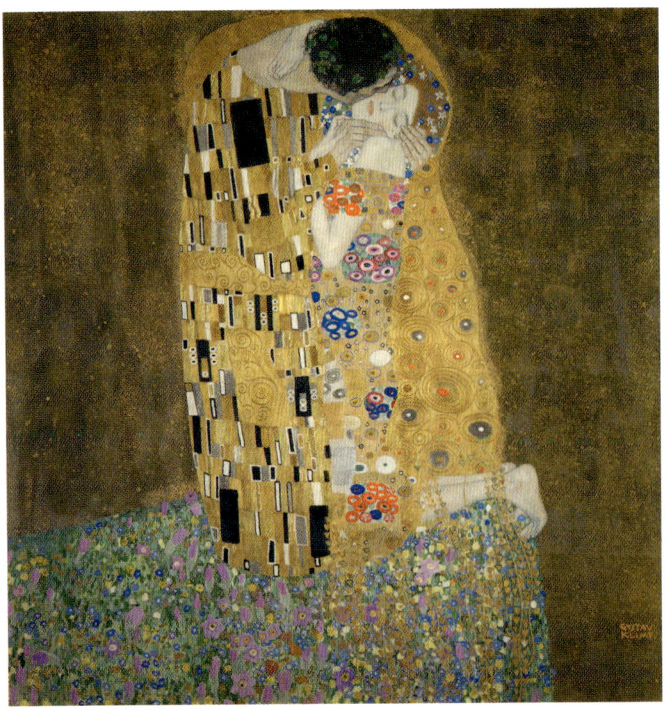

Gustav Klimt, *The Kiss*, 1907–08
Osterreichische Galerie Belvedere, Vienna

allegory

When symbolism appears throughout a narrative, and figures, objects and entire scenes carry meanings beyond the literal, an artwork becomes an allegory. Turning ideas into stories, inviting viewers to uncover layers of moral, philosophical or abstract significance and to interpret meanings, allegories have been an important element of Western art since antiquity, enabling artists to convey complex themes, such as virtue, vice, love, death or justice, especially in periods when direct expression was limited by political or religious constraints.

A clear example of allegory in art is *Primavera* by Sandro Botticelli (below), in which individual symbols, such as the orange trees associated with marriage, fertility and the powerful Medici family, operate within a far more extensive allegory of seasonal renewal, desire and the generative forces of nature. Across the painting, there are separate, individual symbols, but as a whole, it functions as a layered allegory in which meaning emerges through the interplay of those symbols, mythological figures, gestures and setting.

In such works, the viewer can read the image at both a surface and a metaphorical level, recognizing that allegory uses symbolic elements but binds them into a coherent framework. While symbolism can remain suggestive, open-ended or poetic, allegory typically conveys a clear, direct narrative, making philosophical or moral ideas more understandable – provided the viewer can decode its visual language.

In a nutshell
Figures and scenes represent abstract ideas, moral lessons or philosophical themes.

Why it matters
Complex messages can be communicated immediately and yet subtly.

Key figures
Hieronymus Bosch, d.1516
Sandro Botticelli, *c.*1445–1510
Pieter Bruegel the Elder, d.1569
Eugène Delacroix, 1798–1863

Make the connection
Renaissance/ Mannerism, pp.16–17
Baroque, p.18
art, p.54
fresco, p.64

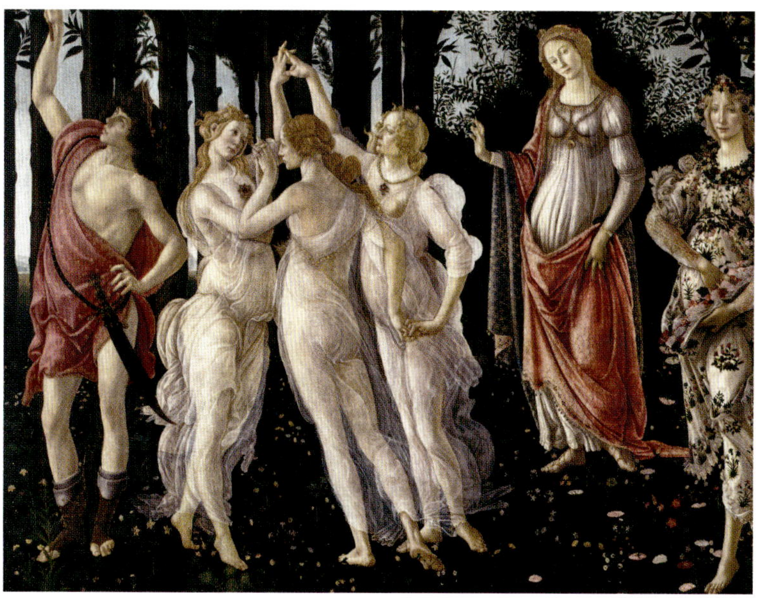

Sandro Botticelli, *Primavera* (Spring), *c.*1478 Gallerie degli Uffizi, Florence

history painting

Traditionally considered the most prestigious genre in academic painting (that is, painting approved by the European academies of art from the 17th to the 19th centuries), history painting depicts significant events from history, mythology, religion or literature. It focuses on subjects that carry moral, political or philosophical weight. These paintings are often significant in scale and dramatic in tone, intended to instruct or stir emotional and intellectual reflection.

While the term 'history painting' might suggest only historical subjects, it actually encompasses far more. Historical paintings typically feature several figures, dramatic compositions, gestures, expressions and symbolism. For example, *The Death of Socrates* by Jacques-Louis David (below) portrays the execution of the Greek philosopher Socrates, as told by Plato; Socrates is depicted as a moral hero who accepts death rather than abandoning his principles. The painting emphasizes the values of reason, sacrifice and civic virtue. In *The Raft of the Medusa* (1818–19) by Théodore Géricault, a real-life tragedy – the shipwreck of the French frigate *Méduse* in 1816 – is transformed into a powerful political and emotional epic. The painting criticizes government incompetence while also exploring human suffering, resilience and hope.

An earlier work, *The School of Athens* (p.66) by Raphael, represents intellectual history, with philosophers gathered in a grand setting. It is not a literal moment, but a celebration of knowledge, reason and the Classical spirit of inquiry.

In a nutshell
Depicts grand, often moral or political narratives from history, mythology, religion or literature.

Why it matters
Once considered the highest form of art, used to educate, inspire and promote cultural ideals.

Key figures
Jacques-Louis David, 1748–1825
Eugène Delacroix, 1798–1863
Théodore Géricault, 1791–1824
Raphael, 1483–1520

Make the connection
Baroque, p.18
Romanticism, p.20
observation, p.94
symbolism/allegory, pp.134–5

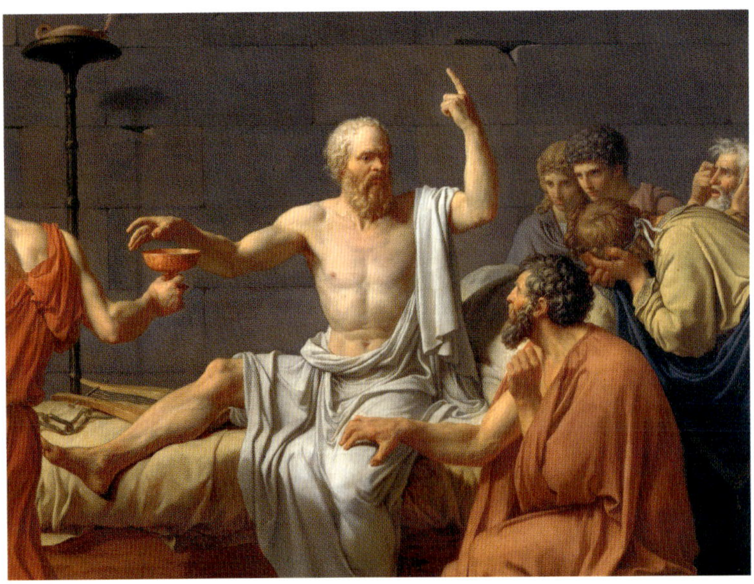

Jacques-Louis David, *The Death of Socrates* (detail), 1787 Metropolitan Museum of Art, New York

genre painting

While history painting depicts impressive, moral or mythological subjects, genre painting explores the ordinary and commonplace: scenes of everyday life in which people eat, work or play. Genre paintings are generally small in scale and focus on quiet observations, subtle commentary or even humour. They were traditionally made for domestic interiors, while history paintings were often commissioned for civic, royal or religious locations.

Genre painting emerged in 17th-century Dutch art, with artists depicting scenes featuring peasants, parties, musical groups or people in taverns. For instance, *A Game of Cards* by Judith Leyster (below) depicts a lively group of people playing cards. The scene suggests themes such as flirtation, humour and deception.

Towards the end of the 19th century, a new focus emerged in genre painting. Artists sought to capture the excitement and fleeting nature of modern life as they observed it in the cities around them. Even the French Impressionists, while mainly focusing on light, painted bustling street scenes and café interiors. During the early 20th century, artists such as Walter Sickert and Edward Hopper painted genre scenes that convey the loneliness often felt in cities.

Confusingly, in art, the word 'genre' is also used to describe different types or broad subject areas of painting. The five 'genres' of painting are history painting, portrait painting, landscape painting, genre painting and still life.

In a nutshell
Depicts scenes of everyday life, featuring ordinary people engaged in daily activities.

Why it matters
Often highlights the complexities and social realities of everyday life.

Key figures
Jean-Baptiste Greuze, 1725–1805
Edward Hopper, 1882–1967
Judith Leyster, 1609–60
Walter Sickert, 1860–1942

Make the connection
linear perspective, p.79
foreshortening, p.85
oil paint, p.125
symbolism/allegory, pp.134–5

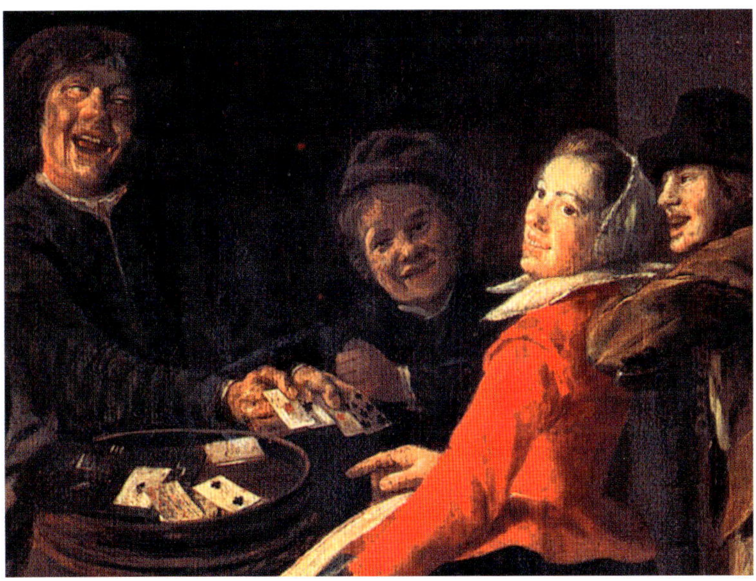

Judith Leyster, *A Game of Cards* (detail), 1633
Musée des Beaux-Arts de Rouen

still life

Works of art depicting inanimate objects, still life paintings and drawings often feature flowers, fruit, glassware, books, tools, food or everyday household items. Still life objects are always inert, yet paintings of them can also be lively with symbolism, technical mastery and emotional depth.

Dating back to antiquity, still life has flourished at different times, particularly in Dutch painting of the 17th century. Artists such as Rachel Ruysch and Jan van Huysum painted detailed floral arrangements, often symbolizing the fleeting nature of life, beauty and time; a concept also known as vanitas. Skulls, wilting flowers and extinguished candles frequently appeared in such works, reminding the viewer of mortality and the passage of time.

Still life can be a means for an artist to explore a technique or approach, or to convey an underlying or secondary meaning, such as domesticity, wealth or religious belief. Artists have also used still life to explore formal qualities, such as light, shadow, shape, perspective, texture, colour or close observation. In Modern and Contemporary art, still life has continued to evolve, as seen in the paintings of Paul Cézanne (see below), which explore the underlying structures of objects and the white still lifes of Giorgio Morandi.

The power of still life painting lies in its ability to transform the ordinary into the extraordinary.

In a nutshell
Still life paintings and drawings depict inanimate objects, exploring form, light or symbolism.

Why it matters
Allows artists to study composition, refine technique and convey deeper meanings.

Key figures
Paul Cézanne, 1839–1906
Juan Sánchez Cotán, 1560–1627
Giorgio Morandi, 1890–1964
Rachel Ruysch, 1664–1750

Make the connection
Cubism, p.36
Photorealism, p.50
tone, p.63
observation, p.94

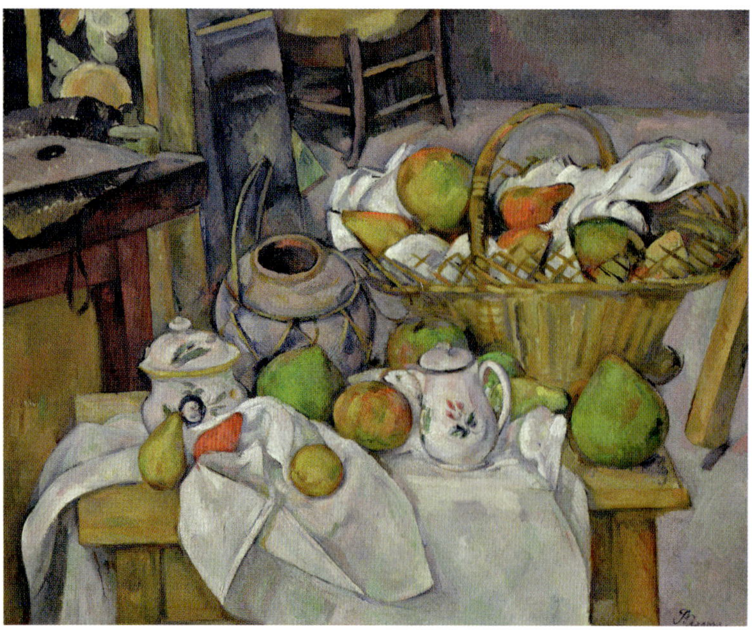

Paul Cézanne, *Still Life with Basket*, 1888–90
Musée d'Orsay, Paris

life drawing

Unlike still life, life drawing involves animate subject matter, as it is the practice of drawing the human figure from a live model. One of the most foundational exercises in art education, life drawing has been central to artistic training for centuries, with the goal of developing an understanding of human anatomy, proportion, movement and expression through direct observation and analysis.

Unlike portraiture, which focuses on the likeness of an individual, life drawing emphasizes the structure and form of the entire body. It involves quick sketches (gestural drawing), as well as longer, more detailed studies. These depict the human figure, nude or clothed, moving or still, and may focus on specific body parts, such as hands or feet. Often, artists follow life drawing with finished paintings, or they use studies from life to depict the clothed figure.

Life drawing sharpens visual perception, improves hand-to-eye co-ordination and helps artists understand the shapes, forms, angles and lines of the human form. As a meditative and expressive process, life drawing encourages artists to respond to the rhythms and gestures of a living body. It is usually, though not always, representational; some artists use life drawing to explore abstraction, emotion or psychological depth.

Life drawing brings immediacy, spontaneity and sensitivity into the creative process – qualities that inform all areas of artistic practice.

In a nutshell
Drawing the human figure from a live model to study anatomy, movement and proportion.

Why it matters
Life drawing sharpens observational skills and serves as the basis for figurative art across disciplines.

Key figures
Lucian Freud, 1922–2011
Michelangelo, 1475–1564
Jenny Saville, b.1970
Egon Schiele, 1890–1918

Make the connection
observation, p.94
charcoal/pencil, pp.112–13
golden ratio, p.131
negative space, p.140

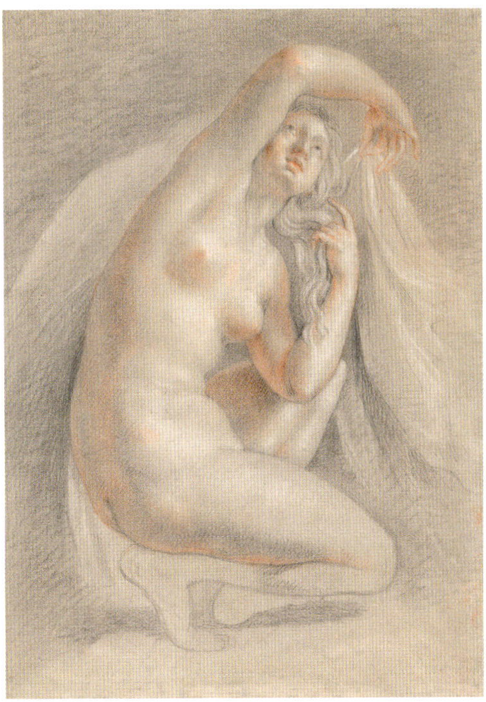

Sir Thomas Lawrence, *A Life Drawing*, c.1789
Yale Center for British Art, New Haven

negative space

A crucial component of visual structure, negative space refers to the areas around and between objects. By observing these spaces, artists can understand and portray proportion, angles, balance and shapes. In simple terms, while the positive shape is the object, the negative space is everything around and between the object.

In fine art, negative space plays a crucial role in drawing and painting, helping artists observe accurately. Focusing on the spaces around a subject can help artists avoid assumptions and see shapes, lines and angles more objectively. Most Ukiyo-e images (see p.26) utilize negative space to convey a sense of harmony. In sculpture and architecture, negative space influences how the viewer experiences depth, structure and composition. Minimalist artists such as Ellsworth Kelly and Donald Judd explored the relationship between form and space. Some artists use negative space to evoke atmosphere or create a sense of light. British sculptor Barbara Hepworth (below) introduced negative space into her 'pierced' works to help viewers see the environment around, through and behind her artworks.

Ultimately, negative space is not 'empty'; it is active and intentional. When artists deliberately incorporate it into an artwork, it helps define an image or object and can help to guide the viewer's eye around and across the composition.

In a nutshell
The empty or unoccupied space around and between objects.

Why it matters
Creates balance, clarity and focus; helps artists use correct angles and proportions, guiding the viewer's eye.

Key figures
Maurits Cornelis Escher, 1898–1972
Barbara Hepworth, 1903–75
Katsushika Hokusai, 1760–1849
Edvard Munch, 1863–1944

Make the connection
line, p.56
drawing, p.59
woodcut, p.72
observation, p.94

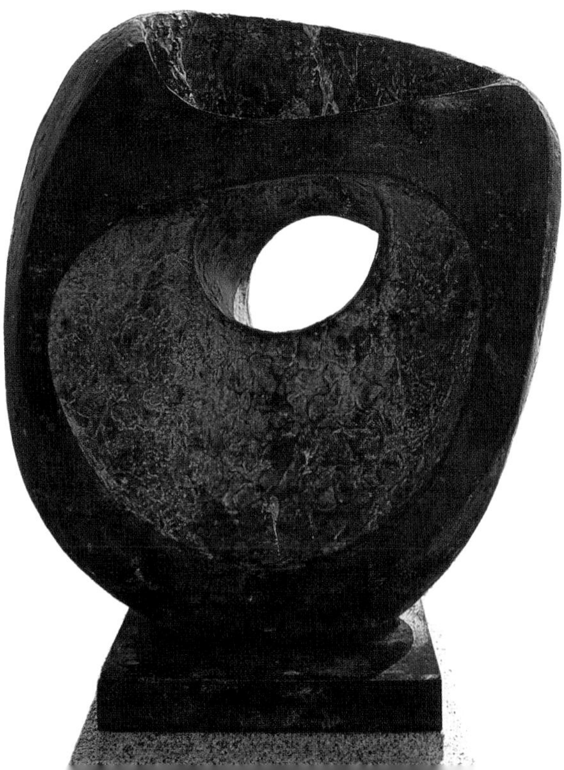

Barbara Hepworth, *Epidauros II*, 1961
Tate, sited at the Malakoff, St Ives

positive shapes

The main visual elements in an artwork, which occupy space and represent the key areas of interest, are the positive shapes. They may include figures, natural elements such as trees or water, objects like fruit or furniture, or even abstract geometric forms. Positive shapes are surrounded by negative space that interacts with them.

Only when an artist uses both positive shapes and negative spaces effectively does a realistic or balanced image emerge. The relationship between the two is crucial to creating visual balance and guiding the viewer's eye. In the work of artists like Henri Matisse (see below), for example, this relationship between solid shapes and the space around them is a bold, expressive tool.

Often, positive shapes serve as the focal points of an image. They draw attention, define the subject and usually carry emotional or symbolic weight. In both abstract and representational art, these shapes are fundamental to storytelling and expression. In realistic art, they might take the form of recognizable figures or objects. In abstract artworks, they may be more ambiguous, but still play a critical role in how meaning is constructed. Positive shapes can be regular and geometric, like rectangles or circles, or more irregular and organic, such as flowing natural contours. Because viewers often associate certain shapes with familiar ideas or cultural references, positive shapes can carry symbolic meaning, reinforcing themes, emotions or narratives within an artwork.

In a nutshell
The primary forms or subjects in a work of art.

Why it matters
Positive shapes establish structure, meaning and visual focus, forming the core of most compositions.

Key figures
Tracey Emin, b.1963
Henri Matisse, 1869–1854
Kara Walker, b.1969
Kehinde Wiley, b.1977

Make the connection
Expressionism, p.30
shadow/tone, pp.62–3
contrast, p.92
observation, p.94

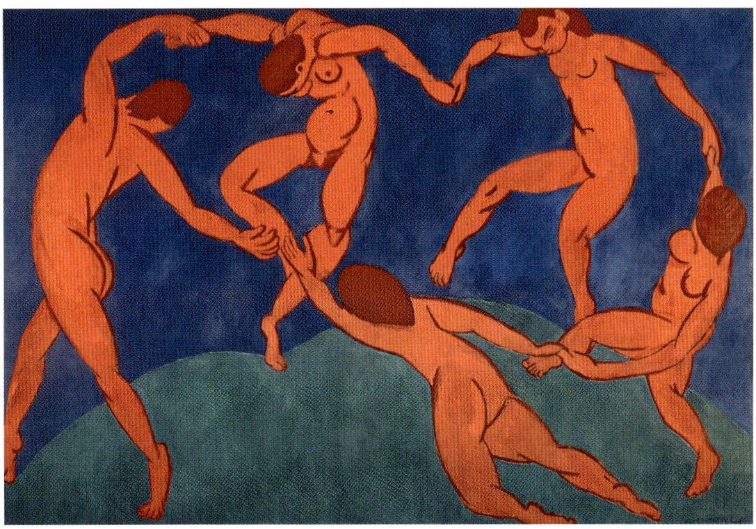

Henri Matisse, *Dance*, 1910
State Hermitage Museum, St Petersburg

Land art

Also known as Earth art or Earthworks, Land art emerged in the late 1960s and early 1970s as a movement in which artists used the natural landscape as both medium and canvas. Rejecting the commercial confines of galleries and museums, artists such as Robert Smithson, Nancy Holt and Michael Heizer created large-scale, site-specific works that directly interacted with the natural world (and continue to do so).

One of the best-known examples is Smithson's *Spiral Jetty* (below), a massive spiral of basalt rocks extending into the Great Salt Lake in Utah, USA. British artists Andy Goldsworthy and Richard Long also create site-specific sculptures in natural or urban settings. These sometimes alter the land itself; alternatively, they specifically do not change the land, leaving it as it was. Land art is deeply connected to themes of impermanence, scale, environmental change and humans' relationship with the natural world.

Unlike traditional landscape painting or sculpture, Land art is not meant to be relocated or sold. It often requires a pilgrimage to experience in person, or it is shown in galleries as photographs and documentation. Many works are intentionally left to erode, decay or change with time and weather, emphasizing nature's power and transience. This can be seen as both a criticism of consumer culture and a celebration of the environment.

In a nutshell
Art that focuses on the environment, often made in the landscape using natural materials.

Why it matters
Challenges traditional art spaces; highlights humanity's relationship with nature and time.

Key figures
Andy Goldsworthy, b.1956
Nancy Holt, 1938–2014
Richard Long, b.1945
Robert Smithson, 1938–73

Make the connection
installation, p.83
observation, p.94
symmetry/asymmetry, pp.108–9
theme, p.127

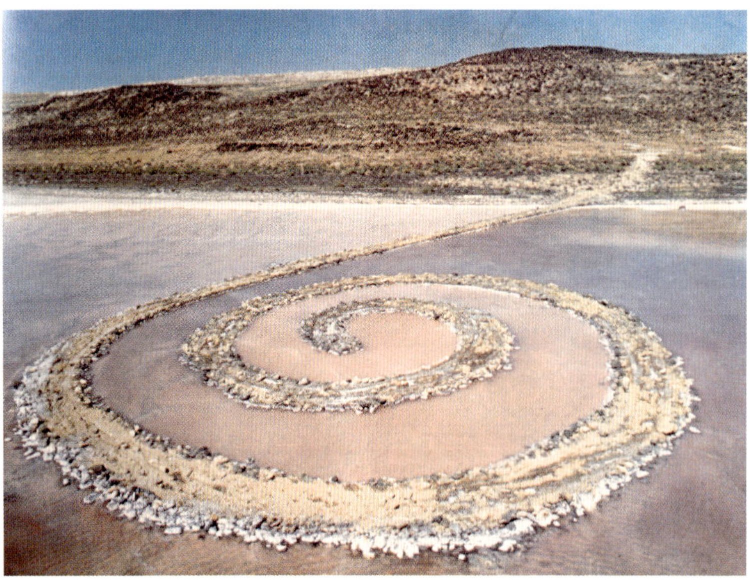

Robert Smithson, *Spiral Jetty*, 1970
Great Salt Lake, Utah

landscape architecture

All around us, landscape architecture shapes the way we experience outdoor spaces. It involves designing and planning environments such as gardens, parks, green urban areas, university campuses and other public or private spaces. Landscape architects integrate natural systems with human needs, aiming for a balance between practicality, environmental health and visual coherence.

Blending art and science, landscape architecture draws on design, horticulture, ecology and engineering. Practitioners often have to accommodate elements such as buildings, water features or circulation routes. They consider factors such as drainage, traffic flow, environmental impact and stormwater management, while also creating habitats for wildlife and spaces for human leisure.

Well-known examples of landscape architecture include the gardens of Versailles, designed in the 17th century by André Le Nôtre; the grounds of Blenheim Palace, created in the 18th century by Lancelot 'Capability' Brown (below); and New York's Central Park, designed in the 19th century by Calvert Vaux and Frederick Law Olmsted.

Although both Land art and landscape architecture use natural materials such as earth, stone and vegetation, their aims differ: Land art creates artworks within the landscape, while landscape architecture serves a practical, functional purpose.

In a nutshell
The design of outdoor spaces, blending aesthetics, ecology and function.

Why it matters
Shapes sustainable, functional environments while supporting natural systems.

Key figures
Capability Brown, 1716–83
Frederick Law Olmsted, 1822–1903
Martha Schwartz, b.1950
Kongjian Yu, 1963–2025

Make the connection
imagination, p.95
theme, p.127
Fibonacci sequence/golden ratio, pp.130–1
creativity/innovation, pp. 132–3

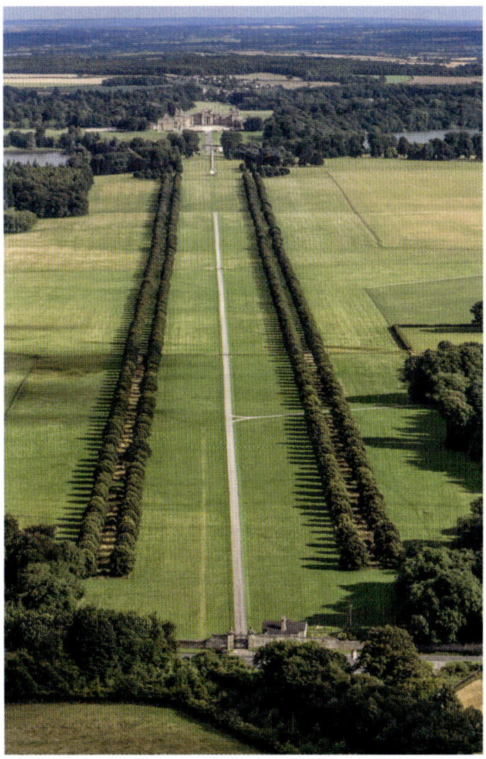

Aerial view of Blenheim Palace and grounds, Oxfordshire, 2007

landscape

A genre of art, landscape depicts scenery. Some artists portray calm, peaceful views, some aim to evoke nostalgia, and others create dramatic or even unsettling scenes.

While landscape painting has held a central place in Eastern art for centuries, it took much longer to gain prominence in Western art. In Chinese, Korean and Japanese traditions, landscape painting, particularly the Chinese *shanshui* ('mountain-water') style, emerged as a major genre in the 10th century. These were visual representations of nature and were also philosophical, often tied to Daoist and Buddhist ideas about harmony, contemplation and the human place within the cosmos.

During the Renaissance in the West, artists began incorporating elements of the natural world into their backgrounds. By the 17th century, landscape had evolved into an independent genre, particularly in Dutch painting. Later, during the Romantic era, it took on deeper emotional meanings, with artists such as Caspar David Friedrich exploring themes like spirituality and the sublime.

Although traditionally associated with depictions of nature, the concept of landscape has evolved to include urban scenes, cityscapes, seascapes and industrial views, highlighting the broad and changing scope of the genre. Landscapes can reflect how humans interact with their environment – whether living in harmony with it, changing it, feeling in awe of it or destroying it.

In a nutshell
Landscape art depicts scenery, mainly natural, often focusing on light, atmosphere, weather, spirituality or drama.

Why it matters
Reflects cultural attitudes toward nature, evokes emotion, and explores human connection to place and environment.

Key figures
Caspar David Friedrich, 1774–1840
Claude Lorrain, 1604/5–82
J. M. W. Turner, 1775–1851
Henry Ossawa Tanner, 1859–1937

Make the connection
Romanticism, p.20
observation, p.94
plein-air painting, p.104
sublime, p.152

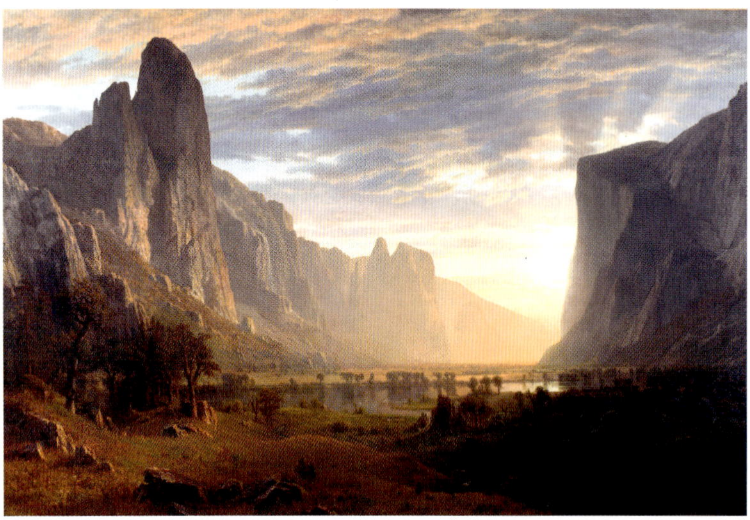

Albert Bierstadt, *Looking Down Yosemite Valley, California*, 1865
Birmingham Museum of Art, Alabam

panorama

A panorama is all about the wide-angle wow factor. Expansive and immersive, panoramas are continuous views that capture broad stretches of landscape or narrative scenes.

First popularized in the late 18th century, the term 'panorama' was coined by Scottish artist Robert Barker to describe his 360-degree paintings, which he exhibited in circular buildings that allowed viewers to stand inside and feel surrounded by the scene. These early panoramas were huge cylindrical paintings, often depicting battle scenes, cities or natural landscapes. The goal was to create an immersive experience, a kind of early virtual reality, where the viewer felt physically transported to another place. They became a form of mass entertainment.

Today, the term 'panorama' in art does not always mean a full, 360-degree image. It can refer to any broad, extended view, including wide-angle landscape paintings or photos, horizontal scroll paintings (common in Chinese or Japanese art), and panoramic cityscapes or seascapes. Panoramas are now less about complete immersion and more about capturing the breadth or expansiveness of a scene.

A landscape painting might be panoramic in scope, or it may focus on a central subject or single viewpoint. While panorama is about breadth of vision, a landscape's primary aim is often to evoke mood, explore composition or spirituality, or express a relationship with nature and the environment.

In a nutshell
A wide, immersive depiction of a scene; originally 360-degree paintings, designed to surround the viewer.

Why it matters
Transformed visual storytelling and prefigured modern immersive media.

Key figures
Robert Barker, 1739–1806
Henri Félix Emmanuel Philippoteaux, 1815–84
John Vanderlyn, 1776–1852
Zhang Zeduan, 1085–1145

Make the connection
atmospheric/linear perspective, pp.78–9
verisimilitude, p.107
subject, p.126
cool colours, p.149

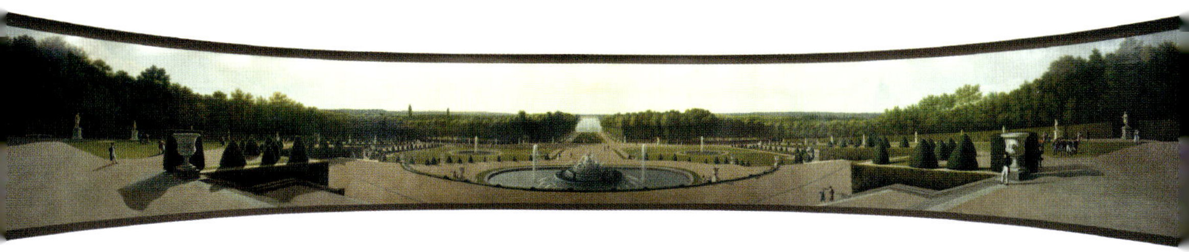

John Vanderlyn, *Panoramic View of the Palace and Gardens of Versailles*, 1818–19
Metropolitan Museum of Art, New York

picturesque

As landscape became a more prominent subject for painters during the second half of the 18th century, definitions of various types of landscape evolved. The aesthetic concept of the 'picturesque' emerged, along with the 'beautiful' and the 'sublime' (see pp.152–3). Each was different. The picturesque was associated with natural irregularity, variety and texture, describing scenes that are visually engaging and rich in detail – neither too smooth and pleasant as in the beautiful, nor too vast and awesome as in the sublime.

Prizing ruggedness, contrast and a sense of natural, unplanned harmony, the picturesque was an aesthetic ideal. Artists including Thomas Gainsborough, John Constable and Claude Lorrain have been described as painting the picturesque: rural scenes, ruins, winding paths and asymmetrical landscapes. Their paintings often convey a sense of mystery, decay and time. The picturesque was also considered in 18th-century landscape gardening; figures such as Capability Brown and Humphry Repton created carefully planned country estates that aimed to appear informal and romantic.

The picturesque reflected the philosophical and cultural values of the Romantic era, including an admiration for nature, a criticism of industrialization and a desire for a more harmonious, intuitive relationship between humans and the land.

Constable's *The Hay Wain* (below) is often considered 'picturesque' because it presents an idealized rural scene that balances naturalism with gentle order and harmony.

In a nutshell
A late-18th- to 19th-century aesthetic concept that valued natural irregularity and variety in landscapes and art.

Why it matters
The blend of nature and art influenced painting, garden design and Romantic thought.

Key figures
John Constable, 1776–1837
Thomas Gainsborough, 1727–88
William Gilpin, 1724–1804
J. M. W. Turner, 1775–1851

Make the connection
Romanticism, p.20
design, p.55
atmospheric perspective, p.78
asymmetry, p.109

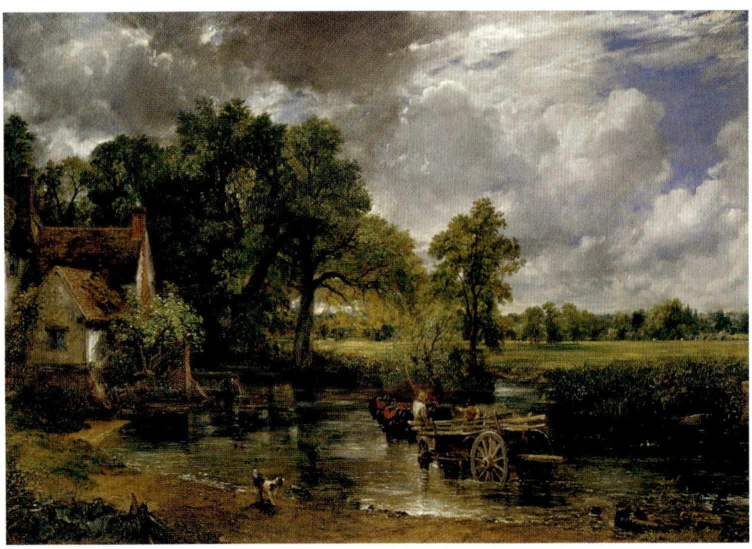

John Constable, *The Hay Wain*, 1821
National Gallery, London

Grand Manner

Characterized by its elevated subject matter, Classical influences and idealized presentation, the Grand Manner refers to a style of painting that emerged in the 17th and 18th centuries. Inspired by the art and philosophy of the Renaissance and ancient Rome, it aimed to depict noble themes with dignity, clarity and grandeur.

In London, the first president of the Royal Academy of Arts, Sir Joshua Reynolds, was a leading advocate for the Grand Manner. He believed that artists should emulate the great masters of antiquity and the Renaissance, such as Raphael and Michelangelo, to elevate the moral and intellectual status of painting.

Key elements of Grand Manner painting include historical, religious or mythological subjects, often featuring idealized figures in Classical poses and dramatic compositions. Portraiture in the Grand Manner also followed these conventions; sitters were often shown in stately poses against grand architectural backdrops, projecting power, intellect or virtue.

Reflecting the values of order and idealism associated with the Enlightenment, the Grand Manner contrasts with the picturesque, which celebrates natural irregularity and emotional resonance.

In a nutshell
A classical painting style focused on noble subjects, idealized figures and formal composition.

Why it matters
Elevated painting's status by aligning it with moral virtue, history and Classical ideals.

Key figures
Angelica Kauffman, 1741–1807
Nicolas Poussin, 1594–1665
Raphael, 1483–1520
Sir Joshua Reynolds, 1723–92

Make the connection
ancient Roman art, p.8
High Renaissance, p.15
linear perspective, p.79
imprimatura, p.101

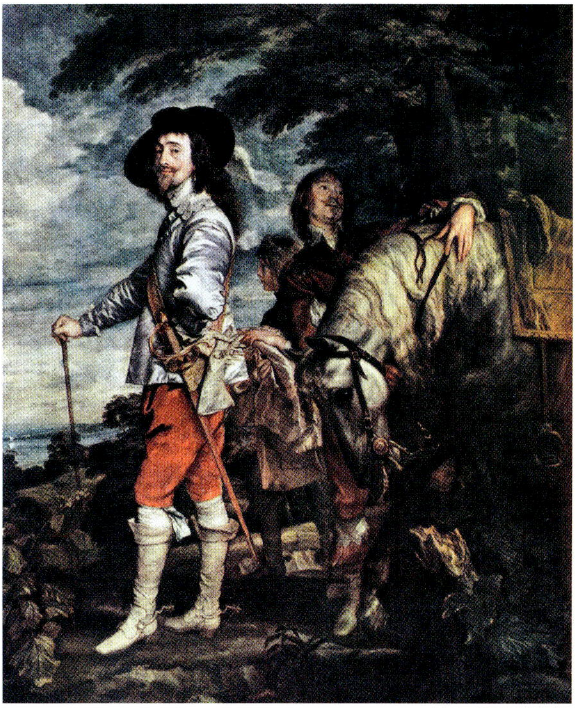

Sir Anthony van Dyck, *Charles I at the Hunt*, *c.*1635
Musée du Louvre, Paris

warm colours

Colours often convey information. For example, through the colours in an artwork, the viewer may be able to determine the time of day, the temperature of the environment or the emotion portrayed. Usually associated with heat, energy and sunlight, warm colours include reds, oranges and yellows. They evoke feelings of warmth, comfort, passion, joy, excitement or love, as well as fear, danger or anger. Because warm colours tend to advance visually, artists often use them to create a sense of depth, contrasting them with cooler, receding tones.

Artists sometimes use warm colours to create a sense of drama or to draw attention to certain areas within a composition. Red, for instance, is often noticed instantly. Warm colours are used to depict sunsets, autumn leaves or scenes bathed in sunlight in landscape art. In portraiture, they can add life and vitality to skin tones. When used in interior design or still life paintings, they can make a space or object feel inviting and alive.

Because warm colours can be intense, they are often balanced with cooler hues, as in J. M. W. Turner's *Burning of the Houses of Lords and Commons*, where golden yellows and fiery reds are used for the blaze and blue-grey elsewhere. Henri Matisse frequently used bold reds, oranges and yellows to infuse his paintings with vitality, emotional warmth and a sense of joyous harmony, as seen in his *Still Life with a Red Rug* (below).

In a nutshell
Including reds, oranges and yellows, these evoke a sense of heat, energy and emotion.

Why it matters
Create mood, direct the viewer's focus and intensify drama.

Key figures
Paul Gauguin, 1848–1903
Vincent van Gogh, 1853–90
Henri Matisse, 1869–1854
Wassily Kandinsky, 1866–1944

Make the connection
contrast/unity, pp.92–3
theme, p.127
creativity, p.132
symbolism, p.134

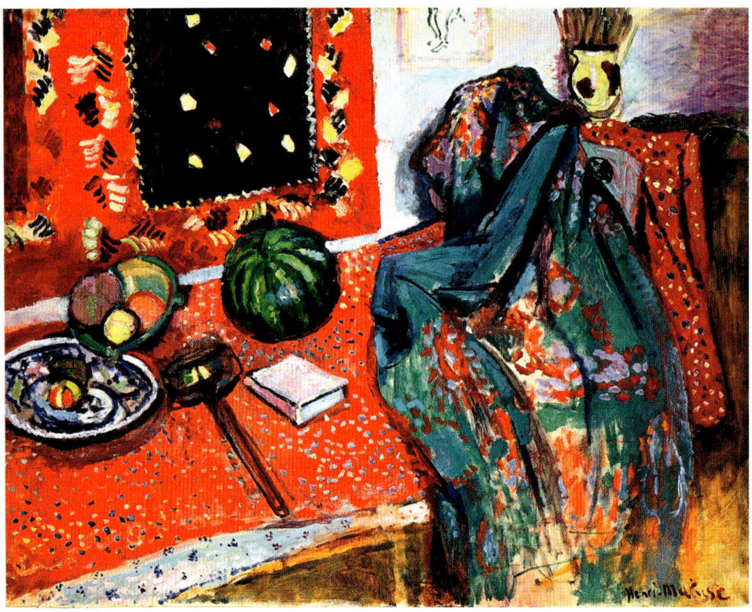

Henri Matisse, *Still Life with a Red Rug*, 1906
Musee des Beaux-Arts, Grenoble

cool colours

Often associated with water and the sky, or with a sense of quietness, tranquillity and composure, cool colours include blue, green and violet, and are located close together on the colour wheel; technically speaking, these are colours with shorter wavelengths than the longer wavelengths of warmer colours. Generally, they evoke coolness and tend to recede in a composition, creating a sense of depth and distance through atmospheric perspective.

Artists often use cool colours to create a peaceful or contemplative mood; they suggest stillness, melancholy or introspection, in contrast to the energy and intensity of warm colours. A scene dominated by blues and greens might evoke, for example, a quiet forest, a rainy day or the gentle hush of twilight. In portraiture, cool colours might be used to highlight shadows or to convey a sense of detachment or calm. In abstract art, cool tones can create a soothing visual rhythm or a meditative space. In *Nocturne: Blue and Gold - Old Battersea Bridge* (below), James McNeill Whistler uses tonal restraint; cool blues and greens dissolve form, creating an atmospheric image where bridge, water and sky merge in meditative harmony.

Cool colours are especially effective when paired with warm colours in a composition, creating balance or visual interest: a figure painted in warm colours against a cool background will usually become the focal point of the entire image.

In a nutshell
Including blues, greens and purples, cool colours suggest calm, distance and serenity.

Why it matters
Soothe the viewer, create a sense of depth and balance compositions.

Key figures
Akseli Gallen-Kallela, 1865–1931
Katsushika Hokusai, 1760–1849
Ernst Ludwig Kirchner, 1880–1938
Pablo Picasso, 1881–1973

Make the connection
Impressionism, p.22
Ukiyo-e, p.26
unity, p.93

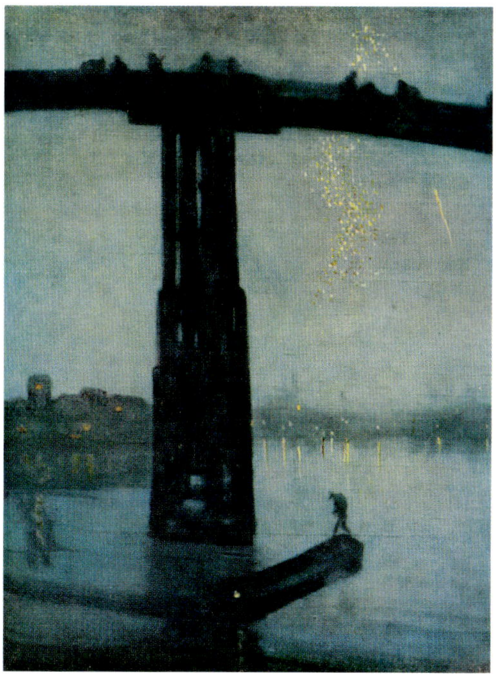

James McNeill Whistler, *Nocturne: Blue and Gold – Old Battersea Bridge*, c.1872–5
Tate

primary colours

Red, yellow and blue are primary colours, meaning that they cannot be created by mixing other colours. Apart from them, every other colour can be made by mixing the primaries in various combinations, sometimes with the addition of white or black. Because they are the foundational building blocks of all other hues, primary colours are essential for any palette in both traditional and modern art.

Primary colours form the basis of the artist's colour wheel (see opposite), which shows the relationships between all colours of the spectrum. Artists use the primaries in various ways, either in their pure form or with touches of other colours, to create artwork that can be both expressive and symbolic. For example, J. M. W. Turner's *The Fighting Temeraire* (below), showing the eponymous *Temeraire* being towed along the River Thames to be scrapped, is a glowing painting, made with only primary colours, white and black.

From 1914, Piet Mondrian began using only primary colours, plus black and white, for all his work (see p.40), believing that they were the purest colours and could transcend cultural divisions. This was part of his broader philosophy of Neo-plasticism, which aimed to create 'universal beauty' through non-representational forms. The simplicity, clarity and purity of primary colours made them central to his art and related art movements, as he sought to reduce visual language to its most essential elements.

In a nutshell
Red, blue and yellow – the foundation of all other colours in art.

Why it matters
Blended, they are the basis of all other colours; used alone, they have intense visual impact.

Key figures
Eugène Delacroix, 1798–1863
Vincent van Gogh, 1853–90
Piet Mondrian, 1872–1944
J. M. W. Turner, 1775–1851

Make the connection
De Stijl/Bauhaus, pp.40–1
contrast, p.92
paint, p.110
oil pastel, p.115

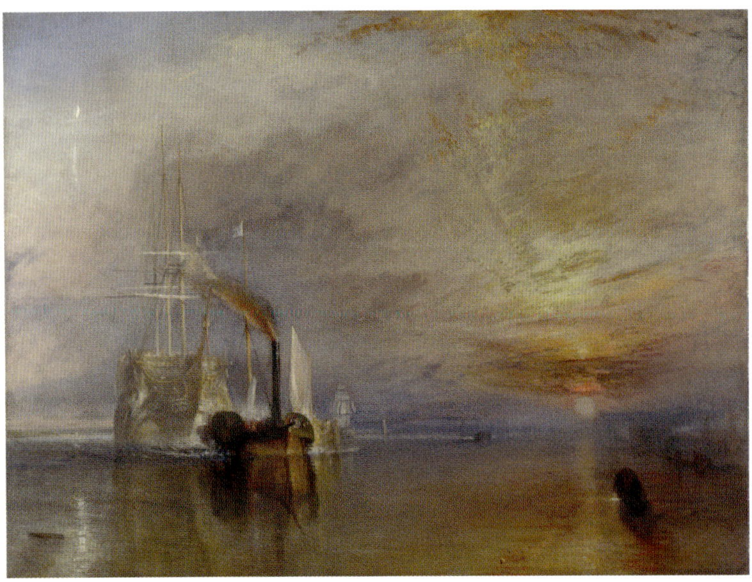

J. M. W. Turner, *The Fighting Temeraire*, 1839
National Gallery, London

complementary colours

Colours situated directly opposite each other on the colour wheel are known as complementary colours. Familiar examples include red and green, blue and orange, and yellow and violet. When placed side by side, these colours appear more vivid, creating a visual intensity far stronger than when they are used alone or next to other hues.

The principle behind this phenomenon is called 'the law of simultaneous contrast'. It was first described in 1839 by the French chemist Michel Eugène Chevreul, in his book *The Law of Simultaneous Colour Contrasts*. While working at the Gobelins tapestry workshop in Paris, he noticed that dyes seemed to shift in appearance when placed beside other colours. He concluded that complementary colours intensify each other when viewed together.

Chevreul's theory inspired many artists. Impressionists and Post-Impressionists such as Claude Monet, Georges Seurat and Paul Gauguin quickly embraced complementary contrasts to heighten the luminosity of their paintings.

While complementary colours enhance each other when placed side by side, mixing them has the opposite effect. The mixture typically results in browns or greys – subtle, muted tones that artists often use to suggest shadows and depth.

In a nutshell
Complementary colours are opposite each other on the colour wheel.

Why it matters
When placed side by side, they enhance each other's intensity. They create visual contrast, balance and vibrancy in art.

Key figures
Paul Gauguin, 1848–1903
Vincent van Gogh, 1853–90
Henri Matisse, 1869–1854
Georges Seurat, 1859–91

Make the connection
Impressionism/Post-Impressionism, pp.22–3
Modernism, p.34
contrast, p.92
pointillism, p.96

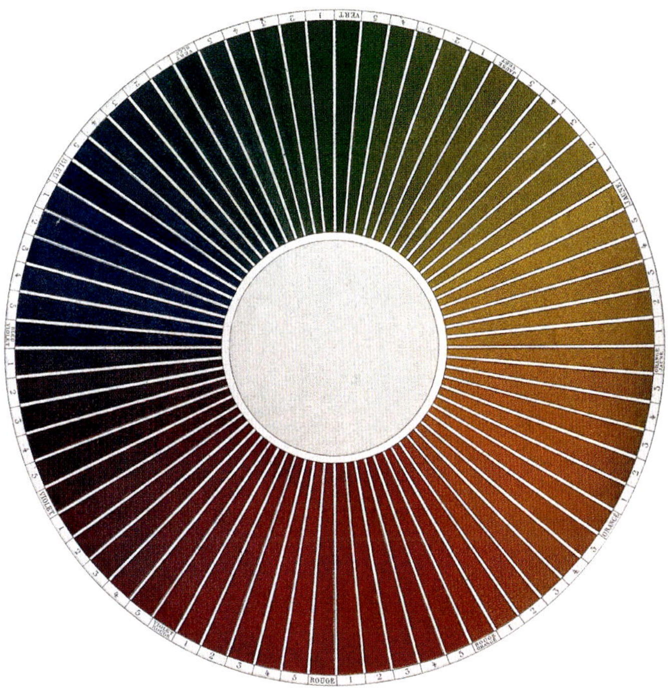

'Optics: a colour-circle', colour aquatint by R. H. Digeon after M. E. Chevreul, *c.*1868.

sublime

A quality that provokes a powerful emotional response – often awe, reverence, or even fear – the sublime, when used in art, is unlike beauty, which tends to soothe or please. In art, the sublime can feel overwhelming, astonishing or unsettling.

The idea of the sublime took shape in 18th-century philosophy, most notably in the writings of Edmund Burke and Immanuel Kant. Burke linked the sublime to dramatic elements of the natural world, such as mountains, storms, deep forests or vast seas, whose scale and intensity elicit fear and wonder. Kant saw the sublime as a mental response to something so immense or unknowable that it surpasses our senses, yet reveals the mind's capacity to grasp ideas beyond physical reality.

During the 19th-century Romantic era, the sublime became a central theme in art. Artists such as Caspar David Friedrich, John Martin and J. M. W. Turner created scenes in which nature dominates, and human figures appear small, encouraging viewers to reflect on the vastness of the world and their place within it.

The sublime is not limited to figurative painting. Installations, abstract and Minimalist art can evoke it through impressions of infinity, emptiness or transcendence, while Contemporary artists often engage themes such as climate change, technology or human vulnerability. Whenever an artwork moves the viewer beyond simple beauty toward a deeper, more expansive emotion, it can be considered sublime.

In a nutshell
The sublime in art captures awe-inspiring, huge, startling or alarming scenes or events.

Why it matters
Aims to stir emotions, challenge opinions and explore the place of humans in the universe.

Key figures
Frederic Edwin Church, 1826–1900
Caspar David Friedrich, 1774–1840
John Martin, 1789–1854
J. M. W. Turner, 1775–1851

Make the connection
Romanticism, p.20
atmospheric perspective, p.78
watercolour, p.122
oil paint, p.125

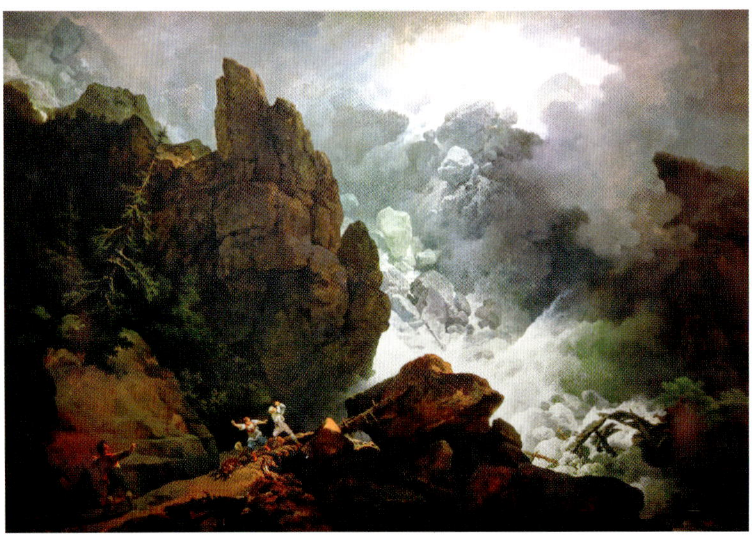

Philip James de Loutherbourg, *An Avalanche in the Alps*, 1803
Tate Britain, London

beauty

Both the sublime and beauty are aesthetic concepts that describe how art affects us emotionally and intellectually. Rooted in philosophical thought, they offer different yet complementary ways of understanding our responses to what we see. Beauty is traditionally linked to harmony, balance, proportion and pleasure. It comforts, delights and invites prolonged looking. The sublime, by contrast, is associated with awe, vastness, power and even terror.

Beauty in Western art has long been conveyed through idealized forms, symmetry and carefully balanced compositions. Ancient Greek and Renaissance art both celebrated proportion and flawless physical harmony as hallmarks of the beautiful. *The Birth of Venus* (below) by William-Adolphe Bouguereau reflects this tradition: its polished technique, graceful figures and controlled composition present an image of classical perfection that strongly appealed to 19th-century academic taste.

Yet beauty is not fixed. The Impressionists found it in fleeting light and atmospheric effects. Modern and Contemporary artists have sought beauty in raw emotions, visible brushwork or unconventional forms that challenge traditional ideals. In today's art, beauty may be smooth or irregular, restrained or expressive.

Ultimately, both beauty and the sublime deepen our engagement with artworks. Each encourages attention, reflection and a heightened awareness of how art shapes our emotional experience.

In a nutshell
Aesthetics that evoke admiration and delight.

Why it matters
Offers comfort and emotional connection, though ideas and ideals of beauty change across different cultures and eras.

Key figures
Sandro Botticelli, *c.*1445–1510
William-Adolphe Bouguereau, 1825–1905
Élisabeth Louise Vigée Le Brun, 1755–1842
Pierre-Auguste Renoir, 1841–1919

Make the connection
Renaissance, p.16
Rococo, p.19
Ukiyo-e, p.26
Art Nouveau, p.32

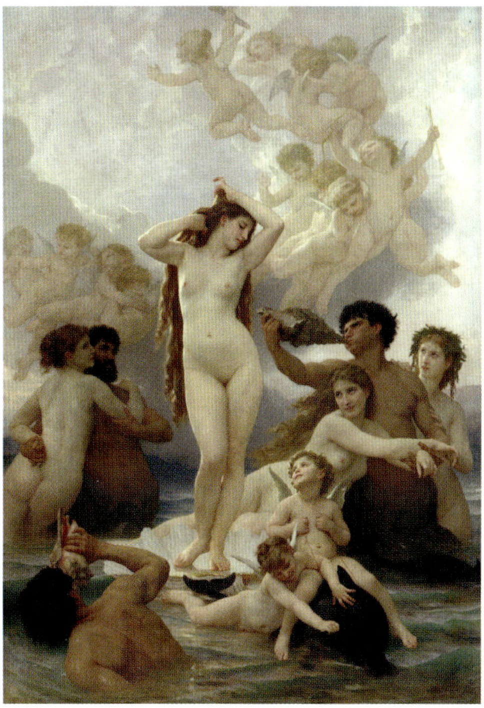

William-Adolphe Bouguereau, *The Birth of Venus*, 1879
Musée d'Orsay, Paris

post–colonial art

In the mid-to-late 20th century, as many nations across Africa, Asia and the Caribbean achieved independence, post-colonial art evolved. From the start, it comprised a range of artistic practices, responding to the political, cultural and psychological legacies of colonialism.

Post-colonial art often explores themes such as cultural identity, trauma and memory, considering how colonial regimes disrupted ancestral traditions, imposed foreign values and fractured Indigenous systems of knowledge. Deeply concerned with confronting historical injustices, the art also plays a central role in reshaping cultural narratives from the perspectives of formerly colonized people.

Yet post-colonial art is not confined to a single style, place or approach. It has developed simultaneously across the world. American artist Faith Ringgold used textiles and storytelling to reflect on African-American identity and history (see below). Ghanaian sculptor El Anatsui repurposes discarded materials into wall installations that invite the viewer to reconsider international trade, consumption and Africa's colonial past and present.

Post-colonial art actively interrogates dominant narratives, and challenges Eurocentric representations.

In a nutshell
Explores identity, memory and resistance in the aftermath of colonial rule.

Why it matters
Reclaims cultural narratives, critiques imperial legacies and gives voice to formerly colonized or displaced communities.

Key figures
El Anatsui, b.1944
Zanele Muholi, b.1972
Wangechi Mutu, b.1972
Yinka Shonibare, b.1962

Make the connection
Expressionism, p.30
Postmodernism, p.35
imagination, p.95
theme, p.127

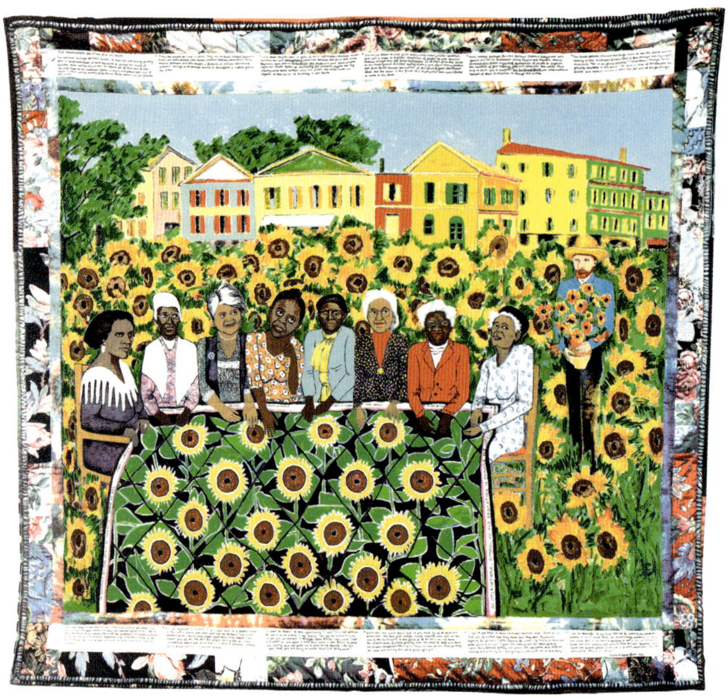

Faith Ringgold, *The Sunflower Quilting Bee at Arles*, 1991
Private collection

decolonization

Unlike post-colonial art, decolonization in art is not only about representation, but also focuses on the redistribution of power. In asking who decides what counts as art and who controls cultural heritage, it reconsiders how art is created, curated, displayed and interpreted, seeking to shift the longstanding traditions of Western art. It supports historically excluded voices and repositions Indigenous and non-Western perspectives.

This movement, which is both artistic and political, challenges the authority of museums and galleries shaped by colonial exploitation and aims to restore more control and presence to cultures and communities whose art was historically marginalized or usurped. Decolonial actions include the repatriation of looted artefacts (such as the Benin Bronzes), the revision of art education curricula, and the decentring of Euro-American perspectives in curatorial practices.

Artists and curators such as South African Zanele Muholi and Australian Brook Andrew embed decolonial strategies in their work by changing colonial narratives, exhibition formats, curatorial voices and institutional hierarchies. Movements like Rhodes Must Fall – a student-led movement that originated on the campus of the University of Cape Town – call for the removal of colonial statues and for a broader transformation in how art and history are taught and displayed.

Building on the ideas behind post-colonial art, decolonization insists that all aspects of the art world must evolve together.

In a nutshell
Refers to the process of challenging and dismantling the dominance of colonial perspectives within artistic institutions, narratives and practices.

Why it matters
Fosters a more inclusive and accurate understanding of global art histories.

Key figures
Kader Attia, b.1970
Candice Breitz, b.1972
Ali Cherri, b.1976
Zanele Muholi, b.1972

Make the connection
creativity/innovation, pp.132–3

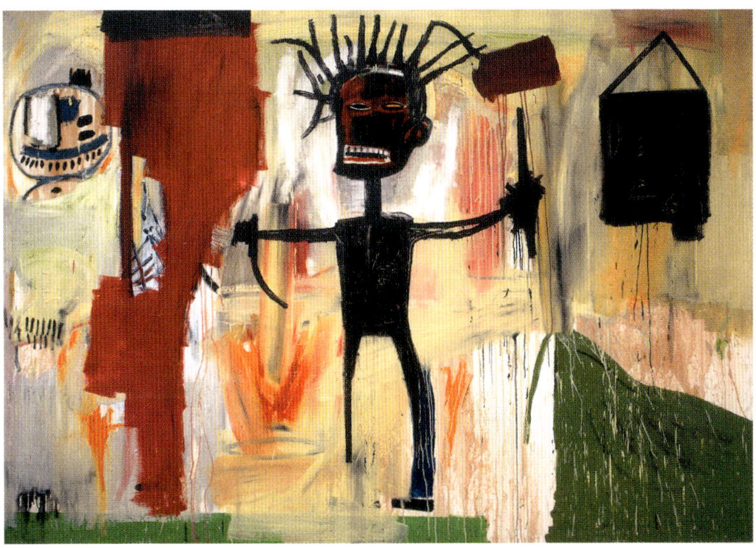

Jean-Michel Basquiat, *Self-Portrait*, 1986
Museu d'Art Contemporani de Barcelona

movers & shakers

Here is a selective list of 20 key figures working across art and design today. They are among the 'movers and shakers' of the art world, each exploring what art is and what it can do now.

Hannah Black Artist and critic whose essays move fluidly between politics, culture and personal voice.

Claire Bishop Art historian and critic whose clear, rigorous writing on participation, spectatorship and digital culture makes complex ideas approachable.

Ben Davis Art critic whose writing connects Contemporary art to economics, class and politics in a clear, journalistic voice.

Catherine de Zegher Curator and art historian known for reframing art history through feminist and ecological narratives.

Okwui Enwezor Curator and theorist whose work reshaped global and postcolonial perspectives in Contemporary art.

Hal Foster Influential art historian and critic associated with *October*, known for incisive analyses of Modernism, Postmodernism and Contemporary art.

Michelle Grabner Artist, educator and writer whose work bridges making, thinking and teaching art.

Boris Groys Philosopher and critic whose short texts on authorship, power and visibility are ideal for curious newcomers.

Amelia Jones Art historian and theorist whose writing on performance, feminism and identity is rigorous but readable.

David Joselit Art historian whose writing on circulation, images and networks gives readers tools to understand contemporary art systems.

Grant Kester Theorist of socially engaged art whose work foregrounds ethics, dialogue and collaboration in clear, grounded language.

Rosalind E. Krauss Foundational theorist of Postmodern art whose work on medium, indexicality and the expanded field remains central to contemporary art history.

Miwon Kwon Art historian best known for her influential writing on site-specificity and institutional contexts.

Pamela M. Lee Art historian connecting Contemporary art to technology, systems thinking and environmental questions.

Lucy Lippard Critic, curator and activist whose essays on Conceptual, feminist and political art remain lively, personal and inspiring.

Ruth Millington Art historian and writer who explores overlooked figures and stories in art history.

Hans Ulrich Obrist Curator and conversationalist whose interviews offer readers an accessible way into contemporary artistic thinking.

Terry E. Smith Art historian whose concept of 'contemporaneity' offers readers a big-picture framework for art today.

Hito Steyerl Artist and writer; one of the most readable and urgent voices on images, power, technology and politics today.

Gloria Sutton Art historian whose research on media art, feminism and exhibition infrastructures opens up how art circulates.

index

Page numbers in *italic* refer to the illustrations

notes & image credits

notes

1. (p.21, Realism) Cited from an exchange described by Courbet's contemporary and biographer, Jules-Antoine Castagnary, in Salon de 1861 (published in *Gazette des Beaux-Arts*, 1861).
2. (p.38, Suprematism) Kazimir Malevich, *The Non-Objective World: The Manifesto of Suprematism*, translated by A. von Riesen, Albert Langen, Munich, 1927.
3. (p.42, Dada) Hugo Ball, 'Romanticism: The Word and the Image' (5 April 1916, Zurich), in *Flight Out of Time: A Dada Diary by Hugo Ball*, edited by John Elderfield, University of California Press, London, Los Angeles and Berkely, 1996.

Quarto

First published in 2026 by Ivy Press
an imprint of The Quarto Group.

One Triptych Place, London, SE1 9SH, United Kingdom
T (0)20 7700 6700
www.Quarto.com

A catalogue record for this book is available from the British Library.

ISBN 978-1-83600-887-3
Ebook ISBN 978-1-83600-888-0

Design by Intercity
Series Editor: Jane Wilsher
Project Editor: Faye Robson
Editor: Róisín Duffy
Senior Designer: Renata Latipova
Senior Production Manager: Alex Merrett

Printed in Guangdong, China TT062026
10 9 8 7 6 5 4 3 2 1

FSC www.fsc.org
MIX
Paper | Supporting responsible forestry
FSC® C016973